ASEAN-CHINA COOPERATION ON REGIONAL CONNECTIVITY AND SUSTAINABILITY

Series on Asian Regional Cooperation Studies

Print ISSN: 2717-5456
Online ISSN: 2717-5464

Chief Editor: GAO Fei *(China Foreign Affairs University, China)*
Deputy Chief Editor: GUO Yanjun *(China Foreign Affairs University, China)*

Track II Diplomacy usually refers to an unofficial process with a government background. It plays an important role in promoting regional cooperation in Asia. The main tasks of Track II Diplomacy are to analyze problems, make policy recommendations, and provide intellectual support for official cooperation. Participants are mainly experts and scholars engaged in policy research as well as the government officials participating in their private capacities. The Institute of Asian Studies (IAS) at China Foreign Affairs University is China's focal point for three most influential Track II mechanisms of this region, namely the Network of East Asian Think-tanks (NEAT), the Network of ASEAN-China Think-tanks (NACT) and the Network of Trilateral Cooperation Think-tanks (NTCT). IAS is proud to launch Series on Asian Regional Cooperation Studies jointly with the World Scientific Publishing, the most reputable English academic publisher in Asia. The purpose of this series is not only to motivate more scholars to get involved in Track II Diplomacy of Asia, but also to increase the recognition of the three networks by reaching out to a wide audience. Based on the platforms of NEAT, NACT and NTCT, this series will invite outstanding scholars to conduct in-depth research on significant and challenging issues in Asian regional cooperation, through conference proceedings, scholarly monographs, textbooks and translations with high academic standards and strong policy relevance.

Published

Series on Asian Regional Cooperation Studies—Vol. 4

ASEAN-CHINA COOPERATION ON REGIONAL CONNECTIVITY AND SUSTAINABILITY

Edited by

GUO Yanjun
YANG Yue

China Foreign Affairs University, China

World Scientific

NEW JERSEY · LONDON · SINGAPORE · BEIJING · SHANGHAI · HONG KONG · TAIPEI · CHENNAI · TOKYO

Published by

World Scientific Publishing Co. Pte. Ltd.

5 Toh Tuck Link, Singapore 596224

USA office: 27 Warren Street, Suite 401-402, Hackensack, NJ 07601

UK office: 57 Shelton Street, Covent Garden, London WC2H 9HE

Library of Congress Cataloging-in-Publication Data
Names: Guo, Yanjun, 1978–   editor. | Yang, Yue, 1976–   editor.
Title: ASEAN-China cooperation on regional connectivity and sustainability /
   edited by Yanjun Guo, Yue Yang, China Foreign Affairs University, China.
Description: USA : World Scientific, 2021. | Series: Series on Asian regional cooperation studies,
   2717-5456 | Includes bibliographical references and index.
Identifiers: LCCN 2021016034 (print) | LCCN 2021016035 (ebook) |
   ISBN 9789811221828 (hardcover) | ISBN 9789811234316 (ebook) |
   ISBN 9789811234323 (ebook other)
Subjects: LCSH: Southeast Asia--Foreign economic relations--China. | China--Foreign economic
   relations--Southeast Asia. | Sustainable development--Southeast Asia. |
   Sustainable development--China. | Trade routes--Southeast Asia.
Classification: LCC HF1591.Z4 A824 2021 (print) | LCC HF1591.Z4 (ebook) |
   DDC 337.1/590951--dc23
LC record available at https://lccn.loc.gov/2021016034
LC ebook record available at https://lccn.loc.gov/2021016035

British Library Cataloguing-in-Publication Data
A catalogue record for this book is available from the British Library.

For any available supplementary material, please visit
https://www.worldscientific.com/worldscibooks/10.1142/11869#t=suppl

Desk Editors: Aanand Jayaraman/Lixi Dong

Typeset by Stallion Press
Email: enquiries@stallionpress.com

Printed in Singapore

Foreword

The Network of ASEAN–China Think-tanks (NACT) was proposed in 2013, and officially launched in 2014. NACT is the only Track II mechanism focusing on promoting ASEAN–China relations recognized and supported by the governments of ASEAN members and China. Five years have passed since its establishment. With unswerving support and substantial contribution from ASEAN NACT members, remarkable progress has been made within just five years. NACT has built a solid three-level working mechanism including Country Coordinators' Meeting (CCM), Working Group Meeting and Annual Conference. On July 3, 2014, the first NACT CCM was held in Beijing, which adopted NACT Concept Paper, and established the principles, purposes and operation mechanism of NACT. On July 4, the Seminar on Building a China–ASEAN Community of Common Destiny and Launching Ceremony of Network of ASEAN–China Think Tanks was held by China Foreign Affairs University in Beijing. Within the NACT framework, a network of "NACT China" research bases has taken shape, and their research work has started. In November 2014, Premier Li Keqiang made it clear in East Asian leaders' meetings that NACT should give a full play of their positive roles and pool wisdom for Asian cooperation.

By the end of 2019, it successfully convened eight working group meetings, six country coordinators meetings and six annual conferences on a wide range of issues of common concern.

The outcomes of joint researches and meetings have been submitted to both ASEAN and China's respective government departments through each member's own channel, which makes important intellectual contribution and support to building a much closer ASEAN–China relation. Also, by the end of 2019, about 100 policy recommendations proposed by both ASEAN and China scholars have been submitted to official levels of both sides for consideration. NACT's work has been highly recognized by the governments, businesses and academia in the region. Vice foreign ministers of the host country and other senior officials attend and address the NACT Annual Conference each year. In 2018 and 2019, NACT outcomes have been successfully submitted to the 21st and 22nd ASEAN–China Summit and noted in both Third Progress Report on the Implementation of the 2016–2020 Plan of Action to Implement the Joint Declaration on the ASEAN–China Strategic Partnership for Peace and Prosperity and the Chairman's statement of the 21st and 22nd ASEAN–China Summit.

In order for NACT joint research to reach out a much wider audience, it was approved by all NACT Country Coordinators in the fifth NACT Country Coordinators Meeting co-hosted by NACT Singapore and NACT China on December 20, 2018 that NACT should start to publish joint researches of all Working Groups from 2019. This book is a collection of research papers contributed by ASEAN and China scholars, some of whom attended NACT Working Group Meeting on Regional Connectivity and Sustainability co-hosted by NACT Malaysia and NACT China in Langkawi Malaysia on April 29–30, 2019.

The agenda for greater connectivity has taken center stage in domestic and international debates in the past decade, for instance, with the creation of One Belt One Road (OBOR) in 2013, which was subsequently renamed Belt and Road Initiative (BRI). BRI, along with Asian Infrastructure Investment Bank (AIIB), aspires to close the gap between the supply and demand of infrastructure globally in the wake of slow economic growth, among other goals.

In the age of globalization, with the push for further trade liberalization and regional integration, efficient physical infrastructure is vital if countries in the region are to increase the size and growth rate of their supply capacity on the ground. Even with a leveled playing field in terms of tariff reduction and elimination of non-tariff barriers, some developing countries were still unable to reap the benefits of free trade, due to the lack of proper infrastructure. As an example, the CLMV countries, including Cambodia, Laos, Myanmar and Vietnam, still lack adequate infrastructure, which may threaten trade activities with extra-regional countries, such as India, which has grown exponentially in the past 17 years from a mere USD 460 million in 2000 to USD 14.5 billion in 2017. This challenge is not just faced by the CLMV countries but also by other ASEAN members and its plus-one-partners to different degrees.

Nevertheless, connectivity projects under the BRI framework go beyond trade facility infrastructure. They include transport, information and communication technology (ICT), energy and even people-to-people networks. In 2017, the Asian Development Bank (ADB) estimated that in order to maintain growth momentum, eradicate poverty and respond to climate change through 2030 and beyond, developing Asia and the Pacific alone will need more than USD 22.6 trillion invested in infrastructure.

To date, a significant number of mega infrastructure projects in the region do not pay adequate attention to the non-economic impacts from these developments even though environmental protection and social sustainability have been emphasized in documents such as "the Vision and Actions on Jointly building Silk Road Economic Belt and 21st century Maritime Silk Road". Admittedly, the real implementation of the policies does not live up to what is expected. This is why it is important to identify the problems so as to make the execution of real projects comply with the principles advocated by China.

As there is a growing demand for infrastructure in ASEAN, it is imperative that the implementation of these projects on the ground mirror the guiding principles. The vision for the ASEAN Connectivity 2025 is to achieve a seamlessly and comprehensively connected and integrated ASEAN that will promote competitiveness, inclusiveness and a greater sense of Community. Apart from people-to-people connectivity, the Master Plan on ASEAN Connectivity 2025 (MPAC 2025) focuses on four other strategic areas, namely, sustainable infrastructure, digital innovation, seamless logistics and regulatory excellence. When it comes to the development of connectivity infrastructure, the MPAC 2025 serves as a guiding document in the planning and execution of a given project in ASEAN. Nevertheless, as the BRI projects within ASEAN are bilaterally negotiated, it is up to the host country to set the appropriate standard and conditions for the execution of the actual project. It is within this platform that the implementation can be monitored to parallel the aspirations of the host country and the guiding principles of the MPAC 2025 and the BRI's vision.

In the race for a more inclusive and sustainable development, the Sustainable Development Goals (SDGs), as part of the UN's 2030 Agenda, have provided guidelines in achieving goals of balancing the three dimensions of sustainable development: the economic, social and environmental. Specifically, Paragraph (21) of the UN 2030 Agenda Document highlights that the new goals and targets have come into effect on January 1, 2016 and will guide the decisions we (the stakeholders) take over the next fifteen years. All of us (the stakeholders) will work to implement the Agenda within our own countries at the regional and global levels, taking into account different national realities, capacities and levels of development and respecting national policies and priorities. All the stakeholders will respect national policy space for sustained, inclusive and sustainable economic growth, in particular for developing states, while remaining consistent with relevant international rules and commitments. The stakeholders will acknowledge also the importance of the regional and sub-regional dimensions, regional economic integration and interconnectivity in sustainable development. Regional and sub-regional frameworks can facilitate the effective translation of sustainable development policies into concrete action at the national level.

The "indivisible and integrated agenda" requires breaking down silos across different policy fields in a unified framework. While the BRI is committed toward achieving the SDGs, there is currently no single policy document related to the BRI that addresses all three pillars of sustainable development. In effect, how the BRI can address sustainable development in an integrated manner remains unclear.

How, then, do we ensure that regional connectivity is created and achieved in a balanced and sustainable manner in the region? How do we ensure that positive spillover effects and minimized negative effects on the economic, social and environmental sectors can be achieved with the development of these infrastructures across the region? What type of assessments and measures are needed on the ground to close the gap between the BRI's policies and how are the projects are being implemented? How can BRI be better aligned with MPAC 2025 by identifying the mutual demands from both ASEAN and China? These are the overarching themes that will be given careful study in this working group.

On both vital and relevant aforementioned questions, the contributing scholars give their ingenious and insightful thoughts from either national or regional perspectives. This book is published at a time of growing debate in the region over connectivity. General discussion has yet to generate specific policy alternatives to benefit all participants. The Working Group Report is also incorporated in this book including innovative and practical policy recommendations on strengthening connectivity between ASEAN and China. If readers use it to debate the relevant issues of our day, this book will have made its mark. With unswerving support from all NACT members who are highly devoted to healthy and sustainable ASEAN–China relations, NACT will continuously endeavor to organize working group studies and produce high quality research outcomes and forward-looking and feasible policy recommendations so as to better serve ASEAN and China governments and peoples as well.

To make this book possible, deep thanks first go to all the contributing authors for their precious time and great efforts. During the long journey to publication, we could not have wished for better and more supportive editors than World Scientific and we have been fortunate to work with them. This book is a product of NACT. It is fitting to dedicate this book to all NACT members. They are in alphabetical order: NACT Brunei (Brunei Darussalam Institute of Policy and Strategic Studies), NACT Cambodia (Cambodian Institute for Cooperation and Peace), NACT Indonesia (Universitas Gadjah Mada of Indonesia), NACT Laos (Institute of Foreign Affairs of the

Lao PDR), NACT Malaysia (Institute of Strategic and International studies of Malaysia), NACT Myanmar (Myanmar Institute for Strategic and International Studies), NACT Philippines (Foreign Service Institute of the Philippines), NACT Singapore (East Asian Institute at National University of Singapore), NACT Thailand (Thai Ministry of Higher Education, Science, Research and Innovation), NACT Vietnam (Diplomatic Academy of Vietnam), and NACT China (China Foreign Affairs University).

NACT China
October 2020

About the Editors

Guo Yanjun is Director of the Institute of Asian Studies at China Foreign Affairs University. As a core member of the Network of East Asian Think-tanks (NEAT) China, Network of ASEAN–China Think-tanks (NACT) China and Network of Trilateral Cooperation Think-tanks (NTCT) China, he has been involved in a couple of Track II diplomacies. He also serves as a research fellow at the Innovation Center on National Territorial Sovereignty and Maritime Rights and the Innovation Center on China's Neighboring Diplomacy. He specializes in the study of regional cooperation in East Asia and international rivers and transboundary water resources management, especially the Lancang–Mekong river water management. He has published relevant writings and articles both at home and abroad in recent years.

Yang Yue is Deputy Director of the Institute of Asian Studies at China Foreign Affairs University. She received her PhD in International Relations from Chinese Academy of Social Sciences. She was a Fulbright Scholar at Georgetown University from 2006 to 2008. Her academic areas include the US electoral politics, the US foreign policy, major power relations in Asia-Pacific region, and cultural diplomacy. She has published books and a series of papers both at home and abroad. As a member of Network of ASEAN–China Think-tanks (NACT) China, she has also been actively engaging in Track II diplomacies in recent years.

Contents

Cambodia's Policy Toward Lancang–Mekong Cooperation: An Assessment

Pou Sothirak

*Cambodian Institute for Cooperation and Peace,
Phnom Penh, Cambodia*

Introduction

During the 17th ASEAN–China Summit held in Myanmar in 2014, Chinese Premier Li Keqiang put forward an initiative to establish the Lancang–Mekong Cooperation (LMC) framework. As a follow-up, the First and Second LMC Senior Officials' Meetings were successfully convened in April and August 2015, respectively. Further commitments were realized at the First LMC Foreign Ministers' Meeting in Jinghong City, Yunnan Province, on November 12, 2015 during which China endorsed a concept paper essentially proclaiming that the LMC will adhere to the spirit of openness and inclusiveness, and thus complement the priority areas of ASEAN Community building,

ASEAN–China Cooperation, and synergize with several existing sub-regional cooperation frameworks including the Greater Mekong Sub-region (GMS) Economic Cooperation Program, ASEAN Mekong Basin Development Cooperation (AMBDC) and the Mekong River Commission (MRC). The LMC is based on the principles of consensus, equality, mutual consultation and coordination, voluntarism, common contribution, shared benefits and respect for the United Nations Charter and international law.

The LMC framework was formally launched at the First LMC Leaders' Meeting in Sanya, China on 23 March 2016 with the participation of leaders from Cambodia, China, Laos, Myanmar, Thailand and Vietnam. The Sanya Declaration was officially formulated, under the benchmark of "A Community of Shared Future of Peace and Prosperity among Lancang–Mekong Countries". On 10 January 2018, the Second MLC Leaders' Meeting was held in Phnom Penh under the theme of "Our River of Peace and Sustainable Development", through which the Phnom Penh Declaration was formulated. Institutionally speaking, in less than three years, LMC could be labeled as one of the most successful regional cooperation frameworks when compared to other existing Mekong mechanisms, addressing a broader range of issues and taking a much more comprehensive approach to the development challenges that confront the region at large as well as the specific needs of all its member states. Currently, LMC's five key priority areas are: (i) connectivity, (ii) production capacity, (iii) cross-border economic cooperation, (iv) water resources and agriculture and (v) poverty reduction.

The heads of states/government of China and the five Mekong countries — Cambodia, Laos, Myanmar, Thailand and Vietnam (CLMTV) — reaffirmed their shared vision that the LMC would contribute to the economic and social development of the sub-regional countries; enhance the well-being of the population; narrow the development gap between members; and support ASEAN Community building as well as promote the implementation of the UN 2030 Agenda for Sustainable Development and advance South–South cooperation. The initiative was also driven by the desire of LMC members to institutionalize cooperation among the six countries to help maintain regional peace and stability, to take advantage of economic complementarities across national markets, and provide greater support for the region's social and economic development.

Despite its concrete inception coming only in 2016, the LMC has had significant economic and developmental influence on the GMS. At the same time, there remains a need to further explore the cooperation mechanism as it relates to coordination between China, the five Mekong member states and external partners. The LMC can be seen as complementary to the existing Mekong mechanisms — which are often constrained by resources — rather than as competitive. At the same time, a more concrete and clear approach to coordination between the LMC and the other existing Mekong mechanisms is needed. The establishment of coordination plans, the fostering of institutional collaboration, the creation of information-sharing platforms, a joint special fund between the LMC and other existing Mekong mechanisms, as well as the jointly hosted Mekong Plus Summit should be considered.

Despite strong political will and the commitments made by each member government in support of the LMC, many regional scholars within the academic community perceive it as Chinese assertiveness or expansionism, seeking to compete with other major powers (the United States, Japan) and to project Beijing's influence in the GMS and Southeast Asia as a whole. One should not overlook criticism from experts who closely follow the development and implications of the LMC framework. Many analysts see a hidden agenda seeking to neutralize mainland Southeast Asia's position on the South China Sea dispute, which would negatively impact ASEAN unity and centrality.[1] Others have even asserted that the Mekong issue could potentially become the largest ASEAN–China conflict after the long-running South China Sea dispute.[2] Others have gone even further, stating that Beijing's strategic objective is to exert control over both the Mekong

---

[1] Vannarith Chheang, "The Mekong Region: A New Strategic Frontier," *ASEAN Focus*, No. 10 (August/September 2016): 12–13.
[2] Catherine Wong, "Is Mekong River Set to Become the New South China Sea for Regional Disputes?" *South China Morning Post*, January 2, 2018, https://www.

River and the riparian countries' development in order to accelerate its rise and to facilitate its "exportation of influence" into ASEAN.[3]

Nevertheless, it is possible to frame the LMC in a different context and focus on more positive aspects. As expressed by a Chinese expert, it was clearly stated that when leaders of the five Mekong countries agreed on the proposed mechanism it was intended that the LMC would be "different" from existing institutions. It was different from existing frameworks in the sense that all the six riparian states put forward this initiative together and reaffirmed their commitment toward concrete projects and actions rather than merely serving as a "talking shop". As a rising power, both politically and economically, China is ready to assist its neighboring countries in order to foster inclusive growth and development. Therefore, the argument goes, the LMC should not be perceived as a competitor or substitute to the existing Mekong mechanisms, but rather as complementary and to seek room for better synergy among the member states. After all, the goal of the LMC, as elucidated in the founding documents, is cooperation for the betterment of the Mekong countries' development and their partnering countries.[4]

As for the structure of the LMC, it is meant to incorporate existing mechanisms through its "3+5+X" vision — i.e. 3 pillars, 5 priority areas, and a better synergized mechanism with Chinese characteristics.

In 2018, as the rotating co-chair of the LMC, Cambodia positioned itself prominently in steering the development of the framework. This chapter seeks to draw more attention to how the LMC has contributed to, and might further contribute to, shaping the geography, environment, politics, society, security and economies of the GMS as a whole and Cambodia in particular. Although the LMC has achieved remarkable success at the institutional level, the comprehensive details of project implementation are quite limited, with certain

---

scmp.com/news/china/diplomacy-defence/article/2126528/mekong-river-set-become-new-south-china-sea-regional.

[3] *Ibid.*

[4] Personal interview conducted in Beijing during research studies in August 2018.

restraints that leave the public with doubts and suspicions in light of this relative lack of transparency.

Cambodia has undertaken to develop in accordance with *The Rectangular Strategy* for the last three phases. At present, the kingdom is in phase four, i.e. *The Rectangular Strategy for Growth, Employment, Equity and Efficiency: Building the Foundation Towards Realizing the Cambodia 2050*, which was adopted in September 2018. It envisages four *Strategic Rectangles*, namely: Rectangle 1 — Human resource development; Rectangle 2 — Economic diversification; Rectangle 3 — Promotion of private sector development and employment; and Rectangle 4 — Inclusive and sustainable developments.[5] As the country strives to become an upper-middle income country by 2030 and a high-income country by 2050, the LMC's five priority areas are indeed parallel to and consistent with Cambodia's national development strategy.

Apart from the Rectangular Strategy, the LMC priority areas also complement some of the objectives in the Industrial Development Policy (IDP) 2015–2025 of Cambodia. The IDP maintains four strategies: (i) attracting foreign and domestic investment; (ii) modernizing and developing small and medium-sized enterprises (SMEs); (iii) revisiting the regulatory environment to strengthen the country's competitiveness; and (iv) coordinating policies including the development of human resources and infrastructure.[6] With these targets, the LMC's priority areas, specifically cooperation in the development of production capacity, emerges as a major component to further facilitate the implementation of the IDP. In the Joint Statement on

---

[5] Royal Government of Cambodia, "Rectangular Strategy for Growth, Employment, Equity and Efficiency: Building the Foundation Toward Realizing the Cambodian Vision 2050: Phase IV of the Royal Government of Cambodia of the Sixth Legislature of the National Assembly," September 2018, http://cnv.org.kh/wp-content/uploads/2012/10/Rectangular-Strategy-Phase-IV-of-the-Royal-Government-of-Cambodia-of-the-Sixth-Legislature-of-the-National-Assembly-2018-2023.pdf.
[6] Royal Government of Cambodia, "Cambodia Industrial Development Policy 2015–2025: Market Orientation and Enabling Environment for Industrial Development," March 6, 2015, http://www.mih.gov.kh/File/UploadedFiles/12_9_2016_4_29_43.pdf.

Production Capacity Cooperation among Lancang–Mekong Countries released in 2016, along with the Sanya Declaration, the LMC leaders agreed that their focus will be on "jointly promoting economic development and industrial transformation and upgrading".[7] Apart from this, the prospects of establishing the Lancang–Mekong Business Council and exploring the development of a service alliance for SMEs, as incorporated into the Five-Year Plan of Action on LMC, are well aligned with the objectives of Cambodia's IDP. If the two initiatives can be put into practice in a timely manner, they will expedite the growth and development of the kingdom's SME sector.

Evaluation of the Lancang–Mekong Cooperation in Cambodia

Some key achievements and notable progress of the LMC in Cambodia include rapid institutionalization as well as project implementation and fund availability. Two major aspects to explore include the speed of institutionalization of the LMC mechanism (at both the national level as well as through Track II diplomatic channels) and the pace of project implementation. It is worth noting that China has pledged support of USD 300 million to the LMC Special Fund for the region to be dispersed over a five-year period.

Among the 132 first-round projects developed, 16 projects are geared toward Cambodia, amounting to USD 7.3 million in funding.[8] Those 16 projects are as follows:

(1) The Buddhist Development Program of Cooperation and workshop on effectiveness of Management of Theravada Buddhism in the countries along Mekong River.

---

[7] Foreign Ministry of People's Republic of China, "Joint Statement on Production Capacity Cooperation Among Lancang–Mekong countries," March 23, 2016, http://www.fmprc.gov.cn/mfa_eng/wjdt_665385/2649_665393/t1350040.shtml.
[8] Ministry of Foreign Affairs and International Cooperation (MOFAIC) of the Kingdom of Cambodia, "Press Release," December 20, 2017, https://www.mfaic.gov.kh/site/detail/16116.

(2) Lancang–Mekong Training-of-Trainers (TOT) Workshop and Publication of the ASEAN Community-Based Tourism (CBT) Standards.

(3) Addressing Land Degradation and Improving Local Livelihoods through Sustainable Land Management.

(4) Forest Restoration and Promotion of Sustainable Forest Use in Southeast Asia.

(5) Promoting an Effective Regional Strategy for Combating Illegal, Unreported and Unregistered (IUU) Fishing in the Mekong countries for Sustainable Fishery Management in the Mekong Region.

(6) Mekong–Lancang ICT Volunteer.

(7) Air Connectivity Enhancement Study in Cambodia, Laos, Myanmar and China.

(8) Enhancing Research and Dialogue on Contract Farming in Lancang–Mekong Countries.

(9) Integrated Community Development Along Mekong River.

(10) Poverty Reduction through Rural Economic Development in Cambodia.

(11) The Lancang–Mekong Symposium on Small and Medium Cultural Enterprises (SMCEs).

(12) Preventing the theft, clandestine excavation, illicit import and export of Cultural Property throughout the Lancang–Mekong Region.

(13) Water quality monitoring system at Mekong mainstream and information center installation.

(14) Joint research and technology development in the risk evaluation, monitoring and early-warning of the three typical vector-borne tropical diseases: dengue, schistosomiasis and angiostrongylosis in Cambodia.

(15) Enhancing China–Mekong Research and Policy Dialogue Program.

(16) Support Program for Scholarship Opportunities to Poor Students to Study in the Field of Science and Technology in China.

The aforementioned projects set out mainly focus on research and development in the LMC's priority areas, including public health care, tourism, water management and general capacity building. These are designed to serve as a stepping stone as the LMC moves into the consolidation phase of the Five-Year Plan of Action (2018–2022).

Most of the 45 first round projects and China's 13 initiatives, which were agreed upon during the 2nd LMC Foreign Ministers' Meeting, either have made substantial progress or have already been implemented.[9] Two-thirds of the USD 1.54 billion of concessional loans pledged in 2016 have been utilized while the other USD 10 billion preferential loans for infrastructure and capacity building have been largely implemented.[10] In Phnom Penh early this year, under the LMC framework, China pledged USD 1.08 billion in concessional loans and a further USD 5 billion in lines of credit to support production capacity and equipment manufacturing cooperation.

So far, the details of the 45 early-harvest projects have remained undisclosed by the governments of the various member states. However, a Chinese scholar claimed that some of those projects are "pre-established" and focus on local livelihood issues, while others are existing infrastructure projects such as the China–Laos cross-border railroad or local power plant construction.[11] Notable LMC signature projects including the Bangkok–Kunming, China–Laos Railway and Siem Reap airport construction are also included within the Belt and Road Initiative (BRI) framework. In addition to these areas, with regard to education cooperation, more than 12,000 students from

---

[9] H.E. Senior Minister Prak Sokhonn, "Interview of H.E. Senior Minister Prak Sokhonn with the Cambodian Institute for Strategic Studies (CISS) on the topic 'Mekong–Lancang Cooperation: Building Peace and Prosperity in the Greater Mekong Sub-Region'," interview by CISS, January 11, 2018, https://pressocm.gov.kh/en/archives/21682.

[10] H.E. Senior Minister Prak Sokhonn, "Interview: Cambodia Highly Values Lancang–Mekong Cooperation Leaders' Meeting, Chinese Premier's Visit: FM," interview by Nguon Sovan, Lu Juan, and Fei Liena, *Xinhua*, January 11, 2018, http://www.xinhuanet.com/english/2018-01/11/c_136887507.htm.

[11] "Breaking the Deadlock," *News China*, March 6, 2018, http://www.newschinamag.com/newschina/articleDetail.do?article_id=3286&section_id=34&magazine_id=2.

the Mekong countries have pursued tertiary education in China since 2016 and about 3,000 officials have attended seminars or training sessions there. In addition, the Lancang–Mekong Vocational Education Base opened in Yunnan and welcomed about 10,000 professionals from their Mekong counterparts. In 2018, China provided the Mekong countries with 2,000 opportunities for short-term workshops and on-the-job education with degrees or diplomas and 100 scholarships for four-year undergraduate studies.[12]

Apart from the first-batch projects, an additional set of 214 projects had been submitted for evaluation.[13] During the second LMC Leaders' Summit, the six leaders also took note of the second round of projects to be supported by the LMC Special Fund 2018 and the Progress Report of the six Joint Working Groups on key priority areas. These additional projects are geared toward the framing of LMC as an institution with a focus on concrete projects rather than — as noted earlier — a "talking shop", i.e. as a project-oriented institution, with special funds allocated to ensure the realization of the projects.[14] Placing the LMC in the context of Beijing's overall regional policy, China has increased its commitment to the South–South Cooperation aid fund of USD 200 million with prioritization of the Mekong area.[15]

---

[12] Lyu Jian, "Increase Cooperation 'Will Benefit Lancang–Mekong Inhabitants'," *The Nation*, February 2, 2018, http://www.nationmultimedia.com/detail/opinion/30337771.

[13] Samdech Akka Moha Sena Padei Techo Hun Sen, "Opening Remarks of Samdech Akka Moha Sena Padei Techo Hun Sen, Prime Minister of the Kingdom of Cambodia and Co-Chair of the 2nd MLC Leaders' Meeting," January 10, 2018, http://pressocm.gov.kh/en/archives/22449.

[14] "Opening Remark by Ambassador Pou Sothirak, Executive Director of the Cambodian Institute for Cooperation and Peace (CICP)," during the Launching Ceremony of the Global Center for Mekong Studies (GCMS), Phnom Penh, Cambodia Center, June 8, 2018.

[15] "Breaking the Deadlock," *News China*, March 6, 2018, http://www.news chinamag.com/newschina/articleDetail.do?article_id=3286&section_id=34&magazine_id=2.

The following are the second-batch projects that have been approved for Cambodia.

(1) Supporting Program for Scholarship Opportunities for Poor Students to Study in the Field of Telecommunication Engineering in China.
(2) The LMC Training Program on Project Management and Sectoral Development of Key Priority Areas.
(3) Poverty Reduction through Rural Economic Development in Cambodia (Phase II).
(4) Integrated Community Development along the Mekong River (Phase II).
(5) Interfaith Dialogue on Sustainable Peace and Development in the Countries along Mekong River (Mekong–Lancang Cooperation).
(6) Mekong–Lancang on Interpreting Natural and Cultural Heritage toward Quality Guiding and Satisfied Tourists-Level I.
(7) Accident Prevention through Cooperation Enhancement in Lancang–Mekong Countries.
(8) Capacity Building for Implementing the National Qualifications Framework (NQF) and Quality Assurance (QA) in Higher Education in Cambodia, Lao PDR, Myanmar and Viet Nam.
(9) Enhancement Capacity Building for Implementing National Protected Area Strategic Management Plan and REDD + Framework in the Lancang–Mekong Sub-Region Countries.
(10) Build Capacity through LMC for Digital Economy.
(11) Mekong–Lancang Cybersecurity Forum and Cyber Drill.
(12) Community-based Transboundary Water and Related Resources Management in the Border Areas of Cambodia and Vietnam and Outreach Experience to the Border Areas of Cambodia and Lao PDR.
(13) The Lancang–Mekong Workshop on Cultural Cooperation Framework.
(14) Harmful Effects of Fake News and Government Action in Dealing with Fake News.
(15) Capacity Development for Sustainable Forest Management in the Lancang–Mekong Economies.

(16) Community Fisheries Co-management: Capacity Building and Sharing Experiences and Lessons Learnt among Mekong Region Member Countries.

(17) Training of Trainers and Lead Auditors for Quality Management Systems (ISO 9001:2015).

(18) Water Diplomacy of the Mekong Basin: Toward a Shared Basin for Prosperity.

(19) Building Regional Partnership for Higher Education Innovation.

The Fourth LMC Foreign Ministers' Meeting in December 2018 has demonstrated further commitment to make concrete the joint building of the LMC Economic Development Belt, which aims to enhance cross-border production capacity and multi-industrial park cooperation. On its part, Cambodia also suggested to look into the possibility of having the LMC International Secretariat established as a one-stop institutional resource and an effective coordinating body.[16]

Attitude of and Demands from Relevant Stakeholders in Cambodia

As discussed previously, the project-based approach taken by LMC has been consistent with Cambodia's national development plan and industrial development plans. This consistency is absolutely necessary in order to ensure that LMC meets the "on the ground" needs of the kingdom as it develops. At the same time, LMC's efforts to fill the funding gaps across multiple areas have resulted in a generally positive view of the initiative from a broader development community in Cambodia. Framing the LMC as an initiative with concrete, measurable results rather than a primary forum for discussion and dialogue has certainly been a step in the right direction as regards gaining support for the initiative in Cambodia and across the sub-region as a

---

[16] Sim Vireak, "Mapping Mekong Cooperation Complementarities and Policy Implications," *Khmer Times*, June 17, 2019, https://www.khmertimeskh.com/506 14730/mapping-mekong-cooperation-complementarities-and-policy-implications/.

whole. Moreover, there are clear positive externalities as regards perceptions of the LMC in light of the provision of capacity-building and training initiatives for Cambodian citizens both in the kingdom as well as in China.

At the same time, three more complicated issues remain to be resolved in order to better facilitate "buy in" from local stakeholders across a wide variety of sectors. First, the lack of concrete mechanisms for cooperation (coordination mechanism) with other donors and sub-region-wide development institutions limits positive evaluation of the program by development stakeholders in the kingdom who are simply unaware of the LMC program and how it may complement their own initiatives. The absence of clear coordination mechanisms leaves the LMC open to criticism including lack of adherence to the development of best practices and the sort of critiques/suspicions discussed previously. Such shortcomings could also provoke fears or risk a backlash with other major powers such as Japan, the U.S. and other countries that have interests in the Greater Mekong area. This is a key challenge for Beijing as it seeks to incorporate the LMC into its larger BRI.

Second, the absence of full transparency and accountability with regard to project development, implementation, monitoring and evaluation results in a significant lost opportunity for the promotion of LMC initiatives and the highlighting of the holistic benefits gained for Cambodia through participation in these initiatives. Absent from such transparency and accountability, local analysts, media and academics are unable to be brought into the process as these individuals simply do not have the requisite data in order to evaluate and explore the effects of LMC in Cambodia. This will remain a significant barrier to the promotion of LMC until it is resolved and leave the mechanism open to criticism by local actors who will compare these negative deficiencies to the approach taken by other sub-regional institutions which are already well established and well known in the region.

Third, the LMC must avoid the tendency to create a perception that its programming is grounded in a model of debt diplomacy or that it creates economic dependency. This perception (as discussed in more detail in what follows) has become widespread among many observers in Cambodia. The absence of a clear, multi-pronged public diplomacy strategy for the LMC continues to result in negative views of the LMC. At the same time, this perception on the part of local stakeholders widens and deepens the existing trust deficit between recipient countries and China.

Challenges Faced by Cambodia in Lancang–Mekong Cooperation

Various drawbacks and challenges need to be seriously considered as the LMC moves forward. First, LMC is still new and young in nature. At this point in time, there exists no clear-cut framework. The three main publicized LMC documents, such as the Sanya Declaration from the First LMC Leaders' Meeting, the Phnom Penh Declaration from the Second LMC Leaders' Meeting and the Five-Year Plan of Action on LMC (2018–2022) all serve as guidelines rather than concrete plans. Second, there is the unequal distribution of projects, which can potentially lead to mechanism dysfunction due to the inadvertent creation of potential mistrust and misunderstanding. Third, limited information and engagement among relevant stakeholders and the public at large remains a problem. The awareness of LMC is still minimal due to the limited disclosure of information, and in-depth project specifications remain unknown.

Another critical challenge is the blurred distinctions between projects listed as derivative from Sino-Cambodia bilateral deals, the LMC and the BRI in projects such as China-invested airports in Siem Reap, Koh Kong and Phnom Penh among others, making cost-benefit analysis and risk assessments difficult. It is also confusing for governmental departments and relevant agencies to provide pragmatic coordination in order to facilitate project implementation. If the current conditions continue, this might not only slow implementation but could also trigger bureaucratic competition for the projects. In addition, one major public concern is the unsustainability of Chinese investment without proper socioeconomic assessment and compensation. China has already gained a bad reputation in Sihanoukville and Bavet, leading to public discontent and social unrest. Even the Chinese Ambassador to Cambodia has acknowledged negative incidents and called for Cambodia's government to take more serious actions against Chinese nationals who violate the country's laws.[17]

There is also an overwhelming concern over potential debt-trap diplomacy, as the large majority of LMC's financial assistance is under the category of concessional and preferential loans, rather than grants. According to the Ministry of Economy and Finance, Cambodia's total foreign debt was USD 9.685 billion in late 2017, of which USD 6.377 billion was borrowed from other countries on a bilateral basis.[18] Of that bilateral debt, China alone owned USD 4.052 billion, or around 63%.[19] Although Cambodia's debt levels remain quite healthy in the context of the country's USD 20 billion GDP last year, this striking figure could have serious implications for Cambodia's foreign policy and territorial integrity. The recent handover of Sri Lanka's strategic Hambantota Port in a 99-year lease to China in exchange for USD 1.12 billion debt repayment has raised many debates and provided lessons for other loan recipients to take into consideration.[20] While the "debt trap" narrative has considerably weakened in recent years and a recent UNDP panel discussion in Phnom Penh had scholars from China and the United States reach consensus that the debt trap issue is not an issue for Cambodia at

---

[17] Hor Kimsay and Bredan O'Byrne, "Chinese Embassy Admits to Issues in Sihanoukville While Lauding Overall Impact of Investment," *The Phnom Penh Post*, February 8, 2018, https://www.phnompenhpost.com/business/chinese-embassy-admits-issues-sihanoukville-while-lauding-overall-impact-investment.

[18] Cambodia, Ministry of Economy and Finance, "Cambodia Public Debt Statistical Bulletin," March 2018, http://www.mef.gov.kh/documents/shares/publication/public-debt-bulletin/Cambodia-Public-Debt%20Statistical-Bulletin-Volume%205.pdf.

[19] *Ibid.*

[20] Reuters Staff, "Sri Lanka Hands Port Formally to Chinese Firm, receives $292M," *Reuters*, December 9, 2017, https://www.reuters.com/article/sri-lanka-china-ports/sri-lanka-hands-port-formally-to-chinese-firm-receives-292-mln-idUSL3N1O908U.

present, the debt trap framing remains salient in the eyes of many stakeholders and the population at large.

Recommendations and Directions for Future Cooperation

In order to drive the LMC forward to become a successful subregional platform that can fuel further growth, build more trust and confidence among its member states and facilitate more positive coexistence with other Mekong mechanisms, the following proposals should be considered:

- The LMC, being a relative newcomer, should engage in mutual and transparent collaboration with the Mekong River Commission, the GSM, ASEAN and other initiatives focused on the development of the Mekong river basin to mitigate the negative environmental, social and financial impacts that could hamper the development of greater prosperity in the region.
- The rule of cooperation among the six member states should be made clear and creative in order to attract other external actors by leveraging LMC to wield greater influence in the region amid growing interest from other regional actors, such as the Japanese-led Mekong cooperation initiative or the U.S.-led Lower Mekong Initiative. Thereby, the LMC can look forward to playing a more active and positive role in water resources management and cooperation in the region, making other powers more receptive to China's growing role in regional affairs.
- The third pillar of the LMC framework on "Cultural and People-to-People Exchanges" should be prioritized.
- The LMC should prioritize grants over loans, especially in the aspect of human capital and production-capacity development.
- More careful socioeconomic assessments should be made by LMC donors and investors.
- Accurate information on the specifications of each project should be publicized with much greater transparency than at present.

- Relevant ministerial stakeholders should intensify their efforts to create a comprehensive LMC website to serve as an information-sharing platform for public consumption.
- Greater emphasis should be placed on coordination efforts of dual-track diplomacy between Track I and Track II with relevant governmental agencies and departments working on Mekong-related issues.

© 2021 World Scientific Publishing Company
https://doi.org/10.1142/9789811234316_0002

Chapter

2

The Belt and Road Initiatives and the Master Plan on ASEAN Connectivity 2025: Connecting the Dots, Integrating the Region

Pich Charadine

*Cambodian Institute for Cooperation and Peace (CICP),
Phnom Penh, Cambodia*
*Global Center for Mekong Studies
(GCMS-Cambodia Center), Phnom Penh, Cambodia*

Introduction

Geographically, the Association of Southeast Asian Nations (ASEAN) comprises the peninsula states (Cambodia, Laos, Myanmar, Thailand and Vietnam) and the maritime states (Brunei, Indonesia, Malaysia, the Philippines and Singapore). Economically, the region of Southeast Asia is divided into two tiers where Brunei, Indonesia, Malaysia, the Philippines, Singapore and Thailand occupy the first tier with higher economic development whereas Cambodia, Laos, Myanmar and Vietnam reside in the second tier bearing the less-developed status. Despite the diversity in cultures, customs and traditions, ASEAN has embraced the inter-regional connectivity mechanisms, initiatives and partnerships to enhance the economic, political and socio-cultural cooperation of the region.

In 2016, striving to stimulate a closer regional integration, ASEAN adopted the Master Plan on ASEAN Connectivity (MPAC) 2025, which serves as a strategic document and plan of action to enhance the region's physical infrastructure, institutions and people-to-people relations.[1] The development of the MPAC has highlighted the need to contribute toward a more connected, competitive and resilient ASEAN as it brings communities, services and capitals closer together as envisioned in the ASEAN Charter. The primary challenge though is the demand for enormous financial resources and the coordination of institutional mechanisms.

In recent years, China has launched its most ambitious development scheme — the Belt and Road Initiative (BRI), which entails five focal key points, including policy coordination, infrastructure construction, unimpeded trade, financial integration and people-to-people bond.[2] It further rests on three main pillars, including utilizing the industrial capacity, encouraging a network of economic interdependence, and fostering regional stability and prosperity.[3] The BRI also emphasizes the logistics and transport networks, using roads, seaports, railway trails, pipelines, airports, transnational electric grid and fiber optic lines. ASEAN is a strategic location for implementing the BRI since all ASEAN member states have already signed up

---

[1] ASEAN, *Master Plan on ASEAN Connectivity* (Jakarta: ASEAN Secretariat, 2016), accessed on November 7, 2019.

[2] "Vision and Actions on Jointly Building Silk Road Economic Belt and 21st-Century Maritime Silk Road," Embassy of the PRC in the Republic Azerbaijan, March 30, 2015, accessed on August 5, 2018, http://en.ndrc.gov.cn/newsrelease/201503/t20150330_669367.html.

[3] Vannarith Chheang, "Cambodia Embraces China's Belt and Road Initiative," *ISEAS Perspective*, no. 48 (2017).

for this initiative.[4] The MPAC 2025 emphasizes five strategic areas: sustainable infrastructure, digital innovation, seamless logistics, regulatory excellence and people mobility.[5] The concurrent existence of the MPAC 2025 and the BRI is the ideal complementarity to further explore the prospective regional connectivity and beyond.

This chapter will layout the discussion on the correlations between the BRI and the MPAC with regards to its opportunities, challenges and some policy recommendations of how to move beyond the past setbacks.

BRI and MPAC: Contemplation of Opportunities

The BRI and MPAC strategies are paralleled in the effort to strengthen cooperation, interconnectivity, sustainable infrastructure and regional supply chains. On the one hand, the shared objectives make ASEAN a great development partner for China's BRI; and for China, the MPAC is a great example of how the utilization of the BRI's strategy can support region-wide connectivity and beyond. China and ASEAN partnership kickstarted in 2003 and has since flourished into a multitude of opportunities for each member state and ASEAN at large. During the 21st ASEAN–China Summit in 2018, the ASEAN–China Strategic Partnership Vision 2030 was adopted, elevating the relation to a new height on all fronts: economically, politically and socially. The 16-year strategic partnership between ASEAN and China has extended to joint maritime and military exercises, a network of cooperative organizations spanning cultural, economic and political concerns. Economically, China and ASEAN have already created a platform through which the ASEAN–China Free Trade Area (FTA) would prosper. In the first half of 2019, ASEAN was China's second largest trading partner. All of these

---

[4] China's State Information Center, *Belt and Road Big Data Report 2017* (Beijing: CSIC, 2017).
[5] ASEAN, *Master Plan on ASEAN Connectivity* (Jakarta: ASEAN Secretariat, 2016), accessed on November 7, 2019.

engagements have created a diverse means for an initiative like the BRI to be comprehensively integrated into ASEAN.

Looking primarily into China's BRI prospects, President Xi Jinping looks at the initiative as a core foreign policy to elevate China's global power projection, which will enhance China's political identity and expand its economic outreach globally. With efficient allocation of resources, greater market integration, better policy coordination and cohesive regional cooperation, the BRI has the potential to become a very successful 21st Century Maritime Silk Road.[6] Historically, connectivity has been interpreted as economic mastery, but looking at the BRI, the proposed connectivity would utilize infrastructure development, trade, investment zones and concrete development projects. The five focal points that the BRI has proposed indeed align with that of the MPAC. By bridging the two initiatives, both actors are then able to strengthen collaborative dialogue, joint contribution and mutual benefits.

At ASEAN's current stage, the regional organization has fallen short in all-round member state infrastructural development of which the total spending accounts for only about USD 55 billion. Southeast Asia would require USD 157 billion annually to cope up with the demands, leaving an infrastructure gap of USD 102 billion. In a recent ADB report entitled "Meeting Asia's Infrastructure Needs", approximately USD 3 trillion is expected to be required between 2016 and 2030 for infrastructure investment across the region.[7] With this huge deficit, ASEAN member states have looked up to China as a key development partner. Overall, the investments have been fortuitous in some capacities, but on the flipside, they have created an increasing debt burden for the recipient countries. From this experience, the MPAC stakeholders question the reliability and validity of the opportunities that BRI–MPAC partnership has to offer. Hence,

---

[6] P. Sothirak, *China's Belt and Road Cooperation with ASEAN and Cambodia* (Phnom Penh: Selected CICP Publications 2016), 15–20.

[7] "Financing ASEAN's Infrastructure Demand," *The ASEAN Post*, July 15, 2018, https://theaseanpost.com/article/financing-aseans-infrastructure-demand.

the feasibility to proceed has been undertaken with cautious and strategic planning to ensure its sustainability aspects. Nevertheless, major progresses have already been made between the two sides such as an Expressway from Phnom Penh to Sihanoukville, Thailand–China Railway (Phase II), China–Singapore New International Land-Sea Trade Corridor, Jakarta–Bandung High-Speed Rail, Laos–China Railway and the Light Rail Project in Hanoi.[8]

While the BRI and MPAC are both opening up some of the remote and economically underdeveloped Chinese provinces to be connected to Southeast Asia region, there is also the anticipation that this partnership attempts to expedite the internationalization of the RMB.[9] While the BRI's short-term implication of the RMB is rather limited, toward the completion of the BRI projects, the bilateral and multilateral trade and investments would create further internationalization of RMB in the foreign markets in the long run.[10]

Competitiveness of ASEAN is something that the region has strived for in order to become a prominent organization in the international arena. With competitiveness comes an increase in trade opportunities; it is therefore expected that the total merchandise trade of ASEAN will increase from it being the sixth largest economy in the world to the fourth by 2050.[11] ASEAN also has benefited largely from its maritime share of the main global trade route as 90% of the global trade is shipped through this area annually. For China, ASEAN has long served as an alternative transport route for its landlocked provinces. With standardized trade regulations, many of the ASEAN member states will strengthen the reliability of regional supply chains, enhanced trade routes and increased industrial competitiveness.

---

[8] "Friendship the Way Forward for ASEAN–China Ties," *The Bangkok Post*, July 30, 2019, https://www.bangkokpost.com/opinion/opinion/1721187/friendship-the-way-forward-for-asean-china-ties.

[9] HSBC, *Belt, Road and Beyond: Understanding The BRI Opportunity* (Hong Kong: HSBC, 2018).

[10] CIMB ASEAN Research Institute, *China's Belt and Road Initiative and Southeast Asia* (Kuala Lumpur: CIMB, 2018).

[11] *Ibid.*

The World Bank Group estimates that if fully implemented, the BRI projects would facilitate the increase of global trade from 1.7% to 6.2%, thereby possibly increasing global real income by 0.7% to 2.9%.[12] While China and ASEAN have been two-way beneficiary trade partners for years, the BRI has opened up ASEAN's connectivity to regions and countries that were previously not in connection. The BRI connects on a transcontinental scale; connectivity not only boosts regional opportunities but also offers a host of opportunities to Central Asia, South Asia, Africa and European countries.

In this connection, China and ASEAN have already strengthened their collaboration in financial integration and dialogue. The China–ASEAN Investment Cooperation Fund (CAF) was founded in 2010, as a USD-dominated offshore quasi-sovereign equity fund sponsored by the Export–Import Bank of China. In the last 9 years, CAF has enhanced cooperation in infrastructure, energy and natural resources. This fund has been integral to the coalition efforts between the BRI and the MPAC through investment schemes on different projects in Thailand and the Philippines. With the BRI, ASEAN will be able to achieve immense infrastructure developments. The MPAC has already proposed several infrastructure projects, including ASEAN highway network, Singapore–Kunming Rail Link, the ASEAN Power Grid and the Trans-ASEAN Gas Pipelines. If completed, transportation development projects, like Vientiane–Boten Railway and Gemas–Johor Bharu land bridges, will facilitate the export of goods from ASEAN to China and Europe, respectively.[13] Additionally, completion of the Vientiane–Kunming Railway will alleviate the reliability of by-sea trade. In these aforementioned instances, the BRI's pillar of regional connectivity would provide an opportunity for these projects to be completed. More recently, the BRI's fund has been focused on the Bandung high-speed rail project (USD 5.5 billion investment).

---

[12] World Bank Group, *"Opportunities And Risks of Transport Corridors"* Belt And Road Economics (Washington: WBG, 2019).

[13] CIMB ASEAN Research Institute, *China's Belt and Road Initiative and Southeast Asia* (Kuala Lumpur: CIMB, 2018).

Although the initial BRI projects were focused on the development of physical infrastructure, which has certainly attracted more investments in manufacturing, energy and service industries from regional connectivity, it has also further enhanced people-to-people connectivity visibly through the tourism sector as the Southeast Asian region has since become a top tourist destination for the Chinese and international tourists. Physical infrastructure is vital to the movement of tourism and cultural exchanges of which roughly around 57 million tourists travel between ASEAN and China and almost 4,000 shuttle flights every week.[14]

As stated in the joint statement on synergizing the MPAC 2025 and the BRI on 3 November 2019, regional connectivity, peace and stability, economic prosperity and sustainable development will be the fundamental benefits from the BRI–MPAC strategic cooperation.[15] With standardized initiatives across economic, political and cultural connectivity, the BRI opens more dialogues for policy coordination. In order to coordinate appropriate mechanisms to achieve a sustainable BRI, it is essential for ASEAN's regional proximity to create a structure that all member states will be able to comply with. This may include creating new policy, minimizing trade or investment barriers or synergizing the regional regulation.

There are many facets of opportunities that the BRI–MPAC cooperation pillars hold, however, as both the BRI and the MPAC are still works-in-progress, the range of projects and capabilities of the Silk Road Fund and regional connectivity will be of strategic importance. While opportunities that can be contemplated are vast, the ability to have efficient delivery is contingent on the coordinated planning and decision-making, participatory approach, cooperative

---

[14] Huang Xilian, "Friendship the Way Forward for ASEAN–China Ties," *The Bangkok Post*, July 30, 2019. https://www.bangkokpost.com/opinion/opinion/1721187/friendship-the-way-forward-for-asean-china-ties.
[15] ASEAN, "ASEAN–China Joint Statement on synergizing the Master Plan on ASEAN Connectivity (MPAC) 2025 and the Belt and Road Initiative (BRI)," in *Proceedings of the 22nd ASEAN–China Summit* (Bangkok: ASEAN, 2019).

endeavor, mutually beneficial partnership and shared responsibility by stakeholders.[16]

Challenges and Setbacks

Besides the remarkable achievements of connecting the dots between the MPAC and the BRI, there are also a number of challenges that need to be addressed in order to reach the aspired goal. First of all, a number of initiatives and strategies of the MPAC have not yet been implemented on time. As of 2016, there were two strategies out of 19, and 39 initiatives out of 125, that were completed.[17] For example, with regard to the physical connectivity, the strategy of establishing an integrated inland waterway network was initially expected to be finished by 2012, however, it was still not completed in 2016.[18] In terms of institutional connectivity, all initiatives to facilitate the interstate land transportation of passengers have not been completed.[19]

In the case of Mekong countries, issues related to customs clearance are still pending. The paperwork in Cambodia, Laos, Vietnam and Myanmar is costly, and in some countries, the process of running documents takes tons of time.[20] Moreover, with regard to people-to-people connectivity, a few initiatives were finished in May 2016, however the deadline was around 2015.[21] The interaction of understanding in terms of the socio-cultural community in ASEAN is observed to be limited. Across the region, the general awareness about this

---

[16] "The Master Plan on ASEAN Connectivity 2025 Deliverables for 2018 and ASEAN Connectivity Microsite Launched," ASEAN, November 13, 2018, accessed on October 27, 2019. https://asean.org/master-plan-asean-connectivity-2025-deliverables-2018-asean-connectivity-microsite-launched/.

[17] ASEAN, *Master Plan on ASEAN Connectivity* (Jakarta: ASEAN Secretariat, 2016).

[18] *Ibid.*

[19] *Ibid.*

[20] Manabu Fujimura, Achievements, Lesson Learned and Remaining Issued for Further Connectivity in the Mekong Region. *Outcome report of Regional Conference on Mekong-Japan Cooperation: Progress and Challenges since 2015* (Phnom Penh: Cambodian Institute for Cooperation and Peace, 2018), 63–69.

[21] *Op. cit.*, footnote 1.

association, as well as the history and culture of other member states, is still low. The concern that was particularly shared among scholarly communities and expert groups was that the majority of citizens in ASEAN are not even aware of what ASEAN really is. In the case of Cambodia, although there are some lessons on ASEAN in high school curriculums (for social science classes), most of them are not widely elaborated and comprehensive enough. And yet, for those who choose "applied science track", the general knowledge of ASEAN is not included. Many regard the ASEAN issue as pretty much leader-centric (i.e. top-down approach) and hence, the general public does not share the same sense of importance, thereby putting less emphasis on it.

Second, there is still a huge difference in terms of infrastructure development among the ASEAN countries. The degree of infrastructure development in this region is rather mixed. According to a report from the World Economic Forum,[22] the ranking of infrastructure quality of ASEAN member states is in different groupings. Countries like Malaysia and Singapore were ranked around 20 (Malaysia was ranked 22, while Singapore was ranked 26).[23] Thailand, Indonesia and Brunei Darussalam were ranked between 40 and 60.[24] Vietnam was ranked 79, and the rest were ranked between 97 and 110.[25] It seems as though some Southeast Asian countries have got higher quality infrastructure over the years. A report from the United Nations Economic and Social Commission for Asia and the Pacific (UNESCAP) stated that the mixed proposition of the infrastructure quality in Southeast Asia is the result of significant investment over the past years.[26] Therefore, some countries have suffered from limited investment in infrastructure and have to show more effort in order to

---

[22] Klaus Schwab, "The Global Competitiveness Report," *World Economic Forum* (2017).
[23] *Ibid.*
[24] *Ibid.*
[25] *Ibid.*
[26] United Nations Economic and Social Commission for Asia and the Pacific, *Infrastructure Financing Strategies for Sustainable Development in South-East Asia* (Bangkok: UNESC, 2017).

support regional economic growth.[27] This region has to spend around USD 150 billion per year, which accounts for 6% of the GDP, to reach the infrastructure needs for stable development.[28] Currently, the amount of spending is only half of the demand for infrastructure.[29]

Third, domestic politics can pose a considerable risk that can affect the ongoing progress of the projects that have been approved by previous governments. The transition of leaders can halt the implementation of projects. For example, in the case of Malaysia in 2018, after the establishment of the new government under Tun Mahathir Mohamad, two BRI projects on oil pipelines which cost around USD 23 billion were canceled.[30] Those projects were previously approved and handled by Najib Razak's government. It is observed that Mahathir's administration intended to clear the alleged corruption that was caused by Najib's Malaysia Development Berhad. The rise of such a sentiment could potentially stir the internal political atmosphere as well as the investment climate. Like in the case of Indonesia, President Joko Widodo was once accused of selling the country to China after he invited China to invest in Indonesia.[31]

Fourth, the weakness of some countries' laws and regulations has led to public discontent. In some cases, the local authority is unable to interpret the implementation of the projects; therefore, there could be some negative responses from the local communities. As in Indonesia, the land acquisition was one of the main obstacles that had to be resolved properly. For example, the project of Jakarta–Bandung railway, which is mainly sponsored by the China Development Bank, was delayed to mid-2021 due to the slow process of the land

---

[27] *Ibid.*

[28] *Ibid.*

[29] *Ibid.*

[30] Stefania Palma, "Malaysia Cancels China-Backed Pipeline Projects," *Financial Times*, September 10, 2018, https://www.ft.com/content/06a71510-b24a-11e8-99ca-68cf89602132.

[31] Siwage Dharma Negara and Leo Suryadinata, "Jakarta–Bandung High Speed Rail Project: Little Progress, Many Challenges," *ISEAS Perspective*, no. 2 (2018), https://www.iseas.edu.sg/images/pdf/ISEAS_Perspective_2018_2@50.pdf.

acquisition.[32] It is said that the locals demanded a higher price from the project developers.[33] Moreover, there was still doubt over the land ownership as the awareness about land registration was still limited.[34]

It is also important to note that the increasing dependence on China's money has led to massive debt. At first, the MPAC projects were not implemented smoothly due to limited funds. However, after the Chinese BRI came into play, the concern on Chinese dependency has grown. In every ASEAN country, the stock of Chinese investment in all sectors between 2008 and 2018 was not less than USD 5 billion.[35] Malaysia got the most investment from China during this period, with nearly USD 45 billion.[36] Apart from that, some countries, like Cambodia, are in an increasing amount of debt to China. As of June 2019, Cambodia owed nearly USD 5 billion of debt to China, which is equitable to around 40% of its total debt.[37] ASEAN countries therefore have to take into account the degree of over-dependency so that ASEAN–China relations can prosper in a good way over the long run.

Policy Recommendations

It is important to understand the "how" of connecting the dots between ASEAN's MPAC and the Chinese BRI through "sustainable infrastructure" schemes. However, there is still room for improvement

---

[32] *Op. cit.*, footnote 6.
[33] "Jakarta–Bandung Railway Project Plagued by Land Acquisition Trouble," *Indonesia-Investments*, 2017, https://www.indonesia-investments.com/news/todays-headlines/jakarta-bandung-railway-project-plagued-by-land-acquisition-trouble/item8176.
[34] *Ibid.*
[35] Sheith Khidhir, "Malaysia Tells China to Keep it Coming!" *The ASEAN Post*, August 14, 2019, https://theaseanpost.com/article/malaysia-tells-china-keep-it-coming.
[36] *Ibid.*
[37] Ministry of Economics and Finance, *Cambodia Public Debt Statistical Bulletin* (Phnom Penh: MEF, 2019), https://mef.gov.kh/documents/shares/publication/public-debt-bulletin/Cambodia-Public-Debt-Statistical-Bulletin-Volume-8-2019.pdf.

toward a more effective strategy in order to implement the projects. As highlighted in the section on challenges previously, the BRI projects have been delayed, undermanaged and disorganized. This impedes the intricate strategic plan previously developed through numerous dialogues between ASEAN and China stakeholders.

First, relevant department(s) within the ASEAN Secretariat need(s) to be strengthened. More mandates should be allocated to this role in order to have a better and efficient check-and-balance system within the ASEAN regional grouping. ASEAN–China comprehensive dialogue should also be strengthened across different levels in both Tracks I and II, from technical working groups to diplomatic working groups, toward multi-stakeholder engagement, in this regard. If needed and feasible, a dedicated department within the ASEAN Secretariat could be established to facilitate the coordination work in relation to MPAC–BRI cooperation scheme, to ensure the efficiency and accountability of the proposed initiatives and to bring more partners on board.

Second, each respective government has to improve their own institutions in order to attract more foreign direct investment. Some countries in the region have yet to establish a more cohesive taxation system properly, while some have not reached the efficiency due to lack of transparency. First of all, an independent anti-corruption agency is needed in every country to tackle the corruption problem. For example, Indonesia's anti-corruption units are separate from the cabinet, unlike most countries in the region. Secondly, each government has to reform some of their institutions in order to secure transparency and accountability. Moreover, states that have undertaken institutional reform policies need to implement and enforce the policies comprehensively, as well as promote awareness among the general public.

Last but not least, with an effective and/or dedicated department within the ASEAN Secretariat that works on MPAC–BRI partnership on top of the applicable institutional reform progress in each respective country in ASEAN, public–private partnerships (PPPs) should be promoted widely across the region in order to enhance more infrastructural investment to cope with the anticipated demands. ASEAN countries shall share best practices with one another in collaboration with the region's longstanding development partners such as the World Bank and the Asian Development Bank (ADB)[38] while at the same time, strengthening one's regulatory framework and smoothening out the linkages between the private sectors so that the investment climate is deemed financially sustainable (and profitable) in the long run.

---

[38] "ASEAN Needs to Re-think Approach to US$2.8 Trillion Infrastructure Gap," *Standard Chartered*, April 03, 2019, https://www.sc.com/en/feature/asean-needs-to-re-think-approach-to-us2-8-trillion-infrastructure-gap/.

Chapter

3

Connecting the Connectivities of the BRI and MPAC 2025 — Perspective and Analysis by the ASEAN–China Centre

Wang Hongliu

ASEAN–China Centre, Beijing, China

Introduction

Globalization has entered a new phase as the world is going through another round of major development, transformation and adjustment. The economic and social well-being of regional countries are increasingly interconnected, while protectionism and unilateralism are resurging, which makes connecting the connectivities more pressing than ever.

Status Quo of Connecting the Connectivities in the Region

ASEAN covers a region of more than 647 million people with a combined gross domestic product of USD 2.8 trillion. It is located at the heart of a dynamic region with the strategic link between the Pacific and the Indian Oceans as well as the three continents of Asia, Africa and Europe.

Connectivity in the ASEAN context refers to the physical, institutional and people-to-people linkages that would serve as the underpinning and lubricant to achieve the goals and objectives of the economic, political-security and socio-cultural pillars of the ASEAN Community. ASEAN member states (AMS) have long recognized the benefits of enhanced connectivity to them all by promoting greater competitiveness, prosperity, inclusiveness and sense of community since its inception in the spirit of the Bangkok Declaration in 1967. In the past decade, AMS have placed great emphasis on the need to strengthen connectivity in the region and taken a series of major steps toward this end, including adopting the Master Plan on ASEAN Connectivity in 2010 which was succeeded by the Master Plan on ASEAN Connectivity 2025 (MPAC 2025) adopted by ASEAN leaders in 2016.

The MPAC 2025, as an integral part of the *ASEAN 2025: Forging Ahead Together*, serves as a guideline for ASEAN's efforts to enhance connectivity and maps out the blueprint to realize connectivity in sustainable infrastructure, digital innovation, seamless logistics, regulatory excellence and people mobility. The vision for the ASEAN Connectivity 2025 is to achieve a seamlessly and comprehensively connected and integrated ASEAN that will promote competitiveness, inclusiveness and a greater sense of community.

As the Rotating Chair of ASEAN in 2019, Thailand has put "connecting the connectivities" high on the agenda. The Thai leadership stressed on several occasions that connectivity is Thailand's core national policy and that Thailand's priorities will include boosting connectivity in infrastructure, simplifying red tape and people-to-people links to make borders around ASEAN more transparent.

Thanks to the commitment and concerted efforts of AMS and their dialogue partners, notable progress has been made on connecting the connectivities in the region. However, much remains to be done to realize the vision of a seamlessly connected ASEAN. For the physical connectivity, the challenges that need to be addressed in the region include improving quality of roads, enhancing air connectivity, completing road networks and linking railways, updating maritime and port infrastructure, narrowing the digital divide, and satisfying the growing energy demand.

On the part of China, Chinese President Xi Jinping put forward the initiative to jointly build the Silk Road Economic Belt and the 21st Century Maritime Silk Road (BRI) during his visit to Kazakhstan and Indonesia in 2013, which is based on the principle of "achieving shared growth through discussions and collaboration". On the Second Belt and Road Forum (BRF) for International Cooperation, the leaders of the countries engaged in BRI envisaged high-quality cooperation in enhancing connectivity by promoting development policy synergy, infrastructure development, unimpeded trade, financial cooperation and people-to-people bond, thereby enhancing practical cooperation for the well-being of all people.

As connectivity also includes areas of policy, trade, finance and people-to-people exchanges both in ASEAN and China, this chapter will mainly focus on infrastructure connectivity and touch upon other areas when necessary.

Both AMS and China have recognized the fact that strengthening connectivity needs long-term and enormous inputs, but it will benefit the development of regional economies and help forge the sense of a shared future. Therefore, in the ASEAN–China Strategic Partnership Vision 2030, the two sides agreed to strengthen the strategic partnership with mutually beneficial cooperation on ASEAN integration and community building, including through capacity building and resource mobilization, synergizing common priorities in the MPAC 2025 and BRI, as part of efforts to synergize the various connectivity strategies in the region in a manner that would be mutually beneficial. At the same time, the BRI is coordinating with the development plans of each and every ASEAN country.

Gratifying results have been achieved in the joint efforts of ASEAN and China on BRI cooperation, especially in the joint building of the 21st Century Maritime Silk Road, in which AMS and China have a strong desire and reached many consensuses.

For instance, Thailand and China have launched joint projects in support of the building of the Eastern Economic Corridor (EEC).

Vietnam and China are focusing on aligning the BRI with the "Two Corridors and One Economic Circle" plan. Both Indonesia and China believe that the BRI is highly compatible with Indonesia's Poros Maritim Dunia (Global Maritime Axis) Strategy and have reached important consensus on synergizing the two development strategies and deepening practical cooperation across the board. The Philippines and China have expressed the readiness to align the Initiative with Ambisyon Natin 2040 (National Ambition 2040). China has also signed MoUs with Cambodia, Lao PDR and other AMS on making relevant cooperation plans. In Vision 2030, the two sides reaffirmed their commitment to enhancing connectivity cooperation, including encouraging airlines from both AMS and China to tap their full potential by utilizing the ASEAN–China Air Transport Agreement (AC-ATA) and its Protocols I and II so as to realize stronger regional connectivity and to work toward the ultimate goal of the full liberalization of the ASEAN–China Air Services regime.

Moreover, notable progress has been made in cooperation projects. Intergovernmental exchange mechanisms at various levels are taking shape. A large number of infrastructure projects, high-speed railways in particular, have been launched.

The digital economy is a new area for cooperation between AMS and China. In Vision 2030, ASEAN and China agree to strengthen physical and institutional connectivity to bring markets closer in line with the strategic objectives in MPAC 2025, as well as improve digital connectivity, including through supporting the implementation of ASEAN ICT Master Plan 2020. China has envisioned a digital Silk Road, that is, to use the digital economy as a key driving force to promote openness, cooperation, communication and sharing of cyberspace. Thailand is working with China's e-commerce pioneer Alibaba to establish a Smart Digital Hub in its EEC project to optimize the cross-border flow of goods between Thailand and other AMS. Malaysia is also working with Alibaba to establish a digital free trade zone. China and ASEAN have also been carrying out more and more cooperation in building smart cities in the region.

In the past decade, the urgency and necessity of accelerating the connecting of connectivities have risen. The world economy is going through profound adjustments, with protectionism and unilateralism resurging, so multilateralism and the system of free trade are under threat.

In this context, it is important to bolster confidence in the future through opening-up and cooperation, and to turn the demands and the willingness of cooperation of all parties into reality to deliver more benefits to the people in the region.

Advantages and Challenges of Connecting the Connectivities in the Region

Advantages

First, AMS generally enjoy political stability and attach importance to economic development.

On the one hand, although AMS have notable differences in religion, language, culture and political background, ASEAN has maintained stable development for many years as a regional organization, which contributes to political stability in Southeast Asia.

On the other hand, as a regional organization with economic cooperation as its core, ASEAN has maintained relatively rapid economic growth and enjoys fast development of trade and investment cooperation with China. China remains ASEAN's largest trading partner for 10 consecutive years. The two-way direct investment has reached a total of over USD 200 billion.

Second, with a time-honored history of mutual exchanges, AMS and China highly value each other's friendship and cooperation. The two sides have maintained frequent high-level exchanges and enjoy a smooth channel for policy coordination. As the mutual visits between ASEAN and China reached 55 million in 2018, both sides are keen to strengthen the interconnection toward a higher level. China is also willing to facilitate larger access to the markets along the route for its strategic partner, ASEAN.

Third, thanks to the joint efforts of AMS and China, significant progress has been made in connecting the connectivities. China's domestic highways leading to Southeast Asia have all reached first-grade standards and above. The Thailand–China railway is the flagship project in bilateral infrastructure cooperation. The Laos–China railway has started construction. The Jakarta–Bandung high-speed railway in Indonesia is also gaining momentum. The "Two Countries, Twin Parks", namely China–Malaysia Qinzhou Industrial Park and Malaysia–China Kuantan Industrial Park, Cambodia Sihanoukville Special Economic Zone, the Rayong Industrial Park jointly developed by Thai and Chinese enterprises and several industrial parks between China and Vietnam, the Lao PDR and Indonesia have all made steady headway. The Myanmar–China oil and gas pipelines, the Laos–China, Vietnam–China, Myanmar–China power grids, Laos–China, Myanmar–China cross-border international optical cables have been built up and benefited the people all along. Water transportation projects including the Lancang–Mekong Navigation Channel, Beibu Gulf Port and the Kyaukpyu Special Economic Zone have entered a new phase of joint development. The New International Land-Sea Trade Corridor, under the framework of the China–Singapore (Chongqing) Demonstration Initiative on Strategic Connectivity, has linked 155 ports to 71 countries and regions worldwide, better connecting the BRI and AMS's development.

Fourth, ASEAN and China enjoy the most full-fledged mechanisms for cooperation on interconnection in the region, as both sides share a strong desire to connect the connectivities so as to benefit from each other's large market. Several facilitating mechanisms and regular consultation mechanisms have been established, which are featured by good planning, transparency and accountability.

Over the years, the ASEAN–China framework has proved to be an effective mechanism for leaders of both sides to share their insights of common development and yield fruitful results on deepening practical cooperation. Platforms like ASEAN–China Trade and Economic Ministers' Meeting, Transport Ministers' Meeting, Finance Ministers' Meeting, China–ASEAN EXPO, China–ASEAN Education Cooperation Week and so on serve as well-established channels to bring together major players of both sides to conduct exchanges, make cooperation plans and produce fruitful outcomes in various areas.

ASEAN and China have already signed a series of multilateral agreements on infrastructure connectivity, including the *Connectivity*

Blueprint and *Plan of Action to Implement the Joint Declaration on ASEAN–China Strategic Partnership for Peace and Prosperity (2016 to 2020)*. The two sides have also set up several financing channels, including China–ASEAN Investment Cooperation Fund (CAF), Asian Infrastructure Investment Bank (AIIB), the Silk Road Fund as well as experimental zones for comprehensive financial reform.

In addition, as the upgraded version of ASEAN–China Free Trade Agreement (ACFTA) has taken effect and the Lancang–Mekong and China–BIMP–EAGA (the Brunei Darussalam–Indonesia–Malaysia– the Philippines East ASEAN Growth Area) Cooperation Mechanisms are making steady progress, the path of cooperation between ASEAN and China will become wider, thus making a greater contribution to regional development.

Challenges

First, development level varies among different member states of ASEAN. There are wide disparities in economic development level, political system, ethnicity, religion and culture.

Second, some AMS and China adopt different rules for traffic and customs clearance, which are not easy to unify. For instance, in Cambodia, China, Lao PDR, Myanmar, the Philippines and Vietnam, vehicles keep to the right-hand side of the road, while in Brunei, Indonesia, Malaysia, Thailand and Singapore, it is the opposite, which makes cross-border driving potentially dangerous. The low-level implementation of the Agreement on the Recognition of Domestic Driving Licenses issued by ASEAN Countries also hinders the flow of people across ASEAN. Technical bottlenecks need to be addressed in order to make connectivity more practical.

Third, some Chinese-funded infrastructure projects have encountered obstacles during construction in some AMS. Some projects were or have been delayed due to the host country's policy adjustments.

Fourth, funding shortage still threatens the implementation of the proposed or even existing projects.

Fifth, there is always doubt or worries about the BRI and China's intention among the local community of AMS.

There are other disturbing factors, including the current international trade environment, the influence of domestic politics and non-traditional security threats.

However, in spite of the aforementioned challenges and the fact that the balance of major powers in the world and the region is undergoing changes, China stands firm to uphold multilateralism and has full confidence in the future of ASEAN.

Suggestions on Connecting the Connectivities in the Region

Thanks to the mutual understanding and efforts by both sides, ASEAN–China cooperation has become the most successful and dynamic model in the Asia-Pacific region. The Chinese government has all along attached great significance to developing friendly exchanges with ASEAN by supporting ASEAN's centrality in East Asian cooperation and deepening practical cooperation.

While addressing the 21st ASEAN–China Summit in November 2018, Chinese Premier Li Keqiang stated that the past 15 years have been a momentous journey for China–ASEAN relations. In 2003, China became the first country to establish a strategic partnership with ASEAN. Over these 15 years, China and ASEAN have engaged in all-round, multi-tiered and wide-ranging cooperation which has delivered bountiful outcomes. China–ASEAN relationship now enjoys tremendous vitality and bright prospects.

China has always supported ASEAN community building, with the aim of pursuing common development in the region by joining hands with all stakeholders of ASEAN to press ahead in the cause of connecting the connectivities. To address the aforementioned challenges and maintain a sustainable development of ASEAN–China relations, some keywords are offered herewith, such as green, mutual beneficial, common development, multilateralism, capacity building, resource mobilization, standardization and digital economy tailored to each AMS.

The goal of connecting the connectivities could boost regional development in a win–win, coordinated and inclusive manner.

Connectivity and win–win cooperation have become the strongest voices of the times. Synergizing the connectivity initiatives between ASEAN and China is aimed at achieving an all-round, cross-sector and systematic interconnection network, which should be compatible with the development strategies of all parties.

It should be conducive to tapping the potential of regional markets, attracting investment, creating demand and consumption, enhancing people-to-people affinity and mutual appreciation, which will lead to better interconnectivity and a stronger and more united community of ASEAN itself.

Major concepts of connecting the connectivities

First, there are basic principles for connecting the connectivities, which include prioritizing infrastructure projects to deliver tangible benefits to the people, applying standardization, utilizing new technologies and new industries and encouraging people-to-people exchanges.

Second, as proposed by China, the ASEAN–China cooperation always welcomes the participation from other parties on the basis of full respect toward ASEAN's centrality. In view of the ever-increasing investment from other major players such as the U.S., Russia, India, Japan, the Republic of Korea and Australia, it is encouraged to advance small-scale trilateral or multilateral cooperation. Undoubtedly the people of the region have the right in choosing the most appropriate models of cooperation and paths for future development of their own will, and all the cooperation should benefit the region as a whole.

Third, the BRI is conducive to a win–win outcome. China pays close attention to the green economy, sustainable development and people-oriented projects in pursing development and cooperation while emphasizing people-to-people exchanges. The connectivity projects proposed by China highlight high quality and reliability with a view to delivering long-term benefits to the local community. More small-scale projects with tangible benefits for the people should be carried out in tandem with large-scale projects, which could also gain more public support.

Fourth, it is advised to make the best use of the existing subregional cooperation mechanisms. Efforts should be made to build a Lancang–Mekong economic development belt, establish a cooperation framework with the East ASEAN Growth Area (BIMP–EAGA), support ASEAN Community building, and reach the Regional Comprehensive Economic Partnership as soon as possible.

Finally, coordination is necessary between hard and soft projects (infrastructure link driven by people-to-people exchanges), big and small projects (large infrastructure projects and small projects related to people's well-being) as well as long-term and short-term projects, so as to have a reinforcing effect in an equal, two-way and win–win manner.

Key points to facilitate connecting the connectivities

All relevant parties should implement the consensus reached by leaders of regional countries and try to achieve early harvest. The authorities of AMS and China share the same vision for regional development by embracing win–win cooperation and rule-based free trade while pursuing green and sustainable development models.

First, platforms and channels for deepening ASEAN–China friendly exchanges should be fully utilized with appropriate coordination mechanisms to achieve the utmost effect.

It is necessary for ASEAN to allocate the resources of its member states with proper internal planning and coordination, so as to enhance the compatibility of connectivity projects. From a long-term perspective, ASEAN and China should also consider updating the present coordination mechanism (ASEAN–China Connectivity Cooperation Committee) to a higher level or hold its meetings in combination with important events, the BRF for example.

Second, efforts should be made to expand financing channels by making good use of governmental funds, absorbing social capital from private sectors and strengthening international cooperation.

It is always necessary to seek support from governmental and organizational sources like the China–ASEAN Investment Corporation Fund, the ASEAN Infrastructure Fund, the Silk Road Fund and the

Asian Infrastructure Investment Bank to partially cover the expenses of connectivity projects. At the same time, sub-regional cooperation sources such as the Lancang–Mekong Cooperation Fund could be used to develop projects that could benefit the local people. It is also suggested to make more efforts to raise the awareness and transparency in facilitating the application of the present funds.

It is equally important to attract private capital on a market-oriented basis and ensure the benefits of investors so as to explore multiple channels of raising social funds. It is also proposed to explore ways to work collaboratively with major international players like the World Bank and the United Nations Development Programme to address the funding gap.

A sound portfolio of financing resources demands a proper combination of various channels, public and private, domestic and international, old and new, while jointly exploring ways to increase access to these resources.

Third, unified regulations and technical standards need to be in place, which holds the key to cross-border flow of goods, services and personnel and the implementation of connectivity projects.

Standards should be tailored to the needs of various industries with due emphasis on environmental assessment and trade clearance, embodying the common concepts of "green, sustainable, people's well-being, inclusiveness and coordination". All parties should speed up discussions, reach a consensus and act together in the region so as to maximize the efficiency of cooperation and eliminate technical barriers. Import and export procedures at the customs could be simplified and an inclusive mode of customs clearance should be established, based on mutual recognition of each other's inspection and supervision regulations. It is also important to make cross-border travel seamless through enabling border control policies and procedures. Pre-planning of the connectivity projects should be strengthened and an information and service platform for the standardization of ASEAN–China cooperation should be set up.

Fourth, an innovation-driven strategy should be adopted to increase ASEAN–China cooperation across the board and upgrade the level of management and services.

With the far-reaching worldwide industrial transformation and the rapid development of the global digital economy, new technologies, new industries, new formats and new models have opened up broad prospects for sectoral collaboration as well as social and economic development. It is proposed for ASEAN and China to ride on the momentum of Industrial Revolution 4.0 and jointly work on connectivity projects to upgrade hardware and software facilities by resorting to technological advances. Both sides should also tap into new business models as stimulated by the digital economy and collaborate on projects of mutual interest. Besides, it is necessary to encourage mass innovation and entrepreneurship especially among the youth and channel more innovative human resources to the projects related to people's well-being, which will invigorate vitality to infrastructure development and high-standard connectivity. It is also advised to promote Authorized Economic Operator (AEO) mutual recognition and cooperation between ASEAN and China and explore innovative ways such as Big Data and Cloud technologies to support the development of new trade formats, especially cross-border e-commerce.

Fifth, it is equally important to strengthen ASEAN–China people-to-people exchanges.

People-to-people exchanges serve as an indispensable link to enhance understanding and deepen trust and friendship among people of different countries. It is highly significant to support people-to-people connectivity by giving full play to the role of universities, think tanks, media, cultural and artistic centers, tourist agencies as well as non-governmental organizations.

To this end, both sides should explore ways to promote visa application facilitation in a bid to increase mutual visits. Efforts should be stepped up to promote tourist destinations of ASEAN and China for the peoples of both sides and produce more high-quality tourism products with proper management and supervision mechanisms, thus providing continuous confidence and vitality to the tourism market. In view of the fundamental role that education plays in people-to-people exchanges, it is advised for ASEAN and China to strengthen information sharing, which will be conducive to increasing two-way students' mobility. Efforts should be made on further promoting intercollegiate networking and cooperation in both technical and vocational education and training (TVET) and higher education in support of talent cultivation and training. It is also proposed to increase friendly exchanges to promote mutual cultural appreciation and set up more platforms to facilitate collaboration in the cultural industry.

Sixth, the focus should also be put on sustainable development and green connectivity.

At present, a majority of countries in this region face the challenge of fragile ecosystems and are vulnerable to climate changes. Joint efforts should be exerted to strengthen consensus on low-carbon and climate-resilient development among AMS, narrow current gaps in addressing climate change challenges, support low-carbon development in the region meanwhile maintaining an expanding energy supply to meet the needs of rapidly developing economies.

Last but not least, publicity should be enhanced to rally social consensus and enhance people's participation in interconnectivity.

In this region, there is a far-reaching impact in initiating collaborative projects in infrastructure, education, culture and tourism, with the improvement of transportation and hardware facilities, increased job opportunities, more access to high-quality education and benefits brought by new technologies and innovations. It is true that relevant parties need to formulate a mechanism of benefit distribution, followed by discussions on issues of mutual concern. Positive guidance must be in place so that people can realize that the long-term benefits harvested through interconnectivity far outweigh some possible short-term compromises. The strong role of the governments is necessary to raise the awareness of the people so that they could realize the importance of connectivities in the region.

Programs for Connecting the Connectivities

On Connecting the Connectivities, the ASEAN–China Centre (ACC) is willing to play its role as an activities center, a promo platform and a one-stop Information Centre.

(a) Participating in the NACT Working Group Meeting on Regional Connectivity and Sustainability — Connecting the BRI and MPAC 2025 with the purpose of enhancing the synergy of the two strategies, which was held on April 29–30, 2019 in Langkawi, Malaysia.

(b) Co-hosting the Conference of ASEAN–China Cooperation on Energy Transition and Climate-resilient Development in a bid to explore ways for green connectivity and sustainable development, which was held on August 28–29, 2019 in Bangkok, Thailand.

(c) Attended the Dialogue on Joint Building of the New International Land-Sea Trade Corridor for Strategic Connectivity and an Expert Meeting, aiming at attracting investment to advance the development of the Corridor and the whole region, as a pilot in pursuing connecting the connectivities, which were held on January 8 and May 22, 2019 respectively.

(d) Hosted the Innovation-leading Development: 2019 ASEAN–China Intelligent Industry Conference with the aim of boosting ASEAN–China practical cooperation in intelligent industries along with business matching, which was held on July 25, 2019 in Ho Chi Ming, Vietnam.

(e) Organized ASEAN Smart City Study Visit to Nanning and Guangzhou and held China–ASEAN Smart City Cooperation & Exchange Conference in Nanning, to exchange information and strengthen experience sharing in smart society development with AMS governmental officials, which took place on June 24–28, 2019.

(f) Exploring ways to establish an online ASEAN–China university network, which will be an information platform including educational resources and scholarships for the benefit of students of both sides.

(g) Exploring ways to expand channels of financial guarantee for micro, small and medium-sized enterprises to enter into each other's market.

(h) Continuing giving policy advice to relevant parties in AMS and China on connecting the connectivities, based on the work programs' implementation, wide consultation with the scholars from AMS and China, and feedback on various conferences, seminars, workshops, and so on.

Chapter

4

Building Sustainable Regional Connectivity — A Case Study of Railway Projects in Southeast Asia

Luo Yongkun

*Institute of Southeast Asian and Oceanian Studies,
China Institutes of Contemporary International Relations,
Beijing, China*

Introduction

Since China's proposal of the Belt and Road Initiative (BRI) in 2013 and the declaration of the establishment of an ASEAN Community in 2015, connectivity building has become an important part in China and ASEAN cooperation. Based on the Master Plan on ASEAN Connectivity 2025, connectivity in ASEAN encompasses physical (e.g. transport, ICT, and energy), institutional (e.g. trade, investment, and services liberalization), and people-to-people linkages (e.g. education, culture and tourism).[1] For China, connectivity refers to five areas including policy coordination, facilities connectivity, unimpeded trade, financial integration and people-to-people bonds.[2] Generally speaking, China's BRI and ASEAN's Master Plan shared similar interests in terms of connectivity, especially infrastructure building. The requirement for development has led to a great number of infrastructure building projects since 2015. Although the two sides concentrated on infrastructure projects and achieved success, there were many difficulties, internal or external, encountered by China and ASEAN as well, and some of those difficulties posed challenges to regional connectivity cooperation. Therefore, it is high time both China and ASEAN countries worked jointly to build sustainable regional connectivity.

Connectivity Projects in the Region

In the past decades, China and ASEAN countries have worked together to build mega infrastructure projects in Southeast Asia. These projects include constructions of bridges, hydropower stations, railways, highways and seaports. Up till now, some of the projects have been completed, like the bridges from Surabaya to Madura in Indonesia or the expressway from Kunming to Bangkok, but some are still under construction, for example, the Melaka Gateway in Malaysia. The following part of the chapter will focus on the railway projects.

Now there are five important railway projects underway in Southeast Asia. In Thailand, the China–Thailand Railway, which is Thailand's first high-speed railway from Bangkok to Nong Khai, is being built. The first phase which contains part of the railway running from Bangkok to Nakhon Ratchasima, 252 km (157 miles) from the capital, began in December 2017 and this part of the railway will be open in 2021. The built railway in its second phase, which will be

---

[1] The ASEAN Secretariat, *Master Plan on ASEAN Connectivity 2025* (ASEAN: Jakarta, 2016).

[2] National Development and Reform Commission, Ministry of Foreign Affairs, and Ministry of Commerce of the People's Republic of China, *Vision and Actions on Jointly Building Silk Road Economic Belt and 21st-Century Maritime Silk Road* (NDFC: Beijing, 2015).

355 km (221 miles) long, stretching from Nakhon Ratchasima to Nong Khai, is expected to be 85% funded by international loans and slated to be put into use by 2023.[3] Once completed, the 607 km (378 miles) route will connect with the China–Laos railway, linking China, Laos and Thailand.

In Laos, we are building the China–Laos railway. It is a 414 km (257 miles) link between the Yunnan's provincial capital of Kunming and the Laotian capital Vientiane. The construction started in 2016 and now the line is almost half complete, which puts it on schedule to begin service in December 2021. In July 2019, main sections of the 1458.9-meter bridge over Mekong River were completed, which indicates the China–Laos railway project construction has made major progress.[4] It is expected that trains on the line can travel at up to 160 km/hr (100 mph), cutting the traveling time between the two cities to three hours from three days.[5]

In Indonesia, China and Indonesia are jointly building the railway from Jakarta to Bandung, covering a distance of around 140 km with four stations: Halim Perdanakusuma, Karawang, Walini and Tegalluar. The Jakarta–Bandung railway is a project of 60% of Indonesian consortium and 40% of China Railway International.[6] It will take only 45 min to reach Bandung from Jakarta once it is completed in 2021. As of this writing, progress of the physical construction has reached 65.1% and land clearance is already at 81.7%. The project was 55% finished at the

---

[3] Jitsiree Thongnoi, "China Wants to Fund Thailand's US$12 Billion High-Speed Railway — But is the Kingdom on Track for More Debt Than it Can Handle?" *South China Morning Post*, April 24, 2019, accessed on July 29, 2019, https://www.scmp.com/week-asia/geopolitics/article/3007551/china-wants-fund-thailands-us12-billion-high-speed-railway.

[4] "Main Section of China–Laos Railway Bridge Over Mekong River Completed," *Xinhuanet*, July 28, 2019, http://www.xinhuanet.com/english/2019-07/28/c_138264471.htm.

[5] Xie Yu, "China's US$7 Billion Railway Link to Laos is Almost Half Done, on Schedule to Begin Service in 2021," *South China Morning Post*, March 21, 2019, accessed on July 29, 2019, https://www.scmp.com/business/banking-finance/article/3002518/chinas-us7-billion-railway-link-laos-almost-half-done.

[6] "Groundbreaking of High Speed Rail Project Jakarta–Bandung," *Wika. Co*, January 21, 2016, http://www.wika.co.id/detailpost/groundbreaking-of-high-speed-rail-project-jakarta-bandung.

end of 2019. It is very convenient for local Indonesians with the ticket price at about 200,000 rupiah (USD 19) for a one-way trip.

In Malaysia, China and Malaysia are now building two important railways. One is the East Coast Rail Links (ECRL) from Kota Bharu to Port Klang which is 640 km long with double-track line on double-track formation. The project began in August 2017, but it encountered some difficulties when Tun Dr. Mahathir took office in May 2018. Now the two nations have signed a supplementary agreement on the financing for the ECRL. Based on the revised agreement, the ECRL project will be built with an investment of MYR 44 billion (USD 10.7 billion), nearly two-thirds of the original cost. On July 25, 2019, the project restarted. Apart from the ECRL, China now is building another important railway for Malaysia that is the southern double-tracking railway. The railway, from Gemas to Johor Baru at the cost of 8.9 billion ringgit (USD 2.2 billion), is going to be completed in October 2021. The railway project is contracted to China Railway Construction Corporation, China Railway Engineering Corporation and China Communications Construction Company. Up till July 2018, the 197 km track was already 20% in progress.[7]

Challenges and Opportunities for Sustainability

It is without any doubt that the railway projects mentioned earlier are welcomed and supported by Southeast Asian countries because they will bring economic and social benefits to the local people. But, on the other hand, the projects are sometimes criticized by the local governments, local people or some non-governmental organizations because they have concerns about the projects' ill impact on environment, employment and so on. Speaking of the sustainability of the projects, I would like to say these railway projects do meet some challenges.

First of all, the geopolitical or geo-economic environment both internationally and regionally is not conducive to the sustainable

---

[7] "Malaysia's Southern Double-Tracking Railway Project to be Completed in 2021: Transport Minister," *Xinhuanet*, 30, 2018, http://www.xinhuanet.com/english/2018-07/30/c_137357911.htm.

development of these railway projects. Internationally speaking, the relations between China and U.S. have been in tension. The U.S. tried every means to counter China in economic, technological or security fronts. The unstable Sino-U.S. relations make most of the countries in the world concerned. China and its partners are worried about the uncertain changes on infrastructure building projects. For example, will the U.S. disturb or hype up China's BRI or relevant projects specifically? Regionally speaking, at present, more and more countries are involved in the projects in Southeast Asia. Japan, India, Russia, Australia and even some EU countries are very keen to invest in ASEAN countries. Inevitably, the involvement of these countries in the region will bring more competition. Take the Indonesian case, for example. Japan and China were very interested in building high-speed railways from Jakarta to Bandung, which led to fierce competition between the two countries. Indonesia had to make adjustments to the project. At last, the railway from Jakarta to Bandung was offered to China, and the railway from Jakarta to Surabaya to Japan.

Faced with these challenges, we, however, have to admit the international and regional environment are now improving to some extent. China and ASEAN countries can find some opportunities ahead. On the one hand, China and the U.S. have continued the discussion and negotiation on trade issues. At least, China will make great efforts to maintain win–win Sino-U.S. relations. On the other hand, China and countries in the region work very hard to make a peaceful and stable environment for common development and prosperity. China now has discussed with Japan and India to conduct cooperation in the third country. This is a very effective way for big powers in the region to expand their cooperation and common interests, which means China and Japan or India will find cooperative rather than confrontational interests in Southeast Asia. It will be very helpful for China and ASEAN countries to build sustainable regional connectivity.

Secondly, mutual trust between China and ASEAN countries is improving since the past decades, but more trust and confidence are needed to promote sustainable railway construction under BRI. Generally speaking, since 1991, China–ASEAN relations have witnessed a positive international and regional atmosphere. Our cooperation has achieved great success although we faced some problems such as the South China Sea issue and China–U.S. trading friction. The political mutual trust between China and ASEAN or Southeast Asian countries has greatly improved. China established a Strategic Partnership with ASEAN in 2003 and Comprehensive Strategic Partnership with Vietnam, Laos, Cambodia, Myanmar, Thailand, Indonesia and Malaysia after 2008. But with rapid development of China and the ASEAN Community, China and ASEAN are now facing a new problem. When China proposed BRI in 2013, some countries in the region began to criticize the BRI since they thought China had geopolitical intentions. They believed China aimed to get hegemonic control by virtue of the BRI. Some countries even worried China would expand its military force in the world. For example, Indonesian media *Kompas* commented that China's BRI was a platform for hegemony.[8] In fact, similar perceptions were quite popular in Southeast Asia, which showed that mutual trust should be further enhanced. Otherwise, the lack of trust and confidence will disturb China and ASEAN mega infrastructure cooperation, like railway projects.

Fortunately, in the past two years, with the progress of relations between ASEAN and China, the situation has improved. In 2019, all leaders from ASEAN countries came to China to attend the Second BRI Forum for International Cooperation. They were eager to strengthen economic cooperation with China. Indonesian President Joko Widodo had proposed the establishment of special low-interest funds to facilitate Chinese investment in Indonesia for four investment corridors within the framework of the BRI when he met with his Chinese counterpart Xi Jinping at the G20 Summit in Osaka.[9] In fact, most of the Southeast Asian countries shared similar

---

[8] "Hegemoni Satu Jalan Satu Sabuk," *Kompas*, November 30, 2014, https://money.kompas.com/read/2014/11/30/073200926/Hegemoni.Satu.Jalan.Satu.Sabuk.

[9] "Indonesia Proposes Special Fund for Investments under BRI," *Antaranews*, July 2, 2019, https://en.antaranews.com/news/128195/indonesia-proposes-special-fund-for-investments-under-bri.

perceptions with Indonesia. In other words, BRI has been benefiting more and more countries and people in the region since 2016. At the same time, China and Southeast Asian nations have worked together to strengthen cooperation in the South China Sea by carrying out negotiations on the Code of Conduct (COC) and conducting military exercises with Malaysia, Thailand and ASEAN. China and ASEAN countries now are improving their abilities to manage risks in the South China Sea. It is an opportunity for China and ASEAN to improve mutual understanding and build sustainable regional connectivity.

Thirdly, the changes in domestic politics in Southeast Asian nations may prevent building sustainable connectivity. Political stability is very important for the sustainability of government policies. If the newly elected President or Prime Minister changes policies adopted by the previous government due to power struggle, the country's cooperation plans with its partners will be greatly changed, which may pose a threat to the cooperation projects. In the past years, Myanmar and Malaysia changed their attitude toward China's economic cooperation projects when Thein Sein was elected to be the President of Myanmar and Tun Dr. Mahathir to be the Prime Minister of Malaysia. The changes of the two governments led to suspension or cancellation of the Myitsone Dam Project in Myanmar and the ECRL project and two oil and gas pipelines in Malaysia. Although some of the projects resumed after the discussions or negotiations between China and the relevant government, the suspension or cancellation of the projects does make ill effects on the sustainable construction of the infrastructure projects. On the other hand, the change of some governments may promote the cooperation between China and some countries. For example, Filipino administration under President Benigno Aquino III refused to work with China for cooperation under BRI. But when Rodrigo Roa Duterte took office, Philippines chose to cooperate with China in various fields including infrastructure building and connectivity. The two countries signed a dozen of cooperation agreements, and agreed to align China's BRI with Filipino's plan of *Build Build Build* which covers many infrastructure projects like construction of seaports, airports, highways and railways. The Burmese, Malaysian and Filipino cases show that changes in the political situation are an important cause affecting sustainable cooperation. If there are no consistent policies, the connectivity projects might be suspended.

But what makes us satisfied is that the political situation in Southeast Asia is generally stable compared with the political situation in the Middle East and other regions. Even if some countries changed their governments, the new government can take a positive attitude toward China. In the Burmese and Malaysian cases, although some projects were stopped, the Burmese and Malaysian governments still regard China as a partner for cooperation rather than an enemy or an opponent. Tun Dr. Mahathir repeated many times since he administered Malaysia once more that the Belt and Road idea is great. Malaysia fully supports BRI and believes everyone will benefit from the ease of travel and communication that the development of the Belt and Road project will bring.[10] With more and more successful projects under BRI in the region, Southeast Asian nations have begun to witness more and more benefits from the BRI, and they are eager to cooperate closely with China no matter who becomes the President or Prime Minister. It is helpful for the sustainable development of regional connectivity.

Fourthly, some Southeast Asian countries sometimes complain about the quality and social benefit of China's funded projects in the region. The complaints mentioned by ASEAN countries, such as the inadequate job opportunities for local residents and less attention paid to environmental protection, are important causes of unsustainable development of regional connectivity. Countries in Southeast Asia attach great importance to the development of local community. They support the mega infrastructure projects with the hope of increasing job opportunities, improving people's livelihood and protecting the environment at the same time. For China's funded

---

[10] Chok Suat Ling, "Dr Mahathir Given Honour to Present Speech, Pledges Full Support for BRI," *Straits Times*, April 26, 2019, accessed on July 31, 2019. https://www.nst.com.my/news/nation/2019/04/483090/dr-mahathir-given-honour-present-speech-pledges-full-support-bri.

infrastructure projects in the region, Chinese enterprises and the relevant parties tried their best to improve people's livelihood by offering job opportunities, and took measures to preserve the natural environment. Take railway projects for example. The China–Laos high-speed railway project requires more than 7,000 local workers. The majority of those recruited are Lao workers who reside near the project, and they are digging tunnels and building a bridge across the Mekong River. Thousands have already been recruited to work on the railway in the provinces, including about 2,000 in Luang Prabang. More than 1,000 Lao workers have been recruited in Luang Namtha to build the railway and the workers are receiving monthly salaries of USD 200–800.[11] The Jakarta–Bandung railway project is expected to offer as many as 39,000 jobs to local workers and it offered more than 2,000 job opportunities for locals by the middle of 2018.[12] However, China's efforts have yet to meet the demand from ASEAN countries. Countries like Indonesia, Thailand and Malaysia always keep requesting China to increase job opportunities and improve social welfare.

In recent years, Chinese government has paid much attention to improve the quality of projects alongside the Belt and Road region in order to promote the sustainable development of BRI. Chinese President Xi Jinping in the Second Belt and Road Forum declared China's will of sustainable building of BRI. According to Xi's speech, for the coming years, the Belt and Road cooperation should focus on priorities and project execution, and move forward with results-oriented implementation. The cooperation needs to be guided by the principle of extensive consultation, joint contribution and shared benefits; needs to pursue open, "green" and "clean" cooperation, to launch green infrastructure projects, make green investment and provide green financing to protect the Earth. In pursuing Belt and Road cooperation, everything should be done in a transparent way, and we

---

[11] *Lao-China High-Speed Railway*, accessed on August 1, 2019, https://www.globalsecurity.org/military/world/laos/hsr.htm.

[12] "Jakarta–Bandung High-Speed Railway Enters a New Stage of Full Implementation and Promotion," *Xinhuanet*, accessed on August 1, 2019, http://www.xinhuanet.com/fortune/2018-06/29/c_1123057562.htm.

should have zero tolerance for corruption. At the same time, the cooperation will pursue high-standard cooperation to improve people's lives and promote sustainable development. China will strengthen international development cooperation so as to create more opportunities for the developing countries, and help them eradicate poverty and achieve sustainable development.[13]

President Xi's speech shows China's attitude and determination to improve Belt and Road cooperation to a higher level. It is an opportunity to build sustainable regional connectivity.

Ways Ahead

Based on the aforementioned analysis, though the regional railway projects construction is now facing some problems, China and Southeast Asian nations have also got some opportunities to pursue sustainable development. In order to make our massive projects sustainable, China and ASEAN nations need to create a positive external environment and maintain stable bilateral relations. To this end, we strongly recommend the following proposals:

First of all, China and ASEAN should make people-to-people connectivity a top priority. Apart from the ongoing programs now, China should pay more attention to the role of religion in the Belt and Road cooperation. Both China and Southeast Asian nations need to conduct more interfaith dialogues, increase student and youth exchange programs, and conduct more joint research programs between think tanks. In terms of media cooperation, China should start more programs with local media in Southeast Asia and share more information with the media on BRI and Chinese foreign policy in the local language. At the same time, similar information should be made available on social media.

Secondly, both sides need to increase visits and meetings between national leaders and relevant ministries to improve mutual

---

[13] Xi Jinping, "Working Together to Deliver a Brighter Future for Belt and Road Cooperation," Keynote Speech at the Opening Ceremony of the Second Belt and Road Forum for International Cooperation, April 26, 2019.

understanding and political trust. Political mutual trust is one of the most important factors to guarantee sustainable cooperation. Leaders and ministers from China and ASEAN countries should have frequent visits and meetings for policy coordination. Relevant ministries or organizations should conduct timely consultation and discussion when our cooperation projects encounter difficulties. Under the China–ASEAN framework, foreign ministers, defense ministers and ministers on economic issues should have a regular meeting to exchange views on international and regional situations as well as the ongoing BRI programs in order to ensure smooth policy coordination. At the same time, China should make more efforts to meet and contact local governments in Southeast Asia since local governments in some countries play a key role in promoting Belt and Road cooperation.

Thirdly, it is extremely important to enhance cooperation at the working level. The departments, bodies or joint enterprises in charge of the projects must seriously consider sitting down to jointly discuss on how to implement the relevant cooperation project. Both sides need to set up a comprehensive plan by doing some investigation in person in order to understand both parties' needs, especially the needs of the local community. Discussions should focus on important issues like employment, environment and people's livelihood. Only when the departments at the working level have had enough discussions and investigations can the project start.

Fourthly, China and ASEAN need to further enhance their relationship to maintain the ASEAN-centered regional mechanism. ASEAN centrality is very important when we talk about regional cooperation. For China and ASEAN, we need both bilateral cooperations under BRI framework and cooperation with ASEAN. In the next decades, attention must be paid to implementing the alignment of BRI and ASEAN Economic Community. Lancang–Mekong Cooperation, the East ASEAN Growth Area and New International Land-Sea Trade Corridor must bear early fruit. We need to set up special groups to push forward relevant cooperation.

Fifthly, Chinese enterprises should further enhance understanding of the situation in Southeast Asia, trying to make cooperation projects more beneficial to locals. The enterprises should increase awareness of high quality service, take social responsibility seriously, and contact local people frequently to understand their needs and interests. At the same time, the companies should also work closely with local NGOs and the media. More and more training and education programs related to Southeast Asian conditions including history, religion, culture, ethnic groups and laws need to be offered by enterprises for their employees and managers.

Last but not least, China should try to work with regional powers like Japan, India, U.S., Australia or Russia to jointly invest in Southeast Asia. At present, the leaders of China, Japan and India are in agreement to conduct third-party cooperation. China and Japan held the first China–Japan Third-Party Market Cooperation Forum in 2018. The two countries have agreed to create a "new framework" to jointly move ahead with infrastructure projects in third nations and strengthen a wide range of cooperation ranging from finance to innovation.[14] China and India are now exploring ways to carry out cooperation with third parties in a broader scope. For China and India, it is very necessary to conduct third party cooperation in Indo-China Peninsula, especially in Myanmar and alongside the Mekong River. In fact, apart from Japan and India, more and more third-party cooperation between China and U.S., Russia or Australia should be carried out in order to expand the common interest of the great powers to avoid unnecessary conflict. It is the guarantee for the sustainable development of regional connectivity projects.

Conclusion

Since the implementation of the BRI, China's relations with Southeast Asian countries have achieved great success, especially the cooperation between the two sides in regional infrastructure and connectivity

---

[14] "Japan Pledges to Back BRI Project, Promote Economic Cooperation with China," *Business Standard*, October 26, 2018, accessed on August 1, 2019, https://www.business-standard.com/article/international/japan-pledges-to-back-bri-project-promote-economic-cooperation-with-china-118102601194_1.html.

building. At present, sustainable development is an important issue facing China and Southeast Asian countries in the construction of regional connectivity projects. Both sides face opportunities and challenges, but opportunities outweigh challenges. For China, the key to promoting sustainable connectivity is to further enhance mutual understanding and mutual trust with Southeast Asian countries, strengthen people-to-people relations and enable regional interconnection projects to benefit local people. Chinese companies must further fulfill their social responsibilities, build high-quality projects and interact positively with local communities. China needs to further strengthen cooperation with regional powers to avoid vicious competition and jointly promote regional cooperation.

Chapter

5

Connecting the Master Plan on ASEAN Connectivity 2025 and the Belt and Road Initiative: How to Promote People-to-People Ties

Nur Rachmat Yuliantoro

Department of International Relations
Universitas Gadjah Mada, Daerah Istimewa Yogyakarta, Indonesia

Executive Summary

• On November 3, 2019, the Association of Southeast Asia Nations (ASEAN) and Chinese leaders made a joint statement to synergize the Master Plan on ASEAN Connectivity (MPAC) 2025 and the Belt and Road Initiative (BRI). These two development strategies have their key priorities. Among them are people mobility (the MPAC 2025) and closer people-to-people relations (the BRI). This is important as mutual understanding among people is imperative for greater economic cooperation in the region.

59

- Synergizing the MPAC 2025 and the BRI is expected to produce mutual benefits for ASEAN member states and China. However, this will not be easy as ASEAN has its difficulties in realizing the goals of the MPAC 2025. The synergy between the MPAC 2025 and the BRI is needed to achieve common prosperity in the region, but it will largely depend on the domestic political conditions of ASEAN member states as well as their intra-relations and relations with China.

- The MPAC 2025 has highlighted several measures taken to reinforce people connectivity despite some limitations. It is argued that ease of people mobility will help the connection process of the MPAC 2025 and the BRI significantly.

- The MPAC 2025 and the BRI have similar core purposes: chief among them is encouraging further people-to-people contact. This shall be considered as the main key for the possible success of synergy between both development plans as it can build more trust and mutual understanding.

- Several policy recommendations are offered here: to improve human resources development; to provide more vocational training; to enhance mutual recognition arrangement; to arrange for the increasing number of tourists; to create more opportunities for higher education; to raise awareness of youth issues; to promote the role of certain agents in building mutual understanding; and to support all the practical efforts to increase people's income.

"Connectivity has become a fashionable measure of regional integration."[1]

Introduction

Multilateralism in Southeast Asia received another huge boost on November 3, 2019 when 10 member states of ASEAN and China

---

[1] Sanchita Basu Das, "ASEAN's Regional Integration will be Determined by Better Connectivity in the Future," *ISEAS Perspective*, no. 28(2016): 2, accessed on May 31.

jointly made a statement to synergize two big development plans in the region. At the 22nd ASEAN–China Summit in Bangkok, Thailand, both parties declared that they are ready to enhance their efforts connecting the MPAC 2025 and China's BRI. The joint statement focuses on certain development projects within the expected goals of the MPAC 2025 and the BRI, expanding further common interests as envisioned in, among others, the ASEAN–China Strategic Partnership Vision 2030.

Since 2003, ASEAN has pledged to work further on its framework of regionalism by visioning the ASEAN Community. The ASEAN Community consists of three pillars: ASEAN Economic Community, ASEAN Political-Security Community and ASEAN Socio-Cultural Community. It is within the framework of ASEAN Community that the organization declared the adoption of the MPAC in Hanoi on 28 October 2010.[2] Having physical, institutional and people-to-people connectivity of the MPAC as its base, the MPAC 2025 — announced in Vientiane, Laos on 6 September 2016 — is targeted "to boost the development of the region's infrastructure, logistics, innovation, and skilled labor mobility".[3] The MPAC 2025 has five key areas: sustainable infrastructure, digital innovation, seamless logistics, regulatory excellence and people mobility. To a great extent, these key areas correspond to five major priorities of the BRI (formerly known as One Belt, One Road or OBOR), which are policy coordination, connectivity of infrastructure, unimpeded trade, financial integration and closer people-to-people ties.[4]

On paper, the opportunity to synergize the two development plans looks promising. China is currently the second-largest economy in the world, while given the economic power of the countries of

---

[2] ASEAN, *Master Plan on ASEAN Connectivity* (Jakarta: ASEAN Secretariat, 2016).
[3] Phidel Vineles, "ASEAN Connectivity: Challenge for an Integrated ASEAN Community," *RSIS Commentary*, no. 010 (2017), accessed on January 11.
[4] ASEAN, "ASEAN–China Joint Statement on synergizing the Master Plan on ASEAN Connectivity (MPAC) 2025 and the Belt and Road Initiative (BRI)," in *Proceedings of the 22nd ASEAN–China Summit* (Bangkok: ASEAN, 2019).

The State Council of the People's Republic of China, *Connectivity Set to Accelerate as China, ASEAN Align Development Plans* (Beijing: SCPRC, 2019).

Southeast Asia as a whole, this region has the great prospect of being one of the most prosperous regions in the world. However, the reality on the ground does not look as imagined. The MPAC 2025 and the BRI have their respective problems and challenges, not to mention issues and constraints that may confront the implementation of synergize between them.

This chapter tries to identify efforts to connect the MPAC 2025 and the BRI, especially in strengthening the people-to-people link. With institutional connectivity and physical connectivity, people-to-people connectivity is the major framework within which the MPAC 2025 is expected to function, to the extent that "restrictions on travel for ASEAN nationals within the region are largely a thing of the past".[5] The goals of people-to-people connectivity are, among others, to advance all the initiatives that support education and human resource development, to encourage entrepreneurship, to stimulate cultural exchange and to promote the tourism industry.

This specific focus of people-to-people connection is important as it helps build trust, which is imperative for greater economic cooperation. Trust cannot be achieved without mutual understanding, which in turn shall be developed based on easier mobility and more shared experiences of people in the region. History of ASEAN and China relations tells us that trust-building is not an easy process. While ideology and strategic issues had separated China and ASEAN member countries during the Cold War period, since the early 1990s their relations began to improve, especially in the economic field. According to Huang Haitao, China was the first to use this situation to begin a process of closer and wider interaction with ASEAN, including in the political and security fields. Huang argues "Intensive people-to-people exchanges, to some extent, will help build up foundations to understand each other's real interests and intentions. The multi-level trust-building process will help China and ASEAN countries to have stable and healthy relations in the future, and China's BRI can

---

[5] ASEAN, *Master Plan on ASEAN Connectivity* (Jakarta: ASEAN Secretariat, 2016).

partially realize this goal".[6] The MPAC 2025 and the BRI are expected to complement each other. It is within this framework that this chapter demonstrates what has been done and provides recommendations on improvement and potential for progress in the future.

The Significance of "Synergy"

ASEAN and China relations in the last three decades have focused on developing cooperation and collaboration in politics, economics (investment and trade) and security. Concerning the MPAC 2025 and the BRI connectivity, it might not be wrong to argue that progress in the field of economic development is a shared goal of the parties involved. However, economic progress, the stability of political relations and the maintenance of regional security cannot be reached without trust and mutual understanding, which can be sought through wider connectivity of the people. This type of connectivity "ensures popular support for the entire initiative by promoting cultural and academic exchanges, media cooperation and expanding the scale of tourism".[7] According to Jusuf Wanandi, one of Indonesia's prominent observers of Sino-Indonesian relations, "That is why relations in education, art and culture, sports and youth, are so important for mutual understanding and trust, which in the East Asian context, is particularly critical for the building of regional communities".[8] This indicates that the people-to-people relationship must always be one of the focuses developed in the MPAC 2025 and the BRI synergy efforts.

Zhao Hong writes that linking the MPAC 2025 and the BRI is a strategy that is expected to produce mutual benefits for ASEAN member states and China. Another word for this strategy is "synergy",

---

[6] Huang Haitao, "The Role of Trust in China–ASEAN Relations: Towards a Multi-level Trust Building for China and ASEAN," *International Journal of China Studies*, no. 8(1) (2017): 55–56.

[7] Sanchita Basu Das, "ASEAN's Regional Integration will be Determined by Better Connectivity in the Future," *ISEAS Perspective*, no. 28 (2016): 28.

[8] Ong Keng Yong, "Overcoming Obstacles in ASEAN–China Relations." In *Harmony and Development: ASEAN–China Relations*, ed. Lai Hongyi and Lim Tin Seng (Singapore: World Scientific, 2007).

a concept chosen by China to ensure that BRI's vision and mission and policies are in line with the development plans of partner countries which are involved in this scheme. Among the things emphasized by the document *The Vision and Action on OBOR* issued by the Chinese government in 2015 is to build "mutual understanding among the people along the route … [so the BRI] should be jointly built through consultation to meet the interest of all".[9] Mutual understanding will result in greater trust among concerned parties, which in turn can guarantee shared interests. Zhao adds that it is within the framework of OBOR or the BRI to work on synergies with ASEAN joint development plans. He argues that the synergy between OBOR or the BRI and the MPAC 2025 is necessary for the advancement of development in the region.[10]

For years, China has shown its commitment to work closely with ASEAN in many fields. ASEAN members, on the other hand, have also stated that collectively they welcome China's call to work together for economic development in the region. In 2014, for example, during the 25th ASEAN Summit in Nay Pyi Taw, Myanmar, ASEAN has stated that it welcomes the establishment of Asian Infrastructure Investment Bank (AIIB) initiated by China. The bank is particularly expected to support the MPAC.[11] We can see here that both parties are seeking closer and stronger relations by enforcing their synergy measures. As of today, all 10 member countries of ASEAN are joining AIIB, further clarifying the direction of the synergy between ASEAN and China.

The MPAC 2025 is an ASEAN initiative to strengthen regional integration in many aspects, notably economic development. However, this is not an easy thing considering that ASEAN itself has several obstacles and difficulties. Bruno Jetin noted that the main obstacles

---

[9] The National Development and Reform Commission, Ministry of Foreign Affairs, and Ministry of Commerce of the People's Republic of China, *Vision and Actions on Jointly Building Silk Road Economic Belt and 21st-Century Maritime Silk Road* (Beijing: NDRC, 2015).

[10] Zhao Hong, "Can China's OBOR Initiative Synergize with AEC Blueprint 2025?" *Perspective*, no. 62 (2016): 5.

[11] Sanchita Basu Das, "Can the China-led AIIB Support the ASEAN Connectivity Master Plan?" *Perspective*, no. 30 (2015): 5.

had been the economic disparity and unbalanced development among ASEAN member states themselves, especially between landlocked and coastal countries. ASEAN also does not have enough capital to ensure that all the MPAC 2025 priorities can be met — herein lies the importance of then synergizing with China, which can provide financial assistance through the BRI. Besides, the absence of widely accepted standardized rules and procedures within ASEAN as well as competing political interests contributed to the relative weakness of this regional organization in the effort to pursue the dream of connectivity. The problems posed by the arrival of large numbers of Chinese migrant workers to work on infrastructure projects funded by China also have an impact on the domestic political stability of ASEAN member states.[12] The synergy between the MPAC 2025 and the BRI will largely depend on the domestic political conditions of ASEAN member states, the relations among them and their relations with China.

Synergy has been the keyword for further cooperation on development between ASEAN and China. It is understood that to bring optimal results, both the MPAC 2025 and the BRI need broad support from countries involved, and the support will come from a process of continuous synergy. The Joint Statement document has stated that:

[S]ynergies between MPAC 2025 and the BRI will contribute towards regional connectivity, peace and stability, economic prosperity and sustainable development ... [It is important] to improve connectivity between ASEAN and China by synergizing common priorities in the MPAC 2025 and BRI, as part of efforts to synergize the various connectivity strategies in the region in a manner that would be mutually beneficial ... for the goals of high-standard, people-oriented, people-centered and sustainable development.[13]

---

[12] Bruno Jetin, "'One Belt-One Road Initiative' and ASEAN Connectivity: Synergy Issues and Potentialities," (Working Paper No. 30, Institute of Asian Studies, University of Brunei Darussalam, 2017), 9–11.

[13] ASEAN, "ASEAN–China Joint Statement on Synergising the Master Plan on ASEAN Connectivity (MPAC) 2025 and the Belt and Road Initiative (BRI)," in *Proceedings of the 22nd ASEAN–China Summit* (Bangkok: ASEAN, 2019): 1–2.

To realize the goals of the synergy, leaders of ASEAN member states and China have declared several priorities. These include improving the development of high-standard infrastructure projects in Southeast Asia that can provide more connectivity, strengthening trade and investment in the region, supporting the establishment of the Regional Comprehensive Economic Partnership (RCEP) and other mutually beneficial economic partnership, promoting certain efforts responding to the digital economy, enhancing people-to-people ties and maintaining dialogues and consultations on the available mechanisms.[14]

The Joint Statement has highlighted that the connection between the MPAC 2025 and the BRI is highly needed for common prosperity in the region. However, it should be underlined here that linkage, connection or synergy will not work without trust, and that trust shall be built and developed, among others, through greater people-to-people ties in various levels and activities. Without ignoring the other synergy priorities of the MPAC 2025 and the BRI, building closer people-to-people ties should be given greater importance.

What Has Been Done?

The people-to-people connection can take different forms that will direct corresponding activities and purposes. It may range from mutual exchange among ASEAN member states and Chinese government officials, communication and collaboration of their private sector, further study and training for degrees and vocational expertise, the introduction of cultural richness, to the promotion of tourism and its related industries. All of these can not only realize their own targeted goals but also serve their function as ways to link the MPAC 2025 and the BRI.

It should be noted that strengthening people-to-people connections will get great support from the ease of mobility. In this context, the construction of infrastructure projects and communication networks will facilitate the mobility of the population in ASEAN

---

14 *Ibid.*, pp. 2–3.

member states and the wider regional context. Yet, a Filipino political scientist has warned that several infrastructure projects under the BRI scheme have been subject of criticism from local people due to the lack of job opportunities and potential environmental danger they bring. These projects put local people as "the intended beneficiaries, but who are at greater risks than their governments and elites".[15] Still, in terms of mobility, another issue that needs to be given much attention is the existence of borders as well as national and international laws governing relations between residents of Southeast Asian countries and China. Ease of mobility will help the connection process of the MPAC 2025 and the BRI significantly, but that does not mean having to sacrifice sovereignty as the state's main national interest. In addition to these, a certain economic issue shall also be mentioned as a defining factor for the connectivity in people-to-people ties to proceed: "China's interest in MPAC will thus depend on how much the infrastructure projects can contribute to ASEAN economies' linkages to China".[16]

Before the adoption of the MPAC 2025, several measures showed the existence of cultural relations and people-to-people ties between ASEAN member countries and their partners, especially China. All this reinforces the political, economic and security aspects that have developed between ASEAN and China. However, to involve broader aspects of society than politicians and bureaucrats, business people and security apparatus, more efforts are needed to improve mobility and closer relations of people, with the young generation being the central focus.[17] According to the MPAC 2025 document, several measures have been taken to reinforce people connectivity. These include the development of the ASEAN Curriculum Sourcebook and its

---

[15] "The Belt and Road Initiative and ASEAN: Cooperation or Opportunism?" *Business World*, November 12, 2018.

[16] Sanchita Basu Das, "ASEAN's Regional Integration will be Determined by Better Connectivity in the Future," *ISEAS Perspective*, no. 28 (2016): 7.

[17] Ong Keng Yong, "Further Enhancing ASEAN–China Relations." In *Harmony and Development: ASEAN-China Relations*, ed. Lai Hongyi and Lim Tin Seng (Singapore: World Scientific, 2007): 9.

utilization in different levels of schools, the management of the ASEAN Virtual Learning Resource Centre (AVLRC) website,[18] the growth of initiatives under the ASEAN University Network (AUN) scheme, and the diversification of intra-ASEAN tourism and its related products. Nevertheless, despite several Mutual Recognition Arrangements (MRA) being already in place,[19] made possible with the adoption of the ASEAN Framework Agreement on Visa Exemption, the ASEAN Agreement on Movement of Natural Persons[20] and relevant agreements with China,[21] there have been also limitations in terms of wider mobility of workers and professionals within ASEAN. This has been the case, especially due to the lack of regionally accepted standards and regulations.[22]

Policy Recommendations

The Joint Statement declares that ASEAN and China will "strengthen people-to-people connectivity by supporting cooperation in areas

---

[18] *The ASEAN Curriculum Sourcebook* is important as it helps "to educate primary and secondary school students about ASEAN and what it involves, so they have a greater understanding of the region and its peoples." Meanwhile, AVLRC's main purpose is "to foster greater information and knowledge sharing about ASEAN and its member countries by using IT technology to make it easier to access and share information about the people, culture, history, places of interest, and economies of each ASEAN Member State." See ASEAN–Australia Development Cooperation Program Phase II. (n.d.) ASEAN Connectivity — Key Facts. http://aadcp2.org/wp-content/uploads/ASEAN_People-to-PeopleConnectivity.pdf.
[19] See ASEAN. (n.d.) Mutual Recognition Arrangements in Services — ASEAN Professionals on the Move. https://www.asean.org/wp-content/uploads/images/2015/October/outreach-document/Edited%20MRA%20Services-2.pdf.
[20] Elisa Fornalé, "ASEAN People-to-People Connectivity: The Role of the Mutual Recognition Regime," *European Journal of East Asian Studies*, no. 17(1) (2018): 38–39.
[21] Na Wei, "Exploring the Significance of the Connectivity between China and ASEAN under the One Belt One Road Initiative." In *The 2019 International Conference on Emerging Researches in Management, Business, Finance and Economics (ERMBFE 2019) Proceeding.* ed. Xiaojun Lu (London: Francis Academic Press, 2019): 222.
[22] ASEAN, *Master Plan on ASEAN Connectivity* (Jakarta: ASEAN Secretariat, 2016): 21.

such as education, youth, tourism, human resource, and technical cooperation, media, think tanks and local governments, including building the ASEAN–China Young Leaders Scholarship (ACYLS) as a flagship project, and cooperation on improving people's livelihood".[23] Acknowledging that enhancing people-to-people connection is the key for the synergy between the MPAC 2025 and the BRI, this study would recommend the following for all the concerned parties to consider:

(1) *Improve the development of human resources.* The governments and their related agencies in Southeast Asia can utilize the assistance provided by the Chinese government in efforts to develop human capital and skills of the workers. According to the MPAC 2025 document (p. 32), more workers with sufficient qualifications are what the region needs to be able to deal with the changing times and in turn subsequently reduce inequality and poverty. The BRI should be able to provide adequate access to capacity building for local workers by involving them in the construction of various projects while providing appropriate training for them.

(2) *Provide more training and qualification standards for vocational skills.* The MPAC 2025 has highlighted this issue as one of its main objectives to achieve. As the region will have many infrastructure projects, support from the availability of workers with good and relevant vocational skills is a must. Chinese companies, as part of the government's going out strategy, may play an important role in establishing the link between BRI projects and the need for qualified workers from Southeast Asia. Relevant programs of training need to be carried out for enabling this to happen.

(3) *Enhance the necessary capacity to increase the number of Mutual Recognition Arrangements within ASEAN as well as between ASEAN and China.* ASEAN shall work harder to ensure that the

---

[23] ASEAN, "ASEAN-China Joint Statement on Synergising the Master Plan on ASEAN Connectivity (MPAC) 2025 and the Belt and Road Initiative (BRI)," in *Proceedings of the 22nd ASEAN–China Summit* (Bangkok: ASEAN, 2019): 3.

rules contained in the ASEAN Framework Agreement on Visa Exemption and the ASEAN Agreement on Movement of Natural Persons be implemented. Some relevant rules, after certain adjustment, can also be tried out in the context of connectivity with China. The success in this measure will indirectly have a major impact on the development of some economic sectors, which is a common goal of the MPAC 2025 and the BRI.

(4) *Arrange for more appropriate procedures and standards to increase the number of tourists.* As the MPAC 2025 document argues (p. 62), this policy is intended for "ease of travel to and within the region" for many travelers, including Chinese tourists. Easier procedures to obtain visas (although they are still dependent on an individual country's regulations) may help a lot. No-visa or visa-on-arrival scheme for certain types of traveler, notably short-term tourists, shall be made complementary between ASEAN member states and China. Not to mention that the wide availability of travel information in various forms, in English and corresponding local languages, will be an added value to this ease of mobility as targeted by both the MPAC 2025 and the BRI.

(5) *Increase the number of international as well as ASEAN students studying in reputable tertiary institutions in Southeast Asia, while at the same time provide more opportunities for ASEAN students studying in China.* Student mobility is another important component of people-to-people ties, and more so due to what their education can bring to benefit society. Examples of this measure are the ASEAN International Mobility for Students Program, which just marked its 10th anniversary in 2019, and the China–AUN Scholarship. Ease of procedures and regulations for aspiring international students from either ASEAN member states or China shall be put forth into government policies, in addition to policies of individual universities or colleges. The wide availability of scholarships from ASEAN member states and Chinese governments to their respective students to learn each other's culture in student exchange or degree programs is highly appreciated. It is within this context that cooperation among governments, private sectors and the public in general in ASEAN as well as China to

establish the ACYLS shall be made top education priorities of the synergy between the MPAC 2025 and the BRI.

(6) *Expand the use of available channels, including social media, to raise awareness of youth issues in the region.* The young population is very beneficial for the development in the region, especially in terms of their contribution to economic development. In addition to this, there have been some issues concerning the youth: education, physical and mental health, self-capacity, relationships with other groups in society, and their hopes for the future. The MPAC 2025 and the BRI can work together in encouraging the availability of massive channels of youth awareness and self-development under local regulations and culture.

(7) *Promote the greater role of media, think tanks, and local governments in shaping mutual understanding in the region.* Media reports on each other's culture, exchanges of experts among think tanks, as well as the presence of more sister cities between ASEAN member states and China shall be encouraged for trust-building and closer people-to-people ties as envisaged by the MPAC 2025 and the BRI.

(8) *Support all the practical efforts to increase people's income, especially those who are considered as living below the poverty line.* This particular issue is also of high importance in terms of economic achievement of the MPAC 2025 and the BRI. The number of poor people in Southeast Asia and China is so high that it needs quick and appropriate actions from governments and private sectors to alleviate them. More training on certain occupations and relevant incentives given to successful small and medium-scale enterprises are examples of practical efforts that can be further employed.

Conclusion

The MPAC 2025 and the BRI have similar core purposes: to promote greater connectivity in Southeast Asia by providing more high-quality infrastructure, enabling easier access to trade, investment, transportation and communication, as well as encouraging further people-to-people contact. The latter shall be considered as the main key for the possible success of synergy between the two development plans as it can build more trust and mutual understanding.

Attempted and planned measures for closer and stronger people-to-people ties are important within the context of connectivity as quoted at the beginning of this study. Connecting the MPAC 2025 and the BRI shall have two corresponding long-term goals, namely trust-building and advanced economic development in the region. Without trust and mutual understanding, any government, private sectors, and citizens of ASEAN member states and China understandably hesitate to cooperate among each other, which will hinder the expected results of both the MPAC 2025 and the BRI.

https://doi.org/10.1142/9789811234316_0006

Chapter

6

China–Malaysia Port Alliance: A Case Study of Soft Infrastructure Connectivity

Ngeow Chow-Bing

Institute of China Studies, University of Malaya, Kuala Lumpur, Malaysia

After Chinese leader Xi Jinping put forward the One Belt One Road Initiative (later rebranded as the Belt and Road Initiative [BRI]) during his visits to Kazakhstan and Indonesia in late 2013, Malaysia, under different administrations, has been responding in an overall positive manner. As a result, Chinese companies have increased their involvement in Malaysia's infrastructure sector. Two major BRI infrastructure projects are Malaysia–China Kuantan Industrial Park (MCKIP) and East Coast Rail Link (ECRL).[1]

---

[1] Ngeow Chow-Bing, "Economic Cooperation and Infrastructure Linkage between Malaysia and China under the Belt and Road Initiative." In *Regional Connection under the Belt and Road Initiative: The Prospects for Economic and Financial*

However, other than these mega-infrastructure projects, Malaysia and China also initiated a little known bilateral maritime connectivity mechanism called China–Malaysia Port Alliance (CMPA). CMPA represents the first of its kind for both China and Malaysia. There is no other similar port alliance that China or Malaysia has formed with other countries. It is a kind of "soft infrastructure connectivity". By "soft infrastructure connectivity", the author refers to those efforts aimed at enhancing connectivity and bonding linkage through policy coordination, information sharing, mutual learning, diffusion of best practices, norms and standards, compatible and efficient cross-border management systems, coordination of regulations, and the spirit of good partnership.[2] In other words, while hard infrastructure (ports, rails, roads, industrial parks) makes trade possible, soft infrastructure enables and facilitates greater trade. The role of port authorities, operators, shipping liners, freight forwarding companies is often no less important in international trade than the manufacturers and producers of goods and the hard infrastructure that makes transportation of goods possible. CMPA is created to enhance cooperation between port authorities and operators of both countries. Its success certainly will contribute much to the increased levels of trade, investment and logistics connectivity between Malaysia and China.

In the following sections, the chapter will first provide a brief overview of the development of the port sector in Malaysia, followed

---

Cooperation, ed. Fanny M. Cheung and Ying-yi Hong (New York: Routledge, 2018): 164–191; Ngeow Chow-Bing, "The Five Areas of Connectivity between Malaysia and China: Challenges and Opportunities." In *The Belt and Road Initiatives: ASEAN Countries' Perspectives*, (ed.) Yue Yang and Fujian Li (Singapore: World Scientific, 2019): 117–139.

[2] Economists have pointed out that "soft infrastructure" is often as important as "hard infrastructure" in facilitating connectivity. See Biswa Nath Bhattacharyay, "Strengthening Transport Infrastructure Connectivity Policies for Inclusive and Sustainable Asia." In *The Economics of Infrastructure Provisioning: The Changing Role of the State*, edited by Arnold Picot, Massimo Florio, Nico Grove, Johann Kranz (Cambridge, MA: MIT Press, 2015): 339–354; Tasneem Mirza and Eleanor Bacani, "Addressing Hard and Soft Infrastructure Barriers to Trade in South Asia," *Asia Development Bank South Asia Working Paper Series*, no. 16 (February 2013).

by a section that discusses the origins and content of CMPA. It will then offer an assessment and a brief conclusion.

Ports in Malaysia: An Overview[3]

Malaysia is a trading nation, testified by the fact that total trade comprises about 130% of its national GDP, which also underscores the importance of Malaysian ports as most of the export and import of goods take place through ports. Before 1980s, Malaysia relied on Port of Singapore for the export and import of goods. Since then, the Malaysian government had consciously taken a more concerted effort to spearhead the development of key ports. The major policies on port development included the designation of Port Klang as the National Load Center, the greenfield development of the Port of Tanjung Pelepas, privatization and competition.

The National Load Center was a policy meant to make Port Klang the primary export and import hub for Malaysia. Port Klang is located near Klang Valley, the industrialized and most developed part of Peninsula Malaysia. Years of under-investment and lack of efficiency had undermined the port despite its strategic location, until the government started to seriously build it up since the 1980s.

---

[3] Unless specified, this section is based on the following studies: Chia Lin Sie, Mark Goh and Jose Tongzon, *Southeast Asian Regional Port Development: A Comparative Analysis*, (Singapore: Institute of Southeast Asian Studies, 2003); Hanizah Idris, "Pembangunan Infrastruktur Pelabuhan Utama Malaysia Dalam Konteks Serantau Dan Global (The Development of Malaysian Port Infrastructure in the Regional and Global Contexts)." In *Asia Tenggara Kontemporari* (Contemporary Southeast Asia), ed. Hanizah Idris (Kuala Lumpur: Penerbit Univeriti Malaya, 2006): 133–157; Hanizah Idris, Mohammad Raduan Mohd Ariff and Hanafi Hussin, "Strengthening the Profile of Malaysian Ports and Their Role in the National and Regional Port System." In *The Development of Maritime Sector in Malaysia*, ed. Hanizah Idris and Tan Wan Hin (Kuala Lumpur: Institute of Ocean and Earth Sciences, University of Malaya, 2010): 45–66; Leong Choon Heng and Sung Woo Lee, "Malaysian Port Policy: Concentration or Dispersion?" *International Journal of Maritime Affairs and Fisheries* 4, no. 1 (June 2012): 57–81; Egide van der Heide, "Port Development in Malaysia: An Introduction to the Country's Port Landscape," a report by the Embassy of the Kingdom of the Netherlands in Malaysia (Kuala Lumpur: n.d.).

Under the National Load Center policy, the government invested in and gave policy preferences to make the port competitive and attractive, although it did not mandate that all traders must use the port for export and import.[4] The government also privatized port operations to two private entities: North Port and West Port (each of which is partially owned by foreign companies), while the regulator is Port Klang Authority, a statutory body of the government. North Port and West Port, in terms of operations and ownership, are actually separate entities, and the Malaysian government encourages them to compete with each other, which supposedly will make them more efficient and competitive, avoiding the situation of inefficient monopoly.

The Port of Tanjung Pelepas, which is located not far from Port of Singapore, was developed mainly as a transshipment hub to compete with Singapore. The government poured in substantial financial backing to develop the infrastructure and equip the port with the latest technology. Port of Tanjung Pelepas also benefitted from forming partnership with Maersk, the Danish shipping giant, which propelled its early spectacular growth in the 1990s. As a result of these policies, Port Klang and Port of Tanjung Pelepas have now developed into two major ports, ranked 12th and 18th, respectively, in the ranking of world's busiest ports. Port Klang handled about 12.32 million TEUs in 2018, while Port of Tanjung Pelepas handled close to 9 million TEUs.[5]

Both Port Klang and Port of Tanjung Pelepas are administered under the Ministry of Transport of the central government. Other central government operated ports include Port Penang, Kuantan Port, Kemaman Port, Johor Port, Bintulu Port, almost all of which serve mostly as feeder ports to Port Klang and Port of Tanjung Pelepas. State governments also manage their own ports, but these ports are usually of much lower level of capacity. Some of them have more specialized functions (such as specializing in oil and gas transshipment, or in cruise tourism). Kuantan Port, as the major port of

---

[4] *Op. cit.*, Leong and Lee (2012).
[5] "Top 50 World Container Ports," *World Shipping Council*, accessed on February 11, 2020, http://www.worldshipping.org/about-the-industry/global-trade/top-50-world-container-ports.

the east coast of Peninsular Malaysia, has forged a partnership with Guangxi Beibu Gulf International Port Group (GBGIPG), which is also a major investor in the Malaysia–China Kuantan Industrial Park (MCKIP). Kuantan Port is now undergoing a major upgrading of its infrastructure. Together with the industrialization brought about by MCKIP, the Kuantan Port aims to become a major regional hub for the east coast of Malaysia, Gulf of Thailand and southern Indochina.

Today, Port Klang and Port of Tanjung Pelepas together handle about a quarter of the containers passing through the Southeast Asian region, and account for 3% of world container traffic.[6] However, the goal of successive governments of Malaysia — to rival Port of Singapore as the major regional transshipment hub — is still not realized, as Singapore retains its status as the second busiest port in the world, with a record of handling 36.6 million TEUs in 2018. Industry players pointed out that while both Malaysian ports have made inroads, there are still disadvantages and problems. Competition between North Port, West Port and the Port of Tanjung Pelepas can become excessive, undercutting each other's profits. In addition, the changing landscape of global shipping (with the formation of three major shipping alliances) in the past decade presented a lot of uncertainties and challenges which Malaysian ports had not really fully prepared for.[7]

China–Malaysia Port Alliance (CMPA)

According to Liow Tiong Lai, Malaysia's Minister of Transport from 2014 to 2018, Malaysia first proposed the idea of forming a port alliance back in May 2014 when the then Prime Minister Najib

---

[6] "About RM5b Needed to Expand 3 Malaysian Ports, says RAM Ratings," *The Star*, July 19, 2017, https://www.thestar.com.my/business/business-news/2017/07/19/about-rm5b-needed-to-expand-3-malaysian-ports-says-ram-ratings/.

[7] Kamarul Azhar, "Lacking a National Strategy, Malaysian Ports Lose Out to Singapore," *The Edge*, February 27, 2019, https://www.theedgemarkets.com/article/lacking-national-strategy-malaysian-ports-lose-out-singapore.

Table 1   Members in China–Malaysia Port Alliance (CMPA).

China	Malaysia
• Shanghai International Port Group	• Port Authority of Klang
• Port of Dalian Authority	• Port Authority of Bintulu
• Jiangsu Taicang Port Management	• Port Authority of Johor
• Fujian Fuzhou Port Authority	• Port Authority of Kuantan
• Xiamen Port Authority	• Port Authority of Melaka
• Guangzhou Port Authority	• Port Authority of Penang
• Port and Shipping Authority of Haikou	• Port Authority of Kemaman
• Beibuwan Port Administration	• Port Authority of Sabah
• Ningbo Port Company Ltd.	• Port Authority of Kuching
• Port Administration of Shenzhen	
• Qingdao Port Group Ltd.	
• Tianjin Port Group Ltd.	

Source: First Page of the Website of China-Malaysia Port Alliance, available at: https://cmpa.asia/index.php/en/#

visited China.[8] However, it took until November 2015 for the Memorandum of Understanding (MoU) on CMPA, which was drafted by Malaysia's Ministry of Transport,[9] to be signed by Liow and his Chinese counterpart, Yang Chuantang, under the witness of the then Prime Minister of Malaysia Najib and Chinese Premier Li Keqiang. Premier Li paid an official visit to Malaysia at that time. The alliance originally covered 16 ports from both countries, and a year later expanded to 21 (see Table 1). The purpose of the alliance, as stated in the MoU, is to "enhance the friendship and mutual understanding between Parties by ways of organizing cooperative activities", including port studies, training and apprenticeship, information exchange, technical assistance and mutual port promotion.[10] The first meeting of CMPA was held in Ningbo, China, in July 2016, attended by leading transport ministry officials from both China and Malaysia, and officials of the member ports. Two secretariats of

---

[8] Interview with Liow Tiong Lai, Malaysia's Minister of Transport 2014–2018, Kuala Lumpur, July 8, 2020.

[9] *Ibid.*

[10] A copy of the MoU is available at: https://cmpa.asia/index.php/en/event/edocument/category/8-port-alliance.

CMPA were established. CMPA Malaysia was set up under Port Klang Authority, while CMPA China was established under China Ports and Harbors Association (CPHA), which is headquartered in Shanghai.

The Ningbo meeting also decided to establish an annual joint meeting mechanism and discussed plans of action for implementing the scope of activities outlined in the MoU. Reportedly the meeting also mentioned that CMPA could be a platform to encourage connecting the shipping and logistics businesses from both countries, mutual investment into ports and port management companies, and development of integrated port-industrial park development.[11] It should be noted that business and investment activities actually are not spelled out in the MoU, but could be considered add-on functions of the alliance in the coming years.

Since the first meeting in Ningbo, CMPA annual meeting has been held three times (October 2017 in Kuala Lumpur, November 2018 in Tianjin and August 2019 in Kuala Lumpur). The CMPA meeting is usually officiated by the Minister of Transport of the hosting country, while the visiting delegation is led by a high-level official from the counterpart transport ministry. In addition, the two secretariats also hold several joint meetings every year. These meetings institutionalized the exchanges and ensured the continuity of CMPA. They also allowed CMPA to address issues in a timely manner as both sides moved to implement concrete and specific cooperative projects, review progresses and challenges and plan for major directions.[12]

A curious fact about CMPA's membership is that while on the Malaysian side, the membership is restricted only to port authorities, on the Chinese side, port authorities and port operators (such as Shanghai International Port Group) are both allowed to be formal

---

[11] "Kong: Port Links will Spur Growth," *The Star*, May 27, 2016, https://www. thestar.com.my/news/nation/2016/05/27/kong-port-links-will-spur-growth-deal-with-china-will-boost-trade-ties; "Zhongma Gangkou Lianmeng Zai Ningbo Juxing Shouci Huitan (The First Meeting of CMPA Held in Ningbo)," *China–Malaysia Port Alliance*, accessed on November 22, 2019, http://www.port.org.cn/info/2016/193597.htm.

[12] Interview with K. Subramaniam, General Manager of Port Klang Authority, January 10, 2020.

members of the alliance, mainly due to the fact most port operators are state-owned enterprises that are often considered an extension of governmental bodies rather than purely commercial organizations.[13] Malaysia, however, allows privatized port operators to join CMPA as "associate members". All other stakeholders in port businesses, such as shipping lines, freight forwarding companies, logistics companies, trucking companies, however, are kept outside of the alliance, and this is to ensure that the work of CMPA will remain policy-focused and service-oriented.[14]

Information exchange and sharing

Before CMPA came into being, a common complaint among the ports in both Malaysia and China was that information of the various ports of each country was too scattered and not up-to-date. For both sides, there was basically very little knowledge of the port landscape of the other country, and hence opportunities for cooperation, such as opening up of new routes, were limited. It was felt that a one-stop information center was crucially needed.

To this end, several actions were undertaken. First, the websites of all the participating members of CMPA were to be linked to each other. Second, under the auspice of CMPA, two websites have been launched. The Chinese website is hosted by CPHA's website (http://www.port.org.cn/alliance/index.htm), while the Malaysian (English) website (https://cmpa.asia/index.php/en/) is linked to the website of Port Klang Authority. The two websites serve to publicize and publish the work of CMPA. Third, the Chinese CMPA also publishes a quarterly bulletin *China–Malaysia Port Alliance Information Exchange*

---

[13] *Ibid.* However, this has also created a situation where for Malaysia all the ports have clear boundaries between port management authorities and those business actors, while some participating Chinese members double up as commercial actors as well, and it is not uncommon that during the sidelines of the meetings some of these Chinese port officials would want to discuss business proposals with their Malaysian counterparts.

[14] *Ibid.*

on its website. The bulletin provides quarterly updates and detailed summaries of statistical data, regulations and information related to project investment, shipping and port business among the member ports in China. Fourth, in each joint annual meeting, participating ports from both countries also made presentations of their own respective ports, highlighting their advantages, niche areas, future plans and directions. The direct interactions among members also provided opportunities to clarify misconceptions and to update latest developments. CMPA provides therefore the platform for networking and for the first-hand gathering of crucial port and shipping information.

Training and capacity building

In explaining what benefits that CMPA can bring, Liow, the former Minister of Transport of Malaysia, said that "we are working in many areas … technology transfer, human capacity building, training of manpower from both countries. China is advanced in their port technology, in freight forwarding, container transfers … We are looking at the bottlenecks of our customs and bottlenecks of China's custom".[15] A brief report of the Malaysian secretariat of CMPA in December 2016 stated that Malaysian ports wished to learn from their Chinese counterparts "how to enhance the supply of ancillary service to support shipping lines".[16]

The World Bank maintains two very useful datasets to gauge the level of logistics and port performance. Logistic Performance Index (LPI) takes into consideration the efficiency of the clearance process, quality of infrastructure, quality of logistics services, ease of arranging shipments, tracking system and timeliness as factors in measuring logistics capabilities. According to the Aggregated LPI (2012–2018),

---

[15] Amy Chew, "China, Malaysia Tout New 'Port Alliance' to Reduce Customs Bottlenecks and Boost Trade," *South China Morning Post*, April 9, 2016, https://www.scmp.com/news/asia/southeast-asia/article/1934839/china-malaysia-tout-new-port-alliance-reduce-customs.

[16] CMPA, "China–Malaysia Port Alliance 2nd Quarter Report (October–December 2016)," https://cmpa.asia/index.php/en/event/edocument/category/2-malaysia.

China is ranked 27th in the world with a score of 3.60, while Malaysia is ranked 35th with a score of 3.54 (the first is Germany with a score of 4.19, while Singapore is ranked 5th with a score of 4.05).[17] However, in terms of port's performance, the World Bank maintains the Quality of Port Infrastructure Index, which is derived from surveys of business executives' perceptions, and Malaysia actually scored higher (5.4) than China (4.6) in the 2017 edition of the Quality of Port Infrastructure Index (Singapore had a score of 6.7).[18] Despite the reportedly better performance of Malaysian ports in the Quality of Port Infrastructure Index, the advances that China has made in terms of digitalization and automation of ports (the movement towards "smart ports") and the implementation of environmentally protective measures in port operations ("green ports") have made a great impression on the Malaysian port experts. Port Klang Authority, for example, is planning expansion, and is eager to incorporate advanced systems of automation in port operation and management from China. On the other hand, Malaysia holds advantages in having a sound administrative and legal system. Meanwhile, Malaysia is renowned in the world for its strong maritime shipping law. Chinese ports can learn from Malaysia in areas such as the rule of law, transparency, and the regional business context.[19]

While human resources training and capacity building are promising cooperative activities under the CMPA platform, so far only three training courses have been undertaken. In November 2017, a training course on port regulations, management and operations was conducted in Kuala Lumpur for the Chinese visiting CMPA delegation. In December 2018, Malaysian CMPA delegation attended a week-long training course organized by the Guangzhou Port Authority.

---

[17] See https://lpi.worldbank.org/international/aggregated-ranking, accessed on February 18, 2020. The Aggregated Logistic Performance Index (LPI) combines data from the LPI surveys in 2012, 2014, 2016 and 2018. Reportedly it "reduces random variations" and generates a "'big picture' to better indicate countries' logistics performance."

[18] See https://data.worldbank.org/indicator/IQ.WEF.PORT.XQ?locations=CN-MY-SG, accessed on February 18, 2020.

[19] *Op.cit.*, Interview with Liow Tiong Lai (2020).

Table 2 Malaysia–China–Singapore Liner Shipping Bilateral Connectivity Index.

Year	Index Score and Ranking for Malaysia–China	Index Score and Ranking for Malaysia–Singapore
2015	0.796 (2)	0.800 (1)
2016	0.785 (2)	0.816 (1)
2017	0.761 (2)	0.796 (1)
2018	0.758 (2)	0.809 (1)
2019	0.755 (2)	0.791 (1)

In October 2019, the Malaysian secretariat of CMPA conducted another course, this time focusing on Industry 4.0 and its effect on the shipping industry, for the Chinese CMPA members.

Port and shipping connectivity

According to the Liner Shipping Bilateral Connectivity Index compiled by the United Nations Conference on Trade and Development, for five consecutive years China has been the second most connected country (after Singapore) with Malaysia (see Table 2).[20]

The Liner Bilateral Connectivity Index takes into account the number of transshipments, direct connections, common connections, level of service competition and the size of ship in compiling the index, and the data show that Malaysia and China are quite well connected. Still, in agreeing to form CMPA, it is the goal for policymakers and port authorities from both sides to see more networking opportunities that can bring on greater shipping connectivity. To that end, a number of "sister" port-to-port relationships have been formed. While "sister" relationship between Kuantan Port and Beibuwan Port had existed before CMPA came into being, since the launch of CMPA, more port-to-port relationships, such as Fuzhou Port and Port Klang and Port Malacca, Tianjin Port and Port Klang,

---

[20] Calculated based on the data compiled by United Nations Conference on Trade and Development, accessed on February 20, 2020, http://unctadstat.unctad.org/wds/TableViewer/tableView.aspx?ReportId=96618.

Qingdao Port and Port Klang, Xiamen Port and Port Klang, Guangzhou Port and Port Malacca, were formed.

One presumed implication of forming such relationships is that they could bring more business opportunities, as ports are also in a position to promote their sister ports to their shipping liners clients. Both the individual port-to-port relationships and the whole CMPA network will enlarge the transshipment cargo businesses and bring on more traders for the benefits of the partners and members in CMPA.[21] This is especially crucial for Malaysia, given that Chinese shipping liners have become crucial for both Port Klang and Port of Tanjunge Pelepas in enlarging their businesses. Similarly, Kuantan Port's expansion is premised on the expectation that its sister relationship with Beibuwan Port (and the MCKIP) will significantly increase its businesses in the future.

In addition, through CMPA, Malaysian ports are also learning from China how to create a more efficient and simplified cargo clearance process. LOGINK is China's national electronic exchange platform for transportation and logistics information. In July 2017, a Malaysian port delegation visited LOGINK's office in Hangzhou to understand how it works with North East Asia Logistics Information Service Network (NEAL-NET), in which LOGINK is one of the three founder partners. NEAL-NET serves as a single-window, digital information collaboration system between port authorities that streamlines processes, reduces administrative time and facilitates trade. Through this network, traders only have to report to their port authorities once, and all information will be collaborated and transmitted to their counterparts. A single and standardized cargo clearance process between Malaysian ports and Chinese ports will greatly reduce the time and costs of bilateral trade.

Discussion: Challenges and Prospects

While the MoU of CMPA was signed in December 2015, it came into being only in the Ningbo meeting in 2016. By 2020, it entered its

---

[21] *Op.cit.*, Interview with K. Subramaniam (2020).

fourth year. In reviewing what has been done in the past four years, it is fair to argue that, while not ignoring the progress, perhaps much more could have been done. While in terms of information exchange both sides have had the websites up and running and regularly publishing useful information, the Malaysian side has not really followed up with the commitment to publish quarterly bulletin as the Chinese side has done, perhaps due to the lack of adequate number of staff to cover this. At least for the Malaysian side, there is still a lack of "whole-of-government" concerted action in embracing the potentials and opportunities brought forth by CMPA. CMPA is spearheaded by the Ministry of Transport, but the enthusiasm is not shared across the ministries as well as the agencies under them. Crucially, for Malaysia to fully systemize the kind of automotive port operations that China has, it is critical that some existing regulations governing the customs and clearance process be amended and simplified, and that different government agencies across the board be willing to streamline the process. In terms of capacity building and human resources training, it also seems that more frequent and in-depth training courses could be conducted for both sides.

The many projects launched under CMPA will take some years to see their benefits concertized, but the overall usefulness is clear. In addition, while this is not something stipulated in the MoU of CMPA, a future direction of Malaysia–China port cooperation could involve more investment, and direct involvement of planning, operation and development of ports by China in Malaysia. Malaysian law restricts foreign ownership of Malaysian port operator to 30% equity, but the government made an exception for Guangxi Beibu Gulf International Port Group, which acquired 40% equity in Kuantan Port Consortium, the port operator. As Malaysia's ports plan for expansion, there is a possibility that China will play a bigger and more direct role. The possible expansion of Port Klang is a case in point, which has already drawn the interests of companies from Dubai, Japan, China and so forth. China holds several advantages. As mentioned before, Malaysia is eager to learn the automation system from China, and a direct Chinese investment could allow greater transfer of knowledge and technology in designing automation systems in

Malaysian ports. Moreover, China also has a very good experience in integrating port development with a nearby industrial park. Malaysia is interested in the port-park integration model, and this is why the experience of Kuantan Port and MCKIP will be crucial. In short, while CMPA starts on the basis of port cooperation and soft infrastructure connectivity, it could be a springboard for industrial park and hard infrastructure investment and construction.[22]

Finally, there is also another future implication of CMPA in the sense that it could become a competitive dynamic with the ASEAN Single Shipping Market (ASSM). ASEAN has been devoted to increased connectivity among member states which can be seen in the formulation of ASEAN Economic Community (AEC), the Master Plan on ASEAN Connectivity (2015 and 2025), Brunei Action Plan on strategic transport 2011–2015, and Kuala Lumpur Transport Strategic Plan 2016–2025. ASSM encompasses the ASEAN Port Network of 47 ports, and is an initiative to create a more "efficient and integrated maritime transport sector" and to serve as a "platform for ASEAN countries to upgrade their port infrastructure and capacity in order to serve the ASEAN markets", especially through means of both hard infrastructure construction and "soft infrastructure" policies such as labor market regulations, harmonization of port documentation, development of guidelines of port tariffs, development of electronic information sharing platforms, and development and sharing of port technology.[23] It is in essence similar to (and more ambitious than) what CMPA has set out to achieve between Malaysia and China.

However, unlike CMPA, there is no permanent secretariat that serves ASSM. ASSM has always been a much looser network beset by various challenges. Barriers, ranging from poor infrastructure to differences over customs procedure, laws and regulations, investment

---

[22] *Ibid.*
[23] Andrew Kam Jia Yi and Tham Siew Yean, "Towards an ASEAN Single Shipping Market." In *Connecting Oceans, Vol. 1: Malaysia as a Maritime Nation*, ed. Han-Dieter Evers, Abdul Rahman Embong, and Rashila Ramli (Bangi: Penerbitan Universiti Kebangsaan Malaysia, 2020), 126–127, 147.

restrictions and lack of transparency, continue to affect the development of ASSM.[24] In his interview with the author, Liow Tiong Lai, Malaysia's former Minister of Transport, also recalled that while ASSM discussions were sustained by goodwill and friendship, the actual and concrete improvements were always slow.[25] As a study by Malaysian scholars Andrew Kam Jia Yi and Tham Siew Yean shows, while intra-ASEAN port integration has increased, the better performing ports of medium- and high-income ASEAN countries (Singapore, Malaysia, Thailand, and Indonesia) are having better connectivity with external partners, including China, rather than with the ASEAN ports from the low-income countries. This has further increased the disparity within ASEAN. They have concluded that ASSM has not been very successful, and China's BRI, it was noted, now appears to have greater likelihood to "connect the oceans in Southeast Asia" than "ASEAN's own initiatives".[26]

Conclusion

Compared to the mega-infrastructure projects that tend to attract a lot of headlines, CMPA has captured far less attention. It is an effort by both Malaysian and Chinese governments to enhance maritime "soft infrastructure connectivity" through mutual learning, information sharing and exchanges, technical cooperation, and coordination in policies, standards and practices. Through this kind of cooperative activities, the port operations from both countries could eventually share the same kind of technical processes and methods. At least for Malaysia, CMPA helps improve Malaysia-China trade in terms of improving efficiency and increasing cost-effectiveness. CMPA also

---

[24] Jose L. Tongzon and Sang-Yoon Lee, "The Challenges of Economic Integration: The Case of Shipping in ASEAN Countries," *The Pacific Review* 28, no. 4 (2015): 483–504; Jose L. Tongzon and Sang-Yoon Lee, "Achieving an ASEAN Single Shipping Market: Shipping and Logistics Firms' Perspective," *Maritime Policy and Management*, no. 43(4) (2016): 407–419.

[25] *Op. cit.*, Interview with Liow Tiong Lai (2020).

[26] *Op. cit.*, Andrew Kam Jia Yi and Tham Siew Yean (2020): 148.

serves to enhance connectivity at the people level and build trust and confidence through the frequent interactions among port professionals working on similar issues. It aims to familiarize Malaysian port authorities with Chinese port operations and technologies and *vice versa*, and may also lead to prospective investment and development of ports.

7

Malaysia in China's Belt and Road Initiative — Lessons from a Selected Project

Li Ran* and Cheong Kee Cheok†

*Institute of China Studies, University of Malaya,
Kuala Lumpur, Malaysia

†Adjunct Professor at Faculty of Economics,
University of Malaya, Kuala Lumpur, Malaysia

Introduction

The relationship between Malaysia and China has strong historical roots, from the voyages of Chinese admiral Zheng He who visited Melaka and transited the Straits of Melaka in the 15th century through large-scale migration mainly during the 19th and the early decades of the 20th century up to the outbreak of the Second World War. That war ended these links and the establishment of the People's Republic put China and Malaysia (then the Federation of Malaya) on opposite sides of the Cold War. It was not until 1974 that Malaysia, then under Prime Minister Abdul Razak, established formal diplomatic relations with China, the first Association of Southeast Asian Nations (ASEAN) country to do so. Even so, it took until around 1990 for Malaysia, by then under Prime Minister Mahathir Mohamad, to fully restore economic ties with China.

Significant as the aforementioned developments were for Malaysia, China's role in its bilateral relationship has changed consonant with its rise to great power status. This rise is being and will come to be defined by China's massive Belt and Road Initiative (BRI) announced by Chinese President Xi Jinping in 2013.[1] The BRI consists of two major routes — the land-based Silk Road Economic Belt and the 21st Century Maritime Silk Road. The countries of ASEAN make up one of the major nodes of the latter Road, and have been beneficiaries of a large portion of China's BRI investments. As a founding member of ASEAN, Malaysia also borders the Straits of Malacca, through which reportedly a third of the oil transported by sea from the Middle East moves to Asian markets, including China's.[2] With its strategic importance not lost among China's leadership, Malaysia has been a host to China's outward direct foreign investment (OFDI) that is not all BRI-related.

Among China's OFDI, the implications for Malaysia of China's investments under BRI represent the theme of this chapter. We anchor China's BRI investment in infrastructure using as a case study one of the most controversial projects — the East Coast Rail Link (ECRL) that with a change of government in Malaysia was revised through renegotiation and scaled back. The choice of this as a case study is based on several considerations. First, because the BRI is primarily about connectivity, the ECRL is a suitable candidate. Second, its scale and likely impact makes for it being one of the most important undertakings by Malaysia. Third, because the project represents a new form of collaboration — between two sovereign states without

---

[1] S. Mahmud Ali, *China's Belt and Road Vision: Geoeconomics and Geopolitics* (Cham: Springer Nature Switzerland AG, 2020).

[2] U.S. Energy Information Administration, "The Strait of Malacca, a Key Oil Trade Chokepoint, Links the Indian and Pacific Oceans," August 11, 2017, https://www.eia.gov/todayinenergy/detail.php?id=32452.

the participation of the private sector and other stakeholders — it is interesting and important to trace its likely impact, both positive and negative. And finally, the question of what are the consequences of bypassing the usual checks and balances for the project's governance and institutional support needs to be asked. Would it be captured by vested interests seeking private gains?

Beyond these specific questions, the scale and coverage of the BRI that translate into multiple objectives, the diversity of stakeholders and the dearth of experience during implementation inevitably produce lessons for future BRI projects. We draw project-specific lessons from the much criticized ECRL as well as general lessons from the BRI overall.

This chapter is organized as follows. In the next section, we provide a brief summary of the historical relationship between the two countries. Modern trends, especially in the context of the rise of Chinese OFDI, are previewed. The timing of China's BRI announcement coinciding with Malaysia's reduced economic growth and weak overall foreign direct investment (FDI) performance were good matches between the two countries' supply of and demand for investment funds. Following this, China's involvement in Malaysia's infrastructure projects is briefly reviewed, leading to the ECRL, its specifications and revision after Malaysia's general election. Lessons from the project, both for project planning and execution, and from BRI overall, conclude this chapter.

Malaysia and China from a Historical Perspective

Even discounting the voyages of Zheng He in the 15th century, Malaysia has a history of links with China that spans over two centuries. The discovery of tin deposits in Peninsular Malaysia's Perak and Selangor states in the early 1800s attracted increasing numbers of migrants from primarily the provinces of Fujian and Guangdong where political turmoil and economic hardships made life difficult.[3] Substantial amounts of remittances were sent home by these migrants

---

[3] Yip Yat Hoong, *Development of the Tin Mining Industry of Malaya* (Kuala Lumpur: University of Malaya Press, 1969), 45–55.

to China. But these flows were ended when the Pacific War broke out in 1942. The immediate post-war period saw a brief resumption of remittances to China, but two transitions ended all migration from China — first a political transition in which decolonization in Malaya and the establishment of the People's Republic of China put both countries on opposite sides of the Cold War, and second a demographic transition that saw an increasing proportion of ethnic Chinese who were born and grew up in Malaya/Malaysia as the years passed. A China-supported insurgency mounted by the Malayan Communist Party against the British Colonial Administration and its successor the government of independent Malaya from 1948 to 1960 added to a frosty relationship between the two countries.[4]

It was not until 1974 when Malaysia's second Prime Minister Abdul Razak decided to establish full diplomatic relations with China, the first Southeast Asian country to do so and just 2 years after U.S. President Nixon's meeting with Chairman Mao in Beijing. Despite this establishment of ties, Malaysia placed severe restrictions on trade with China.[5] It was not until the premiership of Mahathir Mohamad that all restrictions in Malaysia–China trade were removed in about 1990.

Prior to that, President Deng Xiaoping had begun his liberalization of the Chinese economy, setting in motion uninterrupted rapid economic growth in China that has lasted for nearly four decades. Malaysia, too, having abandoned import substitution in favor of export promotion, achieved robust economic growth from the 1970s for two decades that earned it membership in the World Bank's "High Performing Asian Economies" (HPAEs).[6] The impressive performance of the HPAEs, together with China's, saw the economic

---

[4] John Swift, *The Palgrave Concise Historical Atlas of the Cold War* (London: Palgrave Macmillan, 2003), 32–33.

[5] "Malaysia's China Policy: The More Things Change … The More They Stay the Same," *The Diplomat*, September 12, 2018, https://thediplomat.com/2018/09/malaysias-china-policy-the-more-things-change/.

[6] The World Bank, *The East Asian Miracle: Economic Growth and Public Policy* (New York: Oxford University Press, 1993).

center of gravity shift from West to East. But for the HPAEs, that growth spurt came to an abrupt halt with the Asian Financial Crisis (AFC) in 1997. Growth never recovered. In the meantime, China in keeping with its gradualist approach only permitted partial liberalization of its international sector with the consequence that it was not severely impacted by the AFC. Indeed, its commitment not to devalue the RMB was seen by Malaysia and other ASEAN countries as a gesture of goodwill.

But the growth story of the 20th century belongs to China. The end of the 20th century and the beginning of the 21st saw several milestones — accession to the World Trade Organization in 2001, recognition that it is the world's factory[7] and the signing of the ASEAN–China Free Trade Area Agreement in 2002. Beyond dominating global exports, and with enterprise reform, China felt sufficiently confident to encourage its enterprises to compete internationally. Thus in 1999, it launched its "going out" strategy that signaled the beginning of China's OFDI.[8] However, until the launch of the BRI, Malaysia did not figure prominently as a destination for Chinese OFDI, having neither high technology industries Chinese enterprises want to acquire nor resource companies for sale, both OFDI priorities for China. The breakthrough for Chinese OFDI would come only with China's launch of BRI as discussed in the following section.

Malaysia's FDI from China since BRI's Launch

Before BRI's launch in 2013, China was encountering an increasingly difficult domestic economic environment. On the one hand, the economic "new normal" China's leaders targeted was for a slower but better quality economic growth that required the acceleration of industrial transformation and upgrading. In its drive for rapid growth, China had accumulated considerable surplus production capacity that

---

[7] Helen Mees, *The Chinese Birdcage — How China's Rise Almost Toppled the West* (New York: Palgrave MacMillan, 2016), 21–32.

[8] China Policy, *China Going Global: Between Ambition and Capacity* (Beijing: China Policy, 2017).

employed low technology. On the other hand, increasing production costs especially for labor combined with shrinking market demand and trade restrictions by European and American countries forced Chinese manufacturing enterprises to consider relocating production overseas. The Southeast Asian region especially Malaysia, blessed with a good transport and communications infrastructure and with a growing middle class, would appear to be a natural choice.

Even before and also after BRI's launch, there was a wave of Chinese companies coming to Malaysia. These investments were in the form of FDI and foreign indirect investment (FII). Common forms of FDI include establishing subsidiaries of Chinese parent companies, setting up factories to produce in Malaysia, setting up China–Malaysia joint-venture companies and international mergers and acquisitions (M&As). There were also FIIs such as Chinese companies (mostly construction companies) winning contracts and Chinese banks providing bank loans to projects in Malaysia.

According to Figure 1, investment flows from China to Malaysia grew steadily from 2012 to 2015 and sharply from 2015 to 2017. However, there was a significant drop in 2018. Due to the change of

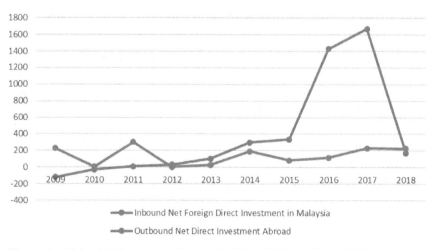

Figure 1 Malaysia's Investment Flow with China (USD million), 2009–2018.
Source: Department of Statistics Malaysia, Official Portal.

Table 1 Accumulated Investment from China in Malaysia (USD million), 2005–2018.

Sector	FDI (32)	FDI + Contract work (76)
Energy	6,820 (35.97%)	12,040 (28.80%)
Real Estate	5,450 (28.74%)	8,090 (19.35%)
Transport	3,100 (16.35%)	13,760 (32.91%)
Total	18,960	41,810

Note: Investment amount of USD 100 million and over only.
Source: China Global Investment Tracker, http://www.aei.org/china-global-investment-tracker/.

government after the general election in May 2018, some mega infrastructure projects such as the ECRL in which China's companies were involved were suspended, renegotiated and downsized. This created considerable uncertainty until the then Malaysian Prime Minister Mahathir attended the Second Belt and Road Forum for International Cooperation and sent a positive signal to potential Chinese investors that the projects would be resumed.

In terms of large investments of USD 100 million and over (Table 1), energy, real estate and transport were the top three sectors that China's investments were involved in in Malaysia. However, if contract work that Chinese companies undertook is counted, the transport sector would rank first, ahead of the energy sector. This shows that for large projects, classification matters. This is well illustrated by the ECRL. Before its suspension, the ECRL was in the category of transport sector by contract work. But after its restart in 2019, the ECRL was considered as an FDI project. Among 32 projects, those from China's state-owned enterprises (SOEs) accounted for about 68%. The Global Investment Tracker Database captured projects with investment of over USD 100 million, which would have been largely undertaken by China's large SOEs (mostly not in the manufacturing sector), so that private enterprises' and manufacturing sector's investment might be underestimated.[9] According to the

---

[9] The presentation and analysis of Table 1 was inspired by Zhang Miao's presentation at a book launch and academic dialogue session in honor of the Late Professor

Malaysian Investment Development Authority (MIDA), China was the biggest investor country in Malaysia in the manufacturing sector for three consecutive years — 2016, 2017 and 2018. In the next section, we look into a controversial case that has particular significance for the BRI.

The East Coast Rail Line (ECRL) as BRI Infrastructure

Both land and sea regional connectivity are important for Malaysia. Land transport infrastructure consists of railways, highways and rail transit that connect Malaysia with the Eurasian continent, while sea transport infrastructure such as maritime ports, cross-sea bridges and undersea tunnels link Malaysia with the whole Asia-Pacific region and beyond. So far, Malaysian transport infrastructure projects that China is involved in include the ECRL, Kuala Lumpur–Singapore High-speed Rail, Mass Rapid Transit (MRT), Light Rail Transit (LRT), Penang Undersea Tunnel, Kuantan Port, Melaka Gateway and TRX Signature Tower.

The ECRL is a railway that Malaysia wants to build in the Malay Peninsula that links the more developed west to the less developed east.[10] In the very beginning, this railway was intended to connect several key cities in Malaysia, including Kota Baru, Kuala Terengganu, Kuantan and Klang. The total planned length of the railway was 688.3 km. The ECRL, to be built by China Communications Construction Company, Ltd. (CCCC), was planned to take five to six years to develop in stages and expected to be completed by 2022.[11]

Lee Poh Ping at Institute of China Studies, University of Malaya, Kuala Lumpur, Malaysia on December 12, 2017.

[10] "Alleviating China's Malacca Dilemma," Institute for Security & Development Policy, March 13, 2013, https://isdp.eu/alleviating-chinas-malacca-dilemma/.

[11] "China Has Offered 89.1 Billion Yuan in Low-interest Loans for the Construction of the East Coast Rail Line of Malaysia," *Guanchazhe*, December 11, 2016, https://www.guancha.cn/Neighbors/2016_11_01_379045.shtml.

In November 2016, the ECRL project agreement was signed between the owner Malaysia Rail Link Sdn Bhd (MRL)[12] and the general contractor CCCC in the presence of the then Prime Minister Najib without an open bid. The contract involved a sum of RM 46 billion. Under the bilateral agreement, the Chinese side would provide RM 55 billion for the project.[13] About 85% of the RM 55 billion was lent by Exim Bank of China at a low interest rate of 3.35%, with an amortization period of 20 years with the first seven years free of repayments, including interest.[14] The Malaysian government was the guarantor.[15] On May 13, 2017, in the presence of the then Malaysian Prime Minister Najib, MRL and CCCC signed the second phase work of the commercial contract in Beijing. This contract involved a sum of RM 9 billion.[16] In August 2017, Chinese State Councilor Wang Yong and Najib attended the opening ceremony. Wang Yong said this

---

[12] MRL is the wholly owned subsidiary of the Minister of Finance Incorporated (MOF Inc.), as well as the project and asset owner of the ECRL project.

[13] "The Actual Cost of the East Coast Rail Line of Malaysia is 81 Billion Yuan, and the Ministry of Finance Requests Drastic Price Cuts," *Malaysiakini*, July 13, 2018, https://www.malaysiakini.com/news/432434.

[14] "China Has Offered 89.1 Billion Yuan in Low-interest Loans for the Construction of the East Coast Rail Line of Malaysia," *Guanchazhe*, November 11, 2016, https://www.guancha.cn/Neighbors/2016_11_01_379045.shtml.

"Najib: Pakatan Harapan Should Publish the Contract Report. Let the People Assess Whether the East Coast Rail Line of Malaysia Should Be Built," *Sin Chew Daily*, August 24, 2018, https://www.sinchew.com.my/content/content_1787058.html.

"The Government Announced That the East Coast Rail Line Would Resume Work with a Cost Cut of 21.5 Billion Yuan," *Malaysiakini*, April 12, 2019, https://www.malaysiakini.com/news/472010.

[15] "Wan Saifu Wan Jan: The Impact of Chinese Investment on Malaysia," *Lianhe Zaobao*, July 10, 2017, https://beltandroad.zaobao.com/beltandroad/analysis/story20170710-777842.

[16] "The Actual Cost of the East Coast Rail Line of Malaysia is 81 Billion Yuan, and the Ministry of Finance Requests Drastic Price Cuts," *Malaysiakini*, July 3, 2018, https://www.malaysiakini.com/news/432434.

railway was a flagship project of BRI jointly built by the two countries. Preliminary design and exploration work were then started.[17]

Malaysia's 14th general election held on May 9, 2018 saw the defeat of the government led by Najib. On July 4, 2018, the new government under Mahathir instructed MRL citing national interest as one of the reasons, to ask CCCC, the general contractor of the ECRL project, to suspend all work commissioned under the engineering, procurement and construction (EPC) contract with immediate effect.[18] On April 12, 2019, the then Malaysian Prime Minister's office issued a notice that MRL signed a supplementary agreement with CCCC to allow the ECRL project to resume work. The ECRL had been reduced to 640 km and its completion date had been pushed back to 2026.[19] The ECRL project resumed work at the Kuala Dungun Tunnel in Terengganu State on July 25, 2019.[20]

Between these two events, what had changed? First, under the original ECRL project, the number of stations planned for Phases 1 and 2 was 24. The number of stations was reduced to 20 with the new alignment. And the northern extension was canceled.[21] Second, taking into account cultural, heritage and environmental issues, the new scheme had its route diverted to avoid the Klang Gate Quartz Ridge[22]

---

[17] "China's BRI and the Timing: Malaysia to Resume the ECRL Project," *BBC News*, April 15, 2019, https://www.bbc.com/zhongwen/simp/world-47934661.

[18] "For the Interests of the State, the Malaysia Rail Link Sdn Bhd Ordered the East Coast Rail Line to Stop," *Malaysiakini*, July 4, 2018, https://www.malaysiakini.com/news/432668.

[19] "Details of Revising the Treaty of the East Coast Rail Line of Malaysia, the Landmark Project of China–Malaysia Cooperation Will Resume Work," *Caixin*, April 14, 2019, http://international.caixin.com/2019-04-14/101403918.html.

[20] "Malaysia's East Coast Rail Line Project Resumes Work," *China News*, July 25, 2019, http://www.chinanews.com/gj/2019/07-25/8907011.shtml.

[21] "Press Statement by MRL to Clarify Certain Misleading Information on the ECRL Project," *The Malaysia Rail Link Sdn Bhd*, April 17, 2019, http://www.mrl.com.my/en/press-statement-by-mrl-to-clarify-certain-misleading-information-on-the-ecrl-project/.

[22] "Details of Revising the Treaty of the East Coast Rail Line of Malaysia, the Landmark Project of China–Malaysia Cooperation Will Resume Work," *Caixin*, April 14, 2019, http://international.caixin.com/2019-04-14/101403918.html.

as well as those parts where land acquisition might pose difficulties, the overall bridge/tunnel ratio had been reduced. Third, the length of the line had been reduced from 688.3 km to 640 km.[23] Fourth, the project would make use of the existing Kuala Lumpur International Airport Express (ERL) and MRT2 lines, known as the Sungai Buloh–Serdang–Putrajaya line, with an interchange at Putrajaya station.[24] Thus, by adjusting the routing direction, distance and work scope, as well as optimizing the design scheme and value engineering,[25] there was a reduction in the overall project cost from RM 65.5 billion to RM 44 billion.[26]

In addition, the cooperation mode for this project had changed. Under the new agreement, the ownership of the ECRL project belonged to the MRL of the Ministry of Finance, Malaysia, while the management, operation and maintenance of the ECRL network was under the joint venture of MRL and CCCC with equal shares.[27] This joint venture would provide technical support and share operational

---

[23] "ECRL Key Facts," *The Malaysia Rail Link Sdn Bhd*, 2019, http://www.mrl.com. my/en/ecrl-key-facts/.
[24] "The Money Saved by the East Coast Rail Line Could Be Used to Build Two Twin Towers, Daim Denies Involvement in the Palm Oil Trade," *Malaysiakini*, April 12, 2019, https://www.malaysiakini.com/news/472042.

"Bypassing Bentong and Gombak and Taking the Way of the State of Sembilan, the East Coast Rail Line Maintains the DualTrack Form," *Malaysiakini*, April 12, 2019, https://www.malaysiakini.com/news/472053.

"Details of Revising the Treaty of the East Coast Rail Line of Malaysia, the Landmark Project of China–Malaysia Cooperation Will Resume Work," *Caixin*, April 14, 2019, http://international.caixin.com/2019-04-14/101403918.html.

"Public Transport Connection Plus Environmental Concern, the Government Decides to Divert the East Coast Rail Line," *Malaysiakini*, April 15, 2019, https://www.malaysiakini.com/news/472349.
[25] "The East Coast Rail Link Has Cut Its Costs by More Than RM20 Billion, But the Transport Minister Says the Scale is Not Shrinking," *Malaysiakini*, July 10, 2019, https://www.malaysiakini.com/news/483265.
[26] "Malaysia's East Coast Rail Link Has Officially Resumed Work with a Cost Cut from RM65.5 Billion to RM44 Billion," *China Value*, July 25, 2019, http://www. chinavalue.net/Finance/Blog/2019-7-25/1814570.aspx.
[27] "FAQ for 2019 ECRL," The Malaysia Rail Link Sdn Bhd, 2019, http://www.mrl. com.my/en/faq/.

risks upon completion of the project. However, the new deal would be more favorable to the MRL side. In practice, when faced with a loss, the two companies would share the burden, but if profitable, MRL would take home 80%.[28] Moreover, a more equitable policy for the Malaysian party was that after the project resumed, the payment to CCCC would be made according to the progress of the project instead of at fixed time points.[29]

The new agreement also included the engineering, procurement, construction and commissioning (EPCC) subcontracts. And according to the old contract, Malaysian contractors would do 30% of the work, that is RM 16.5 billion worth, with the remaining 70% (RM 38.5 billion) would go to the Chinese contractors.[30] One of the revised project specifications was to increase the number of Malaysian contracted projects from 30% to 40%.[31]

The first reason for the revision was the cost of this project. This cost had escalated since it was first signed. In 2014, the then chief executive officer (CEO) of the East Coast Economic Region Development Council (ECERDC) of Malaysia, Jebasingam, first announced the estimated cost of the ECRL at about RM 30 billion. At the end of 2015, HSS Integrated Sdn Bhd (HSSI) conducted a feasibility study for the project and said the 545 km long planned

---

[28] "Share the Loss with the Chinese Side, If the East Coast Rail Link Makes Profit, the Malaysian Side Takes 80%," *The Malaysian Insight*, April 15, 2019, https://www.themalaysianinsight.com/chinese/s/147963?fbclid=IwAR3itpTgaGkAvtoVMJ4jYe m4lVliMzG8x28Vej1JstmEJj2fQLPc9iQT4kU.

[29] "Malaysian Contractors Account for 40% of the East Rail Link Project, Malaysia was Refunded the Advance Payment of 1 Billion," *The Malaysian Insight*, April 15, 2019, https://www.themalaysianinsight.com/chinese/s/147950?fbclid=IwAR3etL NUuRDI1rm3OAuFFFMNzHcDWgonexJtuLDZXEex385ZhQo_jPrTLDc.

[30] "The Cost of the East Coast Rail Link Could Balloon to More Than RM100 Billion," *Malaysiakini*, August 16, 2017, https://www.malaysiakini.com/news/392046.

[31] "Malaysian Contractors Account for 40% of the East Rail Link Project, Malaysia Was Refunded the Advance Payment of 1 Billion," *The Malaysian Insight*, April 15, 2019, https://www.themalaysianinsight.com/chinese/s/147950?fbclid=IwAR3etL NUuRDI1rm3OAuFFFMNzHcDWgonexJtuLDZXEex385ZhQo_jPrTLDc.

route would cost RM 29 billion.[32] In mid-November 2016, the then Malaysian Minister of Transport, Liow Tiong Lai, said the cost had soared from RM 29 billion to RM 55 billion as a result of the rapid devaluation of the ringgit and the increased length of the railway line.[33] On July 3, 2018, the then Malaysian Minister of Finance Lim Guan Eng issued a statement stating that after re-estimation, the ECRL construction cost was not RM 55 billion, but nearly RM 81 billion. He also said the project was unlikely to recoup its operating costs and that the RM 81 billion project did not include the operating deficit, which was difficult to estimate at that time. Only by slashing its costs would the government be able to build the railway.[34]

Significant cost escalation over a short span of time was on its own source of concern. Add to this the Malaysian government under Najib's customary refusal to disclose or allow scrutiny of project details and a trust deficit, whether or not justified, naturally emerged among civil society watchdogs and members of the opposition parties. The Chinese side, seen as being in bed with the government and party to its conspiracy of silence and disregard of civil society concerns, was therefore not trusted even if its statements were factual. And yet, instead of relying totally on the Malaysian government, it was not difficult for the Chinese to independently assess the sentiments of civil society, NGOs or social activists.

The second reason was related to perceptions of the sourcing of work mainly to the Chinese. Civil society groups and the opposition had been vocal in criticizing the project, with sourcing mainly from China as one of the complaints. They had based their perception of Malaysian contractors getting only 30% of the work according to the

---

[32] "Worried the East Coast Rail Link Becomes the Most Expensive Infrastructure in the History, the Opposition Urges Liow Tiong Lai to Explain," *Malaysiakini*, October 13, 2017, https://www.malaysiakini.com/news/398213.
[33] "Liow Tiong Lai Says the East Coast Rail Link is Difficult to Use the Old Valuation, He Argues the Devaluation of Ringgit and Extension of the Line," *Malaysiakini*, November 15, 2016, https://www.malaysiakini.com/news/362974.
[34] "The Actual Cost of the East Coast Rail Line of Malaysia is 81 Billion Yuan, and the Ministry of Finance Requests Drastic Price Cuts," *Malaysiakini*, July 3, 2018, https://www.malaysiakini.com/news/432434.

signed contract and the belief that China stood to gain disproportion- ately from the project. Likewise, denial by CCCC which was seen as being on the government's side did not help its case. And as long as it was seen as a partner of the Malaysian government, its credibility would be questioned. Therefore, it did not matter that on September 24, 2018, CCCC also denied that the company's raw materials and equipment were all imported from China, stressing that in the total length of 688 km of railway engineering, CCCC worked with more than 500 subcontractors, 157 suppliers and 91 consultant companies in Malaysia and sourced materials and equipment locally whenever possible.[35] The Chinese side was battling both fact and perception.

The third reason was political. On January 8, 2019, the *Wall Street Journal* revealed that China offered to help resolve Prime Minister Najib's 1Malaysia Development Berhad (1MDB) case in 2016 in exchange for Chinese companies financing and building the ECRL project.[36] The ECRL, Trans-Sabah Gas Pipeline (TSGP) and Multi-Product Pipeline (MPP) schemes were among those being used to rescue 1MDB and SRC International Sdn Bhd, confirmed Amhari, assistant to the then Prime Minister Najib.[37] As before, the Chinese side officially denied this allegation, but in the face of so many gov- ernance irregularities committed by the Malaysian government and the notoriety 1MDB had acquired, it was a losing public relations battle. There was also a risk of falling into a "debt trap" if Malaysia failed to repay loans backed by its government.

---

[35] "CCCC Denies the East Coast Rail Link's Construction Cost Too High," *Malaysiakini*, September 23, 2018, https://www.malaysiakini.com/news/444347.

"CCCC Clarified That Not All East Coast Rail Link's Materials and Equipment Comes from China," *Malaysiakini*, September 24, 2018, https://www.malaysiakini. com/news/444390.

[36] "The WSJ Reveals That China Uses to Help Solve the 1MDB Case in Exchange for a Railway Plan," *Malaysiakini*, January 8, 2019, https://www.malaysiakini.com/ news/459313.

[37] "The Former Assistant Says Low Taek Jho Follows up with Najib's Instructions Immediately," *Malaysiakini*, September 4, 2019, https://www.malaysiakini.com/ news/490573.

Last but not least, in August 2017, the Malaysian Nature Society (MNS), Pertubuhan Pelindung Khazanah Alam Malaysia (PEKA) and another NGO — Treat Every Environment Special (TrEES) — worried that the ECRL project would not only saddle Malaysia with huge debts but it would also destroy its ecology, and urged the government to suspend the project. In November of that year, in a written response to a question from a member of parliament, the government said that the ECRL would requisition a total of 357 hectares of forest reserves, which were habitats to a variety of wildlife, including leopards, elephants, Malayan bears, Malay tapirs, bison, rat, deer and wild boar. Its impact included the loss and fragmentation of wildlife habitats, animal–human conflict, poaching, difficulty in animal migration and even vehicle collisions with wildlife.[38]

Lessons from the Case Study

Aside from the political economy issues clouding renegotiation of the agreement, there are substantive matters that need to be clarified. One is the management of risks by the contracting parties. In this process, care must be taken to redress the perception that the deal is too favorable to one party, whether in terms of project costs or of benefits. This is not simply about the equal distribution of benefits but also about being seen to share equitably in the project's benefits. Under the revised agreement, a Malaysia–China joint venture was established to share the cost, but 100% ownership still belonged to Malaysia. Moreover, the Malaysian company bears only 50% of the operating losses but 80% of the profit. The risk for the Malaysian side was reduced by the Chinese side's role changing from being only a contractor to an investor plus contractor, i.e. from being involved in FII to being involved in FDI. To its credit, the Chinese side must have realized that for the venture to continue, some concession needed to be given to the Malaysian side. The basis for giving the

---

[38] "The East Coast Rail Link Expropriates Three States' Forests and Invades Animals' Habitats Such as the Malay Tapir's," *Malaysiakini*, November 27, 2017, https://www.malaysiakini.com/news/403459.

Malaysian party added benefits appears to be that the original terms were perceived to favor the Chinese and the new terms were concessions to Malaysia. However, the risk is shared and perceptions aside, the two countries have to cooperate to strengthen the project's risk management, for instance, through professionally estimating the amount of financing needed to reflect the real value of the project, using and disclosing debt sustainability analysis to safeguard debt sustainability, establishing comprehensive fiscal frameworks with proper reporting of government operations, adequate monitoring and management of fiscal risks, multiyear budgets, and transparent procurement practices and so on.[39]

Related to risk management and in the interest of transparency and accountability, the two countries also have to estimate as accurately as possible the infrastructure project's short-term and long-term benefits. Local sourcing including employment (all levels, especially skilled workers), raw materials and equipment, and cooperation with local Malaysian suppliers (mainly building material), subcontractors and consultant companies will benefit the host country in the short term. But the availability of local sources has to be carefully considered. If there is not enough supply of local resources, the home country, China, can stand in to bridge the shortfall, but this has to be spelled out from the outset to avoid accusations of home country favoritism.

The ECRL Industrial Skills Training Programme (PLKI-ECRL) has been planned to provide the rail industry skills training for locals.[40] This flagship initiative in developing and upskilling local talents was suspended with the suspension of the ECRL project and planned to be resumed in November 2019 to benefit more than 5,000 talents in railway construction and railway operation and

---

[39] "Belt and Road Economics: Opportunities and Risks of Transport Corridors," *The World Bank*, June 18, 2019, https://www.worldbank.org/en/topic/regional-integration/publication/belt-and-road-economics-opportunities-and-risks-of-transport-corridors.

[40] "Tripartite PLKI-ECRL Agreement to Benefit Rail Industry and NRCOE," University Malaysia Pahang, November 2, 2017, http://news.ump.edu.my/academic/tripartite-plki-ecrl-agreement-benefit-rail-industry-and-nrcoe.

maintenance.[41] This initiative is of vital importance for China's investment in Malaysia and needs to be explicitly recognized. Even though other flagship FDI projects such as CRRC Rolling Stock Center (Malaysia) Sdn Bhd (CRM) had a very high local to foreign staff ratio of about 80:20 there were insufficient local skilled workers to meet project needs and skilled workers had to be brought in from China. But CRM does train local workers, which is considered as long-term benefits that it brings for Malaysia.

Another implication from the CRM experience is that FDI can create a sustainable ecosystem and promote new supply chains. Through its investment, CRM had envisaged more engagement with the local population mostly small- and medium-sized enterprises becoming better suppliers of spare parts. By training its suppliers so that they can produce more reliable parts and components, CRM forms backward linkages that will nurture a more competitive and diverse market ecosystem.[42] Through training, China will realize transfer of its technology as a long-term benefit for Malaysia.

Another long-term implication is that Chinese greenfield investments can be made where its firms can potentially not only nurture new industry but also scale it up for the host country. The case of CRM in making Malaysia the regional hub in rolling-stock manufacturing is an example of attracting more investors thereby propelling Malaysia into new markets, building areas of new competitiveness, and creating new sources of economic growth. One of the factors behind China's success in promoting rapid innovation is its continental-sized consumer market, allowing domestic firms to quickly scale-up production. China's massive market also enables firms to achieve critical mass to innovate and experiment, kicking off a virtuous cycle of technology-led competition and spill-overs. Concerning

---

[41] "Recruitment Roadshow to Fulfill 70% Local Manpower Requirement for the ECRL Project," *Malaysia Rail Link Sdn Bhd*, November 21, 2019, http://www.mrl.com.my/en/recruitment-roadshow-to-fulfill-70-local-manpower-requirement-for-the-ecrl-project/.

[42] E. T. Gomez *et al.*, China in Malaysia: State–Business Relations and the New Order of Investment Flows (Singapore: Palgrave Macmillan, Forthcoming).

manufacturing rolling stock, the Malaysian market alone appears too small for it to be economically viable. But CRM's vision to make Malaysia a regional hub for the railway industry in ASEAN presents an opportunity for technology acquisition and transfer, helping meet the country's need for technology-led growth. As MNCs step up their investments in ASEAN infrastructure, Malaysia should leverage globally competitive firms such as CRRC. By facilitating technology transfer and know-how, Malaysia can become a net exporter of transportation infrastructure and services.[43]

In the short duration during which Chinese OFDI had ramped up in Malaysia, a number of important lessons have emerged. First, the keenness with which the two countries approached bilateral investment projects might have led to over-hasty conclusion of project agreements without due consideration of project benefits and costs.[44] This and the readiness of officials to please their bosses raise the likelihood of missteps from undue haste in project planning and execution from which lessons can be drawn for subsequent projects and for the BRI overall. And indeed, there were lessons for the case study. It also did not help that as the projects are negotiated between one state and another, there exist no checks and balances provided by civil society against institutional or governance excesses.

From the perspective of specific projects, it mattered which party sets the terms. This is in the interest of institutional transparency and assigning responsibility for project components. For the ECRL, the total project cost, as well as the details of the rail line, were decided by the Malaysian government, which also owned 100% of the project while sharing only a part of the cost. Allegations that the project was grossly overpriced would ensnare Malaysia in a "debt trap",[45] and evidence of high-level corruption were immediately leveled by the

---

[43] *Ibid.*

[44] Daniel R. Russel and Black Berger, *Navigating the Belt and Road Initiative* (New York: Asia Society Policy Institute, 2019).

[45] "Improved ECRL Deal a 'Solution' to Debt Trap Concerns," *The Malaysian Reserve*, April 16, 2019, https://themalaysianreserve.com/2019/04/16/improved-ecrl-deal-a-solution-to-debt-trap-concerns/.

opposition and civil society of both parties. By condoning the Malaysian government's customary non-disclosure of its projects' details, China was criticized as much as the Malaysian government. The opacity regarding project feasibility, debt burdens and suspicions of China's standing on the side of Malaysia's corrupt leadership did not help China's reputation, already targeted by hostile Western media.

In terms of governance, arguably the most important practice is to disclose publicly details of project costs as well as justification for the major components of costs. The dominance of China's SOEs also exposes it to the accusation that Chinese OFDI is motivated by non-economic as much as by economic considerations. Lack of transparency on project rationale only abets this suspicion. The ECRL, with its inflated cost, is an extreme example. Also, despite ample justification as the enterprise of choice, the CRM project, which was awarded to China without competitive bidding, was also seen as the Chinese side being party to the "grabbing hand" of the state.[46]

It is equally important to be explicit regarding the estimated benefits and costs to both parties in a project. For the sake of transparency and objectivity, such estimates should come from credible independent sources. Charges have been leveled that bilateral projects were stacked heavily in favor of Chinese enterprises.[47] Included are such media favorites as employment of mostly Chinese workers, use of Chinese subcontractors and equipment, and the crowding out of local SMEs.[48] Benefits to Malaysia as a host country, such as employment of local workers, skills training, some form of technology transfer, applicable establishment of new supply chains, and creation of backward and forward linkages have seldom surfaced except in government propaganda. Distinction between short- and long-term

---

[46] *Op. cit.*, E. T. Gomez *et al.* (Forthcoming).
[47] "'We Cannot Afford This': Malaysia Pushes Back on China's Vision," *The New York Times*, August 20, 2018, https://www.nytimes.com/2018/08/20/world/asia/china-malaysia.html.
[48] Tham Siew Yean, "Chinese Investment in Malaysia: Five Years into the BRI," *Perspective*, no. 11 (2018).

benefits and costs should also be made. Such disclosure should also help to refute unfounded allegations, including in the increasingly influential social media.

These project-specific lessons can be also applied to other BRI projects. They speak to the need to ensure professional governance in all phases of a project so that critics and skeptics cannot find reasons to doubt the motives of a project and find instances where they stray from what had been officially stated. Beyond these, the Malaysian context also offers lessons for strategic issues that underlie the BRI.

First, in Malaysia's infrastructure projects, by bringing together China's SOEs and Malaysia's government-linked companies (GLCs), a new form of FDI business relations — state–state relations — is forged. Without participation of private sectors, which would have at least ensured financial viability, project success depends entirely on the stability of decision-making and leadership of the two states. The change in government in Malaysia in 2018 caused the initial cancellation and subsequent revision of the project. This has resulted in negotiation time, effort and goodwill to be wasted. Undoubtedly, each state entity would have had to rely on the word of its opposite number to a large extent to ensure project success. But especially for China, it cannot be assumed that other countries' leaderships have the same stability that China has. And while non-interference in another country's internal affairs is a superior alternative to attempting to impose one's preferred system,[49] it runs the risk of ignoring the political realities of that country.

Second, reliance on the host country government for project specifics may be unavoidable, but this does not mean other stakeholders can be neglected. With almost instantaneous communications,

---

[49] A report critical of China's non-interference policy referred to its respecting sovereignty as "ducking responsibility", justifying interference by stating that "developing countries often lack the necessary institutions to support adherence to the rule of law or the application of international standards" (Russel and Berger, 2019: 11). Such a view assumes it is not only a right to interfere but also an obligation to help countries achieve the "rule of law" of their own design.

perceptions, whether accurate or misinformed, but especially the latter, are quickly formed and spread. That criticism is so conveniently leveled against BRI projects by host country civil society or vested interest groups can be understood from the fact that China's SOEs are heavily involved. This means greater effort should be made to engage these other stakeholders in different phases of each project, if possible, during important phases of project execution. To the extent the host government is reluctant to release such information, the role of making transparent the work of Chinese enterprises should be played by the Chinese embassy, which should be equipped with the capability to handle BRI-related affairs.

Conclusion

The closeness in bilateral relations between Malaysia and China reflected a coincidence of needs between the two countries. For Malaysia, the potential FDI from China's BRI arose at a time when FDI overall was falling. The country faced growing competition from countries like Vietnam and its reputation was sullied by scandals like 1MDB, which the government did its best to suppress. For China, success in the negotiation of infrastructure projects under the BRI signifies a successful start to the initiative while increasing its soft power in a region it considers strategically important. But such power needed to be carefully nurtured, with China's very size relative to its partner countries instantly giving the impression that China dominated its partners.

In the case of Malaysia–China relations, the convergence of interests rendered the successful completion of negotiations relatively rapid and painless. But the use of state-to-state projects which characterize many BRI projects poses multiple risks. First, success requires strong leadership on both sides. Malaysia's case shows what happened when the Malaysian government was toppled, necessitating renegotiating of original contracts. Second, negotiation between strong leaders leads one state to rely overly on the power of the leader of the other, to the exclusion and arousing the antagonism of other local stakeholders. Third, exclusion or minimizing the participation of other stakeholders robs projects of valuable insights that can enrich the substance of projects but also checks and balances against missteps during project execution by officials in state entities.

No doubt, these lessons had been learned by the time the Second Belt and Road Forum was held in April 2019. As an example, in the Second Belt and Road Forum, the Chinese government responded to the "debt trap" allegation frequently used in the Western media[50] against the BRI, through China's Ministry of Finance launching a Debt Sustainability Framework (DSF) for participating countries of the BRI to promote their sustainable economic and social development while ensuring debt sustainability.[51] In this Forum, the Chinese government also responded to environmental issues encountered in the construction process of the BRI by putting forward the "Green Investment Principles (GIPs) for the Belt and Road" which called for promoting environmental friendliness, climate resilience and social inclusiveness under new BRI investment projects.[52]

There are also other projects' challenges to overcome. From the case of the Kuala Lumpur–Singapore High-speed Rail project, it is important to strengthen the capacity for multilateral negotiation with third (e.g. Singapore) or even fourth … countries involved in the infrastructure project in the region. Meanwhile, we have to learn to

---

[50] John Hurley *et al.*, "Examining the Debt Implications of the Belt and Road Initiative from a Policy Perspective" (Center for Global Development, 2018), https://www.cgdev.org/publication/examining-debt-implications-belt-and-road-initiative-policy-perspective.

"Belt and Toad Debt Trap Accusations Hound China as It Hosts Forum," *The Financial Times*, 2019, https://www.ft.com/content/3e9a0266-6500-11e9-9adc-98bf1d35a056.

"Beware of BRI Debt Trap," *Bangkok Post*, April 27, 2019, https://www.bangkokpost.com/opinion/opinion/1667904/beware-of-bri-debt-trap.

[51] "Belt and Road Economics: Opportunities and Risks of Transport Corridors," *The World Bank*, June 18, 2019, https://www.worldbank.org/en/topic/regional-integration/publication/belt-and-road-economics-opportunities-and-risks-of-transport-corridors.

[52] "Belt and Road Economics: Opportunities and Risks of Transport Corridors," *The World Bank*, June 18, 2019, https://www.worldbank.org/en/topic/regional-integration/publication/belt-and-road-economics-opportunities-and-risks-of-transport-corridors.

cooperate with third, fourth … countries (e.g. Japan) based on BRI's "win–win–win …" objective. From the case of the MRT2 project, we should be alert that the contract-issuing party (Malaysian government) demands infrastructure development, but fund shortage can delay payment. However, Chinese SOE contractors need construction work and are prepared to advance payment for construction. Attention must therefore be paid to the risk of loss and intense price competition with other Chinese SOEs in contract bidding should be avoided.

https://doi.org/10.1142/9789811234316_0008

Chapter

8

Improving Regional Connectivity Through Synergizing the MPAC 2025 and the Belt and Road Initiative

U Zeyar Oo

Myanmar Institute of Strategic and International Studies (MISIS), Yangon, Myanmar

Introduction

In the era of globalization and advanced technology, countries are one way or another connected with each other geographically, economically and politically. The phenomenon of one side of the world will directly or indirectly impact the other side, and therefore it is widely accepted that the ideology of global connectivity among the countries in the regions around the world should be established for the prosperity and well-being of the global people. Since the former President of the United States of America Mr. Donald J Trump took office, countries around the world have been worried about protectionism that will probably divert from the way the world is moving toward the common goal of global citizens by undermining the global order resulting from the impediment of global trade and economy. However, most countries including traditional allies of the United States are staying on their own agendas in pursuing global cooperation of Belt and Road Initiative (BRI) led by China. The regional organization ASEAN continues boosting its efforts in implementing the action plans of its blueprints and frameworks and has generated the idea of regional connectivity in early days by adopting the Master Plan on ASEAN Connectivity 2025 (MPAC 2025). Under the MPAC 2025, the ASEAN member states are striving to improve the physical infrastructures, institutional and financial infrastructures, and connectivity infrastructures through individual, bilateral and multilateral means. Parallel to that, China has come up with its billions-worth project of BRI with the aim to establish global connectivity involving infrastructure development and investments in countries and international organizations in Asia, Europe, Africa, the Middle East and the Americas with plans to complete by 2049. Although ASEAN is working with its own agenda of the MPAC 2025, its member states are actively participating in China's BRI through multilateral and bilateral arrangements. ASEAN's participation in the BRI is quite critical to China as most ASEAN nations are China's neighbors and strategic partners as well as geographically located around the starting points of the BRI's connectivity linking its economic corridors. Before the BRI was launched, ASEAN has worked through its MPAC 2025, and therefore to some extent ASEAN had gained experiences in implementing the tasks related to necessary infrastructures for the regional connectivity that will facilitate the synergy between the MPAC 2025 and the BRI. By doing so, both ASEAN and China will not only gain economic, social, technological and cultural benefits but also face unexpected challenges such as environmental risks, cultural risks, and institutional risks and so on. On the other hand, due to different regulations and institutional practices and social norms practiced by ASEAN and China as well as individual member states, there will be socioeconomic and cultural issues to be handled by the cooperation of both sides. Anyhow, synergizing ASEAN's MPAC with China's BRI will strengthen bilateral relations supportive to building global connectivity for the well-being of global people. Therefore, this chapter will study the progress and characteristics of ASEAN's MPAC 2025 and China's BRI; then the chapter will look into the status of synergizing the two initiatives, and examine pros and cons resulting from synergizing the two initiatives.

Overview of ASEAN–China Cooperation

China is the first ever dialogue partner acceding to Treaty of Amity and Cooperation of ASEAN (TAC). ASEAN as one of the most dynamic organizations in the region and China as the regional power and global economic giant has been strategically cooperating in all sectors and at various levels through a myriad of bilateral and multi-lateral cooperation mechanisms that include ASEAN–China Summit, the East Asia Summit (EAS), ASEAN Plus Three, ASEAN Regional Forum (ARF) and ASEAN Defense Ministers' Meeting Plus (ADMM-Plus). In recent years, cooperation in strategic partnerships has been intensified, and Plan of Action guiding the way toward a community of shared future was adopted in 2010, which covers various areas including exploring the ways to improve the connectivity between and among ASEAN and China. In 2018, at the 15th anniversary of the ASEAN–China strategic partnership, the two sides jointly announced a 2030 Strategic Partnership Vision, showing how keen the two sides were to promote their strategic ties. Even though ASEAN and China have a different stance on the issue of South China Sea, both sides spare no efforts to settle the contentious issues through diplomatic means of peaceful dialogues as prescribed in TAC. The first reading of the Single Draft Negotiating Text of the Code of Conduct in South China Sea has proved how hard ASEAN and China are working to improve their political and diplomatic cooperation. In the area of economic cooperation, ASEAN and China have estab-lished various mechanisms and arrangements, through which China has been largely investing in the territory of the ASEAN member states that contribute to the economic development of the individual countries. Under the ASEAN–China cooperation mechanism, the two sides have developed effective cooperation in more than 20 fields such as connectivity, finance, agriculture, information and communication technology, human resources development, investment, energy, culture, tourism, public health, environment and sub-regional development. China–ASEAN Free Trade Area was established in 2002 to facilitate liberalization of trade barriers between China and ASEAN member states ensuring China is ASEAN's biggest trade partner and major investor of the ASEAN member states. Chinese investment in economic infrastructures of the ASEAN member states are beneficial to both sides, and are prepared for taking off the economic flight through BRI. However, based on the past experiences, most people from ASEAN countries have concerns about Chinese firms for the absence of practicing the local rules and standards including environmental protection principles of the respective countries. On the other hand, some countries in the region including the ASEAN member states are quite reluctant to obtain loans from China in building the infrastructures as they worry about being trapped in Chinese debt based on the experience in the course of Sri Lanka. Overall, the relationships between China–ASEAN member states are deep, strong and unshakeable in nature, much supportive in working together under the BRI process, and as well as in synergizing ASEAN's MPAC 2025 and China's BRI.

The MPAC 2025 and the ASEAN Connectivity-Related Frameworks

As part of the efforts made to evolve the ASEAN community, ASEAN has drawn a master plan, guiding the ASEAN member states to build the necessary infrastructures comprising physical infrastructure, institutional infrastructure and financial infrastructures, digital infrastructures and people-people relations. The first Master Plan on ASEAN Connectivity was adopted in 2010 through the Hanoi Joint Declaration. Based on the achievements and progress made from the MPAC 2010, ASEAN upgraded to the Master Plan on ASEAN Connectivity 2025 as the successor document in 2016, emphasizing its significance in building the ASEAN community and promoting the synergy with other sub-regional and inter-regional frameworks such as China's BRI. The ASEAN dialogue partners including China and external parties have backed ASEAN with their full support in adopting MPAC 2025 by indicating their readiness to work together with ASEAN in implementing the action lines of the MPAC 2025. To keep the momentum and speed of the progress, ASEAN Connectivity Coordinating Committee is given the task for monitoring, evaluating and reporting the progress and challenges of the MPAC to the ASEAN leaders.

The MPAC 2025 vision of achieving a seamlessly and comprehensively connected and integrated ASEAN and promoting a greater sense of community has reflected the goal of the ASEAN Economic Community (AEC) that envisioned a highly integrated and cohesive regional economy ensuring sustained economic growth. Looking at the MPAC 2025, it focuses on the five strategic areas namely sustainable infrastructure, digital innovation, seamless logistics, regulatory excellence and people mobility. Full participation of the ASEAN member states in implementing the MPAC 2025 will help the region in promoting the movement of people, goods and services, and reducing policy and institutional barriers by harmonizing ASEAN regulations and standards as well as bringing people closer together within the region. However, ASEAN has been striving for the establishment of ASEAN connectivity and integration with the determination to realize the ultimate goal of the ASEAN community. With this sense, the MPAC 2025 will be a key foundation in exploring the integrated and connected ASEAN community.

As part of the MPAC 2025, ASEAN member states have agreed on installing the ASEAN Highway Network (ANH), aiming to reduce the total length of roads so as to facilitate the better movement of goods and services, people-to-people connection and better engagement in cultural and social exchange among the countries. In implementing the AHN, the ASEAN member states are working with their own agendas through bilateral arrangements, in which China is a major financier of those rail links projects. Some ongoing projects of 6,617.5 km long railways that connect eight countries— Cambodia, Lao PDR, Malaysia, Myanmar, China, Singapore, Thailand and Vietnam — have been under way at different levels of construction. On the other hand, ASEAN recognizes the need to promote cooperation in the transport sector for the economic development of ASEAN and integration. Moreover, the transport sector will provide greater support for the ASEAN member states in building the ASEAN Economic Community; therefore, it is also vital for the future of the ASEAN member states. Kuala Lumpur Transport Strategic Plan (KLTSP) upgraded from the achievements of previous Brunei Action Plan (BAP, 2010–2025), which was developed for the continued cooperation in actual physical connection activities. Since the ASEAN member states have been implementing the goals and action lines described in KLTSP steadily and effectively, transport links in air, land and maritime will gradually improve and facilitate better connection leading to economic development of the ASEAN member states.

Establishing reliable and secure electricity infrastructures and power grid in the ASEAN region is another agenda of ASEAN for the regional connectivity. ASEAN member states especially river-rich countries like Myanmar and Laos PDR have been increasing the national hydropower projects so as to fulfill domestic demand and to export to other countries including China in order to earn as part of national income. Launching the ASEAN Power Grid (APG) is generally beneficial to the ASEAN member states by meeting the rising energy demand, improving access to energy services and reducing the costs of developing an energy infrastructure. Apart from that, having the gas pipelines can also be critical in boosting the ASEAN connectivity and the economic development of the ASEAN member states, though such projects entail environmental consequences affecting the local people in the host country.

Together with physical connectivity infrastructures, ASEAN has generated the institutional connectivity to reduce the burden of policy. The Implementation Framework of the ASEAN Single Shipping Market including its Action Plan was also developed, and trade facilitative measures are being undertaken to achieve free flow of goods and services. In 2016, Indonesia and Singapore began exchanging electronic ASEAN Trade in Goods Agreement (ATIGA) Certificate of Origin Form D information in the production environment using the ASEAN Single Window (ASW) enabling infrastructure. Prof. Hidetoshi Nishimura, the President of ERIA, underscored the importance of "digital connectivity" in terms of implementing the (MPAC) 2025, while noting that enhancing "physical" connectivity remains one of the biggest challenges in ASEAN in achieving an advanced digital economy. Looking at these arrangements, ASEAN has been working very hard to improve digital connectivity to reduce the institutional burdens and to expedite the flow of goods and services and to ease some financial procedures among the ASEAN member states. However, due to the gap in economies and technology among the ASEAN member states, it is hard to say that the countries can fully participate while developing the digital trade and market.

ASEAN is home to diverse cultures, and promoting cultural infrastructures is one of the primary goals of establishing the ASEAN community. Several steps need to be taken to improve social and cultural infrastructures, and among others the most fundamental step ASEAN has taken is developing the ASEAN Curriculum Sourcebook for primary and secondary schools, through which ASEAN students can share and learn from each other's cultures. Moreover, ASEAN has established the ASEAN University Network (AUN) at the postgraduate level for cultural engagement. However, there are still challenges the ASEAN member states are facing due to different curriculum and standards practiced among the institutions, limited budgets and language barriers.

In terms of tourism, the steps have been taken to encourage intra-ASEAN tourism through the concerted development of tourism products to raise the incentives of the global tourists to come and visit ASEAN region. Although new funding vehicles such as the Asia Bond Fund (ABF), the ASEAN Infrastructure Fund (AIF), and the Asian Infrastructure Investment Bank (AIIB) have emerged, more private-sector investments in infrastructure are essential and necessary. According to some reports, ASEAN member states are in need of financial assistance to fulfill their aims of establishing ASEAN connectivity as described in the MPAC 2025. Before the emergence of the BRI and China's indirect ways of involving in the MPAC 2025, ASEAN's planned physical infrastructure projects were pending to be implemented due to financial necessity. Therefore, synergizing with the BRI is another way of reinforcing the implementation of the MPAC 2025.

Impacts of the BRI

In 2013, Chinese President Xi Jinping announced the launch of both the Silk Road Economic Belt and the 21st Century Maritime Silk Road, infrastructure development and investment initiatives that would stretch from East Asia to Europe. The project, eventually termed the BRI, is one of the most ambitious infrastructure projects ever seen in human history. As mentioned by President Xi, China's BRI intends to establish regional connectivity that facilitates seamless trade flow, cultural, social and economic integration leading to the prosperity of the people of the regional countries. However, experts see the BRI as one of the main planks of Chinese statecraft under Xi, alongside the Made in China 2025 economic development strategy. CFR's Elizabeth C. Economy wrote, "Under Xi, China now actively seeks to shape international norms and institutions and forcefully asserts its presence on the global stage". Nayan Chanda, former editor of the *Far Eastern Economic Review*, called the BRI "an overt expression of China's power ambitions in the 21st Century", arguing that Beijing's goal is to remake the global geopolitical balance of power. Some held the view that the BRI is a Chinese response to the United States' policy of "Pivot to Asia Pacific" focusing on Asia, launched by the Obama administration in 2011. Many Chinese people interpret that this policy is formulated to contain China by expanding U.S. economic ties in Southeast Asia. In a 2015 speech, retired Chinese General Qiao Liand described the BRI as "a hedge strategy against the eastward move of the U.S."

After attending the Second Belt and Road Forum, many countries in the region along the routes of the BRI have joined China to participate in the BRI process as they believe that the BRI will bring national development. However, some powerful countries like the United States, Japan, India and some other Western countries have come up with their contrary views of China's BRI as China is projecting its power to influence the region by using economic, social and political clout through the BRI projects, which will change world trade order and shake regional balance. Some countries situated along the routes of the BRI, and some traditional allies of the United States have hesitated to join China. Some small states including littorals and island states are worried that China's loans being lent to them for constructing the infrastructures will probably put them into the so-called Chinese debt trap while leveraging its influence on vulnerable emerging markets. A new report of Rhodium Group, which reviewed 40 cases of China's external debt renegotiations, paints a different picture. Key findings of the report suggest that in most cases, debt renegotiations and distress among borrowing countries are common. The sheer volume of debt renegotiations points to legitimate concerns about the sustainability of China's outbound lending. Much has been assumed that more cases of distress are likely to take place in the future as many projects under the BRI are launched with the loans. Anyway, most of the countries in need of infrastructures and economic development are quite positive to see the BRI as the regional driver in promoting socioeconomic development of the countries around the world. Therefore, such countries are very enthusiastic to join the BRI for the national interest of their own countries and for the well-being of their own people because China is spending its money on all infrastructure projects through its BRI financial infrastructure such as the AIIB. Having received Italy as the 130th nation participating in the BRI is a kind of credit earned to China since Italy is the biggest European economy and first member of the Group of Seven (G7) bloc of advanced countries.

Compared to other participating countries and organizations, ASEAN and its member states are in the list of first organization and countries that join the BRI. Currently, ASEAN and its individual member states have a set of bilateral agreements with China and most of them are being implemented with the funding of China under the BRI cooperation framework. According to Wu Haitao, China's deputy permanent representative to the United Nations, China has signed more than 190 documents on cooperation with over 160 countries and international organizations and has jointly established 82 cooperation parks overseas with participating countries, creating more than 300,000 jobs with a total investment of more than USD

30 billion in six years since it was launched. He also said that the Second Belt and Road Forum for International Cooperation released a list of 283 concrete results. Participating enterprises signed project cooperation agreements worth more than USD 64 billion. He also suggested that the BRI should be fully aligned with the United Nations' 2030 Agenda for Sustainable Development and help accelerate the achievement of the Sustainable Development Goals worldwide.

According to the World Bank, if the BRI is completed, the BRI transport projects could reduce travel time along economic corridors by 12%, increase trade between 2.7% and 9.7%, increase income by up to 3.4% and lift 7.6 million people from extreme poverty. However, some criticized that the BRI will present risks to many major infrastructure projects: debts, governance risks, environmental risks and social risks. CFR's Alyssa Ayres and Elizabeth C. Economy and Johns Hopkins's Daniel Markey said that the BRI projects have been built with low interest loans as opposed to aid grants. In some BRI investments, there is a lack of transparency in the bidding process and as a result, contractors have inflated costs, leading to canceled projects and political pushback.

Looking at the outlines of the BRI show that it prioritizes five areas of cooperation: policy coordination; facilities connectivity; unimpeded trade; financial integration; and people-to-people bonds. Most of the BRI projects focused on building road, rail, marine or air links. During the Second Belt and Road Forum held in Beijing in April, Yi Gang, the governor of the People's Bank of China, said that the Chinese financial institutions have bankrolled USD 440 billion worth of infrastructure projects within the BRI countries. He added that 11 Chinese banks had set up 76 country-level institutions in 28 BRI countries, while 50 banks from 22 BRI nations had established branches in China by the end of the previous year. According to BRI research consultancy, diverse funding channels such as BRI bonds, private capital investment and public–private partnerships (PPP) as well as state-owned enterprise (SOE) investment are expected to be critical elements in attaining the success of the BRI, so as to fully fund the total BRI project volume of estimated USD 4–8 trillion.

Being an industrialized country, China has become one of the major polluters as well as the caretaker responsible for environmental conservation. China has been actively participating in the climate change mechanisms under the framework of the United Nations and other global and regional mechanisms. China is one of the main participants of the Paris Agreement and is ready to take part in such a global arrangement. Keeping such a globally responsible role, China has formulated a set of environmental standards, rules and regulations to be practiced and followed by the Chinese firms which run outbound investment around the globe. Moreover, developing green energy projects is a key aspect of the BRI. The BRI International Green Development Coalition comprises 25 countries, several UN organizations including the United Nations Environment Programme (UNEP), academic institutions and businesses that have launched a number of initiatives. In general, constructing the railway links, establishing the special economic zones, building the seaports, setting up the pipelines and installing the infrastructures under the BRI will entail environmental consequences more or less. Regarding the operators and Chinese firms performing in the BRI-related projects in foreign countries, some are quite unfamiliar with the environmental protection standards, rules and regulations of the host countries, causing environmental risks to the local population. Criticisms have been raised against Chinese firms exercising their own environmental standards rather than following the local regulations.

Nevertheless, China has accordingly pledged to follow the laws and norms of the host countries for all BRI projects; so, in principle, the policies of these host countries provide minimal protection against the environmental risk that comes with every infrastructure project. But policy, capacity, resources and assets to enforce the restrictions can vary and often are inadequate to address these risks.

Synergizing the MPAC 2025 and the BRI Initiative

As aforementioned, ASEAN and China have been strategic partners since the early days of ASEAN, cooperating in all forms and at various levels. Not only with ASEAN but also with the individual member states, China has maintained a good, deep and strong relationship that is beneficial to both sides. As compared to other economic powers such as the United States, the EU, Japan and India, China runs more outbound investments in most ASEAN member states, and is currently the biggest trade partner of ASEAN. Although there are criticisms about Chinese economic influence on the neighboring countries and its presumed assertiveness over the South China Sea issue, the relations between the ASEAN member states and China have been significantly increasing.

Under ASEAN's MPAC 2025 and China's BRI, China is intensifying its outbound investment in the ASEAN countries by undertaking financial assistance in implementing the physical infrastructures projects; railway links, special economic zones, sea ports, gas pipelines, hydropower and power grid. Since the inception of the BRI in 2013, the ASEAN member states have embraced this China-led initiative and made an effort to transform it into a source of national development of the individual member states and to support the socioeconomic development of ASEAN by synergizing the MPAC 2025. For some ASEAN member states, China is the largest foreign investor, largest bilateral donor, largest trading partner, largest buyer of domestic goods and services such as agricultural products, gas and hydropower electricity and so on. Accompanying the BRI, the physical infrastructure and connectivity projects that have been pending to be implemented by the ASEAN member states under the framework of the MPAC 2025 are able to move forward with China's financial assistance, mostly in the form of project loans, under the framework of BRI. However, there have always been pros and cons in pursuing physical infrastructure projects. China's BRI-related infrastructure projects have entailed both positive and negative consequences for the host country and its local people. There are a number of instances where China-led infrastructure projects have directly employed thousands of locals and generated income for the host countries leading to its national development. On the other hand, these projects have been criticized for exposing the locals to environmental risk.

However, ASEAN is the key director and important participant in the BRI. In the past five years, a large number of cooperation projects between China and ASEAN countries have been incorporated into the BRI cooperation framework. Thus, it is believed that by synergizing the MPAC 2025 with the BRI, ASEAN and its member states will have the headwind in implementing the BRI-related projects as compared to the other countries participating in the BRI. Actually, the MPAC 2025 is consistent with the goal of the BRI to promote regional connectivity, and if the two initiatives are successfully synergized, ASEAN and its member states will get more support from China thereby meeting the sustainable development goals of both sides. Generally speaking, ASEAN and China will receive political, economic, social, geographical and institutional advantages if the MPAC 2025 and BRI initiative are fully incorporated and synergized, but there are challenges as well. Given the examples of some the Chinese firms led by infrastructure in some ASEAN member states particularly in Myanmar, some cases are found to involve high risks — social risks such as land acquisitions and resettlement, environmental risks such as land erosion and deforestation, cultural risks such as differences in traditions and customs between foreign and local people, institutional risks such as the gap between local and foreign environmental and social standards, governance risks such as corruption in the bidding process of the projects due to lack of transparency. Nevertheless, such risks can be solved accordingly through the practical cooperation mechanisms introduced to synergize the MPAC 2025 and the BRI.

Conclusion

Based on the findings from the study, ASEAN and China as the major players in the region should continue to promote the cooperation for strategic partnership for the interest and well-being of the people of not only ASEAN member states and China but also of other countries in the region. ASEAN and China should increase their efforts in exploring the ways to a community of shared future benefiting both sides. ASEAN and China should enhance cooperation and collaboration in synergizing the MPAC 2025 and the BRI to improve regional connectivity that facilitates seamless trade flow, cultural, social and economic integration leading to the prosperity of the people of the regional countries. Although there are risks and challenges in implementing the BRI-related infrastructure projects, ASEAN, particularly the individual ASEAN member states, and China should carefully study those challenges and accordingly seek solutions through the existing practical cooperation mechanisms. If the MPAC 2025 and the BRI are successfully synergized, the returns are much more than the risks to follow. Thus, ASEAN should continue to maintain the momentum of cooperation in synergizing the two initiatives and to make its utmost efforts in incorporating the MPAC 2025-related infrastructure projects into the BRI cooperation framework.

© 2021 World Scientific Publishing Company
https://doi.org/10.1142/9789811234316_0009

Chapter

9

Myanmar as a Link in ASEAN–China Physical Connectivity

Khin Ma Ma Myo

Department of International Relations, University of Yangon,
Myanmar

Introduction

ASEAN has planned to upgrade its connectivity as a key step to not only realize intra-ASEAN integration but also to expand its external relations. It introduced the Master Plan for ASEAN Connectivity (MPAC) to achieve a well-connected ASEAN by enhancing regional and national physical, institutional and people-to-people connectivity. ASEAN needs financing and technical resources for these plans and is willing to cooperate more with dialogue partners including China. At the same time, China has launched the Belt and Road Initiative (BRI) which is a web of infrastructure including rail links, road network, airports, inland and sea ports, energy pipelines and telecommunications. MPAC and BRI have commonalities in prioritized areas. In fact, both sides have agreed to enhance economic relationships including connectivity and further extend their economic and social ties. Under these circumstances, Myanmar is geographically located between China and ASEAN region and has maintained closer cooperation. Regional highways, sub-regional transport networks and railways pass through Myanmar. Moreover, there are several connectivity projects under BRI and China Myanmar Economic Corridor (CMEC). Based on this backdrop, objectives of the research are to find out how Myanmar can stand as an integral link between ASEAN and China and to highlight its transport cooperation with regional institutions and neighboring countries. Due to ASEAN–China cooperation in connectivity and various transport projects, Myanmar would be surely a link and the trade and logistic hub between ASEAN and China.

Connectivity becomes a priority for both national development and regional integration in the age of globalization and free trade. It is also a cornerstone of regional economic growth especially in East Asia, which is a region with emerging economies and developed countries. In East Asia, ASEAN countries in particular have taken efforts to find new drivers of regional economic growth, and to create domestic interests by energizing regional integration.

Connectivity is very important for ASEAN's efforts to realize a community through highways, railways, ports, logistic and customs arrangements. It has achieved not only regional integration among its members but also closer strategic cooperation with dialogue partners in Asia. To create the potential of interlinked production networks and markets, ASEAN outlined a broader perspective on physical connectivity especially with its big neighbor, China.

China introduced the BRI in 2013 to improve connectivity and cooperation on a transcontinental scale. By the end of October 2019, it had signed cooperation agreements with more than 137 countries across the globe and 30 international organizations on jointly building infrastructure, connectivity and economic zones. China and ASEAN have had close cooperation for years based on China–ASEAN strategic partnership. BRI would further deepen their cooperation and mutual prosperity. Infrastructure development is necessary for both and the smooth physical connectivity is key to their goals. To realize the goals, Myanmar is a crucial spot as a transport network between China and ASEAN countries. Its domestic transport routes are links between China and ASEAN region and its strategic location is crucial for regional physical connectivity. Besides, regional highways, national highways, trilateral highways, deep sea ports, economic zones and cross-border routes through Myanmar are very useful for regional trade routes and serve as a transport network.

Based on the circumstances, it is interesting to analyze the role of Myanmar in ASEAN–China physical connectivity. The objectives of the research are to find out how Myanmar can stand as an integral link between ASEAN and China and to highlight its transport cooperation with regional· institutions and neighboring countries. The first section briefly highlights ASEAN–China connectivity and Myanmar's position in the region. The second section explains overview of its transport network. Its cooperation in bilateral and regional connectivity arrangements are examined in the third section.

ASEAN–China Connectivity and Myanmar

ASEAN is a regional organization of 10 member countries which are situated well between the India and Pacific Oceans and between South and East Asia. The large markets and production bases are across its borders. Its members have been attracting foreign direct investments, upgrading industry and technology and integrating more into the world economy. Its aim to build an ASEAN community needs advantages for efficient integration and for bridging development gaps. The integrated transport network is vital to realize these advantages and to enhance a single market for production, tourism and investment. The smooth connectivity does support economic growth of many of its members.

Connectivity in ASEAN includes physical, institutional and people-to-people linkages. ASEAN Transport Action Plan (ATAP) 2005–2010 is formulated to cover maritime, air, land transport and facilitation. ASEAN Strategic Transport Plan (ASTP) 2011–2015 is prepared. Moreover, ASEAN has ASEAN Economic Community

(AEC) blueprint initiatives and Master Plan on ASEAN Connectivity.[1] ASEAN has implemented upgrading existing infrastructure and constructing new infrastructure including road network, in land and deep sea ports, rail links, bridges and airports, improving logistic facilities, digital divide and power sources.

ASEAN has planned to upgrade its connectivity not only to realize intra-ASEAN integration but also to expand its external relations. It is trying to gain global flows including digital flow, free flow of goods, service, investments, skilled labor and information. The MPAC 2025 is designed to achieve a well-connected ASEAN by enhancing regional and national physical, institutional and people-to-people connectivity. At the same time, some cooperation frameworks such as ASEAN Transport Facilitation Agreements and sub-regional arrangements are carried out to support regional connectivity.[2] To realize its plans, ASEAN is willing to actively cooperate with dialogue partners including China.

China has planned the BRI, which is a web of infrastructure including rail links, road network, airports, inland and sea ports, energy pipelines and telecommunications. It would enhance physical interconnectivity and economic interactions across Eurasia, Africa and 60 countries. MPAC and BRI have commonalities in priority areas. China's grand plans would support interconnectivity between ASEAN and China and among ASEAN member countries. Similarly, ASEAN's connectivity network would bring about China's closer interactions with ASEAN countries and successful implementation of BRI.

The MPAC has pushed China and ASEAN to explore more substantive cooperation. The pursuit of connectivity brings countries to facilitate access to trade, investment, tourism and people-to-people exchanges. MPAC is a system of roads and railways to link ASEAN members and of ports for vessels and short sea shipping to link Southeast Asian countries with one another. Similarly, the BRI is sure

---

[1] ERIA Study Team, *ASEAN Strategic Transport Plan 2011–2015: Final Report* (Jakarta: ERIA, 2013), E-1, www.eria.org.

[2] ASEAN Secretariat, *Master Plan for ASEAN Connectivity 2025* (Jakarta: ASEAN Secretariat, 2016), 31–32.

to support the ASEAN nations in advancing regional connectivity. Railway projects in Malaysia, Thailand, Laos and Cambodia proved the outcomes. Moreover, China has been ASEAN's largest trading partner and fourth largest investor. On the other hand, ASEAN has been China's third largest trading partner and investor since 2011. BRI would make China boost its economic relations with member countries. They could support China's plans for developing planned infrastructure networks of BRI.[3]

ASEAN and China issued joint statement on further deepening the cooperation on Infrastructure Connectivity on 13 November 2017 at the 20th ASEAN–China Summit in Manila. They recognized five major strategic objectives of MPAC and five major priorities of BRI.[4] Moreover, ASEAN–China Strategic partnership Vision 2030 reiterated their commitments for synergizing common priorities in MPAC and BRI through mutually beneficial connectivity strategies.[5]

Among ASEAN countries, Myanmar has unique opportunities for its geographic position. It is best located in Indo-Pacific region. Geographically, it is a gateway between East Asia and South Asia. It borders with China, ASEAN and South Asian countries which accounts for the market of 2.748 billion. Myanmar stands as a natural land bridge between transport and trade networks of China and ASEAN on the one hand and those of South Asia on the other hand. The country is naturally likely to be a transportation and logistics hub for the region. Cross-border links, therefore, are very important for material, institutional and people-to-people connectivity.[6]

---

[3] "New Silk Road's Impact on ASEAN," *International Policy Digest*, accessed on April 24, 2018, https://intpolicydigest.org/2018/04/24/new-silk-road-s-impact-on-asean/.

[4] "Joint Statement between ASEAN and China on Further Deepening the Cooperation on Infrastructure Connectivity," *ASEAN*, November 13, 2017, https://asean.org/joint-statement-asean-china-deepening-cooperation-infrastructure-connectivity/.

[5] "ASEAN–China Strategic Partnership Vision 2030," *ASEAN*, November 14, 2018, http://asean.org/storage/2018/11/ASEAN-China-strategic-partnership-vision-2030.

[6] *Global New Light of Myanmar*, November 28, 2014, 1–3. https://www.burmalibrary.org/sites/burmalibrary.org/files/obl/docs20/GNLM2014-11-28-red.pdf

As for Myanmar, ASEAN and China are the two closest friends in the world. China has been the top trading partner, donor and investor. The two countries have strategic partnership status with good neighborliness policy. Besides, China is the key supporter diplomatically for Myanmar in the international community. President Xi Jinping praised Myanmar's engagement with the BRI during a state visit of President U Htin Kyaw in April 2017, in Beijing. He stated that China is willing to connect strategically with Myanmar, and push for cooperation in trade, investment, infrastructure, energy, agriculture, water conservancy, electric power, finance and border economic cooperation.[7]

Myanmar's location favors it to connect with two economic corridors under the BRI that makes its role unique geopolitically. In fact, Myanmar is connected to China Indochina Peninsula Economic Corridor along with sub-corridors, Greater Mekong sub-region (GMS) and Lancang–Mekong Cooperation networks. Since 2012, Myanmar had been engaged under the BCIM Economic Corridor in terms of China's regional economic development framework.[8]

Most of the ASEAN countries are major economic partners and Myanmar's relationship with these countries has been cordial and active. Like all ASEAN states, it has participated and carried out regional agreements and frameworks including the MPAC. It also joins ASEAN–China partnership and other regional arrangements. The ASEAN Connectivity Coordinating Committee helps to facilitate the National Transport Master Plan. Myanmar government believed that the country could become a transport and logistics hub for the region in future.[9]

---

[7] "China, Myanmar Stress Win–Win Cooperation to Advance Relations," *Xinhua*, April 11, 2017, http://www.scio.gov.cn/32618/Document/1547473/1547473. htm.

[8] Thompson Chau, "Myanmar Stakes in Two Belt and Road Economic Corridors," *Myanmar Times*, August 3, 2017, https://www.mmtimes.com/business/27084-myanmar-s-stakes-in-two-belt-and-road-economic-corridors.html.

[9] *Global New Light of Myanmar*, November 28, 2014, 1.

The internal roads networks became upgraded with union high-ways, expressway, strategic highways and access to neighboring countries with ASEAN Highways, Asian highways, BIMSTEC highways, Tripartite highways, GMS Corridors, Kaladan Multi-Modal Transit Transport, bilateral highways from Laos, Thailand, China and India. Besides, new bridges are constructed across major rivers. Its dried ports are improving. Deep-sea ports would be attractive for world commercial sea lanes and maritime trade routes. Moreover, railways are trying to upgrade while new Muse–Kyaukphyu railways, Muse–Mandalay railways and Singapore–Kunming Rail Link (SKRL) are being constructed. Trade routes from India to China go through Myanmar within one day while goods from the Middle East can reach Danang from Dawei sea port within hours. The building of smooth connectivity would make Myanmar, India, China and ASEAN countries enhance advantages for more cooperation, trade on goods and services and people-to-people exchanges.

Myanmar has been improving its transportation sector since it lags behind ASEAN standard. The Asian Development Bank (ADB) stated in 2016 that 20 million people need basic road access while 60% of highways and most railways are in poor conditions. The number of vehicles in Yangon has doubled and the traffic congestion becomes quite problematic. The investment would be more than USD 50 billion to upgrade the transport networks from 2016 to 2030.[10] The transportation cost for goods and passengers needs to be reduced by 30%. It is essential to have foreign investment, and financial and technical assistance for building and upgrading roads, railways, ports, airports and logistic facilities.[11] ASEAN–China connectivity plans are helpful for Myanmar under the circumstances. China has been supporting the sector under BRI while ASEAN, UN–ESCAP and ADB provided assistance for transport networks.

---

[10] ADB, *Myanmar Transport Sector Policy Note: Summary for Decision Makers* (Manila: ADB, 2016), 1. https://www.adb.org/publications/myanmar-transport-sector-policy-note-summary-decision-makers.
[11] Thet Zaw Win, "Status of Road Transport and Transit Facilitation in Myanmar," February 6, 2018, Bangkok, UN-EASCAP.

At the same time, sub-regional arrangements also contribute to domestic network and ASEAN–China connectivity via Myanmar.

The Overview of Myanmar's Transportation Network

The successive governments of Myanmar laid down national policy to provide efficient transport network among states and regions. Myanmar governments since 1988 upgraded all four modes of transportation and constructed new facilities. Under the current National League for Democracy (NLD) government, the Ministry of Transport and Communications (MOTC) takes responsibility for the transport sector and cooperation with various ministries in implementing the Master Plan. The objective of the government's transport policy is to develop roads, bridges and residential buildings and implement uniform development on the sub-national level.[12]

The processes for the formulation of Master Plan started in December 2012 and completed in 2014 by the assistance of JICA. The National Transport Master Plan (2015–2040) (NTMP) was formulated and intended to provide life with a safe, efficient and affordable transport service. The plan has three pillars: strengthening road maintenance and improvement, strengthening public transport development and strengthening traffic management. It was designed to implement 10 major corridors across Myanmar (see Figure 1).[13] Apart from NTMP, the government outlined Master Plan for Arterial Road Network Development (2015–2040), Urban Transport development Plan of Great Yangon (YUTRA) (2016–2040), National Strategy for Rural Roads and Access (2016–2030) and National Logistics master Plan (NLMP).

NLMP was prepared from 2016 to 2018. It is a strategic and workable logistics development master plan by adding and

---

[12] "Interview with Union Minister of Construction U Han Zaw," *Global New Light of Myanmar*, April 5, 2019, https://www.moi.gov.mm/moi:eng/?q=news/5/04/2019/id-17243.
[13] "National Transport Master Plan," February 12, 2019, https://openjicareport.jica.go.jp/pdf/12230728_01.pdf.

Figure 1 Development Corridors of National Transport Master Plan.
Source: Ministry of Transport and Communication, 2017.

supplementing the existing national NTMP. Its aim is to develop infrastructure to handle 85% of increase in cargo movement to and from Myanmar of around 312 million tonnes. Its priorities are regional and international connectivity, domestic connectivity, economic benefits and consistency with economy policies.[14] It is based on six logistics corridors across Myanmar. They are as follows: (1) North–South Logistics corridor between Yangon and southern China, (2) South-east logistics Corridor to Thailand, (3) Trans-Myanmar Logistics Corridor connecting Kyaukphyu in Rakhine State with Tachileik in Shan State, (4) Myanmar–India Logistics corridor,

---

[14] Htike Htike, "Status and Future Plan for National Logistics Master Plan," Ministry of Transport and Communications of Myanmar, November 30, 2017, https://www.unescap.org/sites/default/files/Myanmar%20-%20Logistics.pdf.

Table 1   Projects for Sustainable Transport.

No.	Sector	Projects
1.	Road	48
2.	Rail	14
3.	Maritime	15
4.	Inland water	33
5.	Air	32
Total		142

Source: Ministry of Transport and Communication, Nay Pyi Taw, 2017.

(5) Main River Logistics Corridor and (6) Coastal Marine Logistics Corridor.

The NLD government sets its strategies for improvement of transport sector with private–public partnership (PPP) and foreign direct investment. Myanmar Sustainable Development Plan (MSDP) (2018–2030) calls for PPP to support all types of infrastructure. The significant investment from foreign firms can be seen in recent decades. China, India, Japan and some countries have great interests to invest in highways, urban transport, in-land ports, maritime transport infrastructure, airports, etc. The projects for sustainable transport in Myanmar have been carried out as in Table 1.

One of the priorities of the government is to upgrade railways. Myanmar has the most extensive railway system in ASEAN with 6110,481 km in total route length. Its rail system could be traced back to the colonial era under the British. The rail transport service is so poor that majority of people avoid taking railways. Thus, the NLD government highlighted the upgrading of Yangon–Mandalay route which is the major route for passengers and trade. Moreover, Yangon Circular railway project has been implemented to improve railways, stations and reduce travel time by Japan International Cooperation Agency (JICA). It is expected to be finished in 2022.[15]

---

[15] "Yangon Circular railways project," JICA (n.d.), https://www.jica.go.jp/english/our_work/social_environmental/id/asia/southeast/myanmar/c8h0vm000090rovi.html.

Road transport is the major mode of transport, used by 86% of passengers for communication and 90% of freight. It is another area of focus for the government. The Ministry of Construction has upgraded 144 roads including 536 km of concrete road, 576 km of tar road and 1657 km of nylon-tar road. The government aims to upgrade 42,000 km to ASEAN Class III and provide 90% of rural population with access to all-weather roads by 2030. The rural roads accounted for 55,500 miles.[16] The Yangon–Mandalay express-way and the Myanmar–Thailand road around Dawei Special Economic zone (SEZ) have also been upgraded. ADB has supported two highway projects corridor towns and highway modernization project.[17]

The aviation market is booming in Myanmar as the country opens tourism and economy. The Civil Aviation Master plan is still being prepared. Among 69 airports, 32 domestic airports can become operational. There are three international airports and a new international airport, Hanthawaddy, that are being discussed for investment. Moreover, Heho, Kawthaung and Mawlamyine domestic airports are renovated.

Myanmar has a total length of 2,832 km of coastline and four river systems. The major ports for trade are in Yangon which manage 9% of trade from abroad. Its potential to build new sea ports is high. It shares Mekong with China and other Mekong countries. The government has stated to upgrade inland dry ports and logistics facilities. The eight potential dry ports are proposed by Myanmar to Economic and Social Commission for Asia Pacific (ESCAP) while nine sea ports are likely to be developed along the coastlines.[18] Its location near the world commercial sea lanes can create advantages for major commercial ports if deep sea ports in Dawei, Malamyein and Myeik are constructed. Kyaukphyu and Dawei deep sea ports have started construction although there are several issues for detailed plans.

---

[16] "Interview with Union Minister of Construction U Han Zaw," *Global New Light of Myanmar*.

[17] *Myanmar* (Manila: Asia Development Bank, 2019), www.adb.org.

[18] *Op. cit.*, Htike (2017).

Myanmar's Cooperation in Bilateral and Regional Connectivity Arrangements

Myanmar has bilateral, sub-regional and regional cooperation in the transport sector. Its bilateral cooperation is of two types. The first type is cooperation between Myanmar and the neighboring states and the second type is cooperation under regional arrangements. Myanmar has connectivity with neighbors — particularly Thailand, Laos, China and India since history and has developed efficient transport routes.

Myanmar and Thailand developed rail links under the Singapore–Kunming Rail Links (SKRL). Both governments have planned to build Thailand–Myanmar Rail link and Dawei-Phu Nam Rom–Kanchanaburi rail line. The two plans have not been realized yet due to feasibility issues. Dawei–Phu Nam Rom–Kanchanaburi line is a road and rail link from Kanchanaburi to the newly constructed Dawei Deep Sea port.[19] Bridges are needed to smooth out transport and trade routes. The second Myanmar–Thailand Friendship bridge was opened in March 2019 on the Asian Highway between Myanmar and Thailand. The road transport with Thailand is mostly connected with regional highway plans including Asian highways, ASEAN Highways and Tripartite Highway.

Myanmar has new rail roads with China under SKRL and China–Myanmar Economic Corridor (CMEC). Muse–Kyaukphyu rail transportation project was launched in 2011 after signing the MoU between China Railway Engineering Corporation (CREU) and MR. But the MoU expired in 2014 and failed to implement the construction works.[20] In November 2017, Chinese Foreign Minister Wang Yi announced China's proposal to build the Y-shaped CMEC after a meeting with State Counselor Daw Aung San Suu Kyi in Nay Pyi Taw. He claimed that the economic corridor would enhance investment in development and trade under Chinese–Myanmar cooperation

---

[19] "Myanmar Railways," *Report of Myanmar Railways* (Yangon: Myanmar Railways, 2010), 2.

[20] Thida Min, "Infrastructure Development in Transport and Communication Sectors in Myanmar since 1988," (PhD diss., University of Yangon, 2013), 17.

as part of the BRI.[21] In February, a 15-point MoU at the working group level was signed.

Chinese Ambassador to Myanmar Hong Leng stated in September 2018 at the National Day reception that China and Myanmar are working together to promote projects such as the Border Economic Cooperation Zone, Kyaukpyu Special Economic Zone and Yangon New City and connectivity infrastructures such as roads, railways and power grids. He believed that China–Myanmar Economic Corridor would create the construction of the economic belt along the Irrawaddy River, leading to development opportunities for both countries.[22] Under the CMEC, the Muse–Mandalay railways project was signed in October 2018. The project would link the rail route between Mandalay to Muse which has been under feasibility and ground survey.[23] Other projects included Ruili–Kyaukphyu–Yangon Road, construction of Kwanlon Bridge and a highway and railroad connecting Chinshwehaw and Lashio (Figure 2).[24]

Myanmar has transport links with not only China and ASEAN countries but also the Indian subcontinent. India was willing to build India–Myanmar rail link which would be on the proposed route of Trans-Asian Railways Network (TRN). It intended to connect Myanmar with the northeastern states of India, which has been planned since 2004.[25] The rail link is between Tamu of Myanmar and Moreh. India's Northeast Frontier Railways had completed the second phase survey to connect Tamu in 2014. Through the route, Myanmar becomes India's key entry into ASEAN countries.[26] Kaladan

---

[21] "*Wang Yi: China Proposes to Build China-Myanmar Economic Corridor*," November 20, 2017, http://www.fmprc.gov.cn/mfa_eng/zxxx_662805/t1512583.shtml.

[22] "Ambassador Hong Lian's Speech at 2018 National Day Reception," September 29, 2018, http://mm.china-embassy.org/eng/xwdt/t1662822.htm.

[23] Khin Ma Ma Myo, "Myanmar's Transportation Network with Regional Connectivity," *Mekong Connect*, no. 1(2) (June 2019): 20.

[24] "China–Myanmar Economic Corridor and New Company Act," *Xinhua Finance*, August 9, 2018, http://en.xfafinance.com/html/Lancang-Mekong/Economic/2018/362799.shtml.

[25] *Op. cit.*, Min (2013), 17–18.

[26] Narendra Kaushik, "India's New Gateway to ASEAN," *Bangkok Post*, November 24, 2014, https://www.bangkokpost.com/print/445087/.

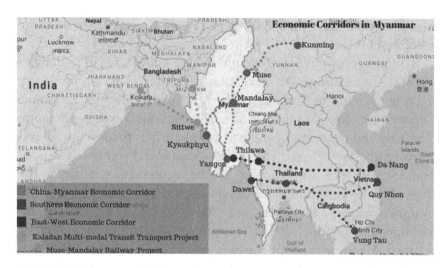

Figure 2   Projects on CMEC.
Source: buildersguide.com.mm.

Multi-Modal Transit Transport Facility over Kaladan River has been the major agreement between the two countries and concluded in April 2008. The project is to upgrade Sittway Port for international commercial shipping, and to connect eastern India's Port of Kolkata and state of Mizoram with Sittway of western Myanmar.[27] Its connectivity with India is beneficial for ASEAN and China to extend their markets through better regional transportation network. In fact, Myanmar is a gateway of these countries to South Asia (see Figure 3).

Myanmar has actively participated in the regional and sub-regional plans in various sectors. It is geographically a crucial transit in regional transport mechanisms. It has been a part of the Asian Highway and ASEAN highway projects for more than a decade. The Asian Highway project is a major road transport project between Myanmar and ESCAP and was established along the 145,000 km of routes through 32 countries.

Myanmar signed the draft agreement on Asian Highway in 2004. There are four sections passing through Myanmar linking major

---

[27] *Op. cit.*, Min (2013), 90.

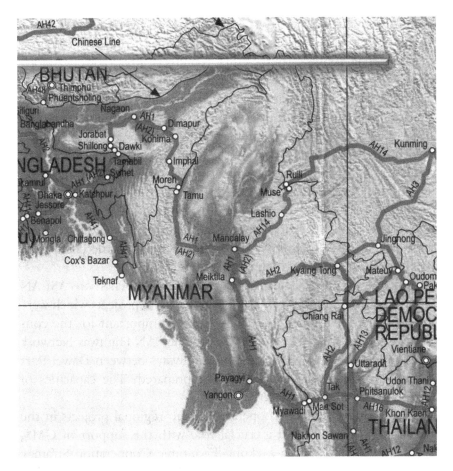

Figure 3 Asian Highways Network in Myanmar.
Source: Win (2018).

highways and border areas of China, Laos and Thailand. The total road length inside Myanmar is 2,932 km. Moreover, the AH1 is located in the East–West Economic corridor of Greater Mekong Sub-region (GMS). Thai–Myanmar friendship bridge on AH1 and border control facilities have also been completed.[28] Figure 3 shows that Myanmar has connectivity with China and ASEAN states through

---

[28] *Op. cit.*, Win (2018), 20.

Asian Highway. The four routes — AH1, AH2, AH3 and AH 14 — can be seen in the figure covering the distance from South Asia to Vietnam. The longest route, AH1, connects Myawaddy–Yangon–Mandalay–Tamu and is 1577.358 km long.

ASEAN Highway is a major road link among 10 ASEAN member countries. The Highway route consists of 23 designated sections and is 38,400 km long. Seven routes with the total length of 4,534 km pass through Myanmar. They link Myanmar with Thailand, Laos, Vietnam, China and India. Myanmar signed ministerial understanding on the development of ASEAN Highway Network project in 1999 and steps 1 and 2 were done in 2000 and 2004. According to Step 3, it is necessary to upgrade national routes to at least Class I or primary road standards by 2020. Figure 4 shows the position of Myanmar in the ASEAN highway network.[29]

ASEAN member states set out the Master Plan on ASEAN Connectivity 2025 (MPAC 2025) to continue 52 projects which were not completed in MPAC 2010. Myanmar is important for the construction of AH123, AH1 and AH2 of the ASEAN Highway Network (AHN). Moreover, railways lines and highways between Dawei Port and Kanchanaburi of Thailand will be prepared. The capacities of Yangon port will also be upgraded.[30]

Myanmar has actively cooperated in sub-regional projects in the transport sector. It played a crucial role with the support of GMS, Ayeyarwady–Chao Phraya-Mekong Economic Cooperation Strategy (ACMECS), BIMSTEC and Lancang–Mekong Cooperation (LMC) for the development of transport infrastructure.

GMS Transport Sector Strategy (2006–2015) was outlined to develop nine corridors as GMS corridor network. The first sub-regional GMS road is implemented with the support of the ADB. Five out of nine corridors pass through Myanmar and they are the North–South Corridor (Kunming–Bangkok), East–West Corridor

---

[29] Aung Myint, "ASEAN Land Transport Connectivity and Status MRA in Myanmar," *Nay Pyi Taw*, February 10, 2016.
[30] *Op. cit.*, Win (2018), 79–81.

ASEAN Highway Network Plan

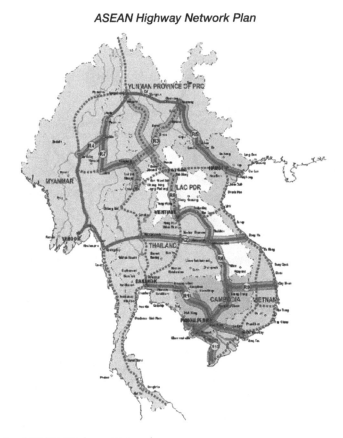

Figure 4   ASEAN Highway Network.
Source: ASEAN Transport Cooperation Framework Plan (ASEAN Secretariat, 1999).

(Malamyine–Danang), Southern Corridor (Dawei–Quy Nhan/Vung Tau), Northern Corridor (Gangheng–Tamu), and Western Corridor (Tamu–Mawlamyine). These routes show that Myanmar could easily link with China, Thailand, Cambodia and Vietnam. There are 14 transport projects for Myanmar under the GMS Transport Sector Strategy 2030.[31] Figure 5 shows that cooperation with GMS

---

[31] *GMS Transport Sector Strategy 2030*, GMS Secretariat, October 2017, https://www.greatermekong.org/sites/default/files/Transport%20Sector%20Strategy%20 2030.pdf.

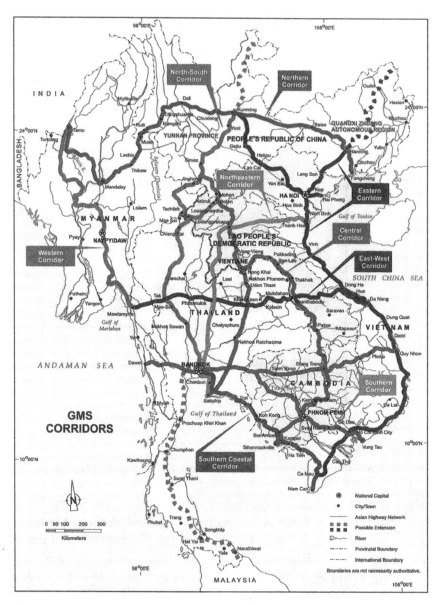

Figure 5   GMS Corridors.

Source: GMS.

corridors has helped Myanmar become a major transit option among China and ASEAN members in Mekong.

Another cooperation is Ayeyarwady–Chao Phraya–Mekong Economic Cooperation Strategy (ACMECS). The ACMECS 2019–2023 Master Plan primarily focuses on the connectivity among five member countries by upgrading the East–West and North–South Corridors of the GMS. Its flagship projects started its study on the Facilitation of Cross-border Movements of goods and passengers among Laos, Myanmar and Vietnam. The Laos–Myanmar Friendship bridge was proposed to be built under the ACMECS plan to connect the highway between Myanmar and other ACMECS countries. It was constructed in 2013 to link Xienglab Township in Laos to Tachilek District in Myanmar with the support of both the governments. It was officially opened on May 11, 2015.[32] The bridge became an integral part of the GMS Northern Economic Corridor, linking Vietnam's Haiphong Seaport and Myanmar's Kyauk Phyu Seaport through Laos. Moreover, Myanmar government upgraded Wan Pong check point as the international border entry point in Tachilek between Laos and Myanmar.[33]

Under the Mekong-Ganga Cooperation (MGC) Initiatives, the Tripartite Highway between India, Myanmar and Thailand (IMT) was agreed in 2003. The Highway covers 1,360 km from Maesot in Thailand to Moreh in India border town, through Myanmar. The two crossings were opened in 2018. The Moreh–Bagan–Mae Sot highway is intended to enhance connectivity, trade, investment and tourism among three countries. It is also a link between Northeast India and Southeast Asia. The project initially started as MGC project, but was later included in the BIMSTEC transport sector.[34]

---

[32] Laos Ministry of Finance and Planning, "Friendship Bridge between Laos and Myanmar Officially Opened," http://www.investlaos.gov.la/index.php/news-and-events/item/9-the-friendship-bridge-between-laos-and-myanmar-is-officially-opened.
[33] Ei Ei Thu, "Laos–Myanmar Border Gate Received International Status," *Myanmar Times*, November 8, 2018, https://www.mmtimes.com/news/myanmar-laos-border-gate-receives-international-status.html.
[34] ASEAN Secretariat, *Master Plan on ASEAN Connectivity 2010*, (Jakarta: ASEAN Secretariat, 20182011), https://www.usasean.org/system/files/downloads/MPAC.pdf.

One of the major regional railway projects is the Singapore–Kunming Rail Link (SKRL) project which stretches from China to Singapore, linking China, Myanmar, Cambodia, Laos, Malaysia, Thailand, Singapore and Vietnam. It started as a flagship project of the ASEAN–Mekong Basin Development Cooperation (AMBDAC) at the fifth ASEAN Summit in 1995. It is a circular rail route, linking 5,000 km through China Yunnan, and seven ASEAN countries. It has six alternative routes. Myanmar stands as the transit point in the major rail route.[35]

Furthermore, Myanmar has participated in the Bangladesh–China–India–Myanmar (BCIM) multi-modal corridor project. The sea and land routes from Kolkota to Kunming pass through Myanmar and Bangladesh. It also actively joined the LMC and one of its priorities is connectivity.

Conclusion

Myanmar is located at the junction between South Asia and Southeast Asia, and between the Indian Ocean and southwestern China's land-locked Yunnan province and occupies a unique geographical position. It is one of the two direct access points to the Indian Ocean for China. In the age of globalization, cooperation in all areas needs good connectivity across borders. The efficient transportation reduces poverty, narrows development gaps and improves well-being of people. Besides, good connectivity beyond borders enhances friendship and understanding among peoples thus creating mutual benefits. ASEAN and China are striving to achieve their regional integration plans with all the neighboring states. At the same time, the country has opened up for trade and cooperation in the democratic transition. Myanmar government hopes that external needs and internal changes pave the way for the country to become a transport and logistics hub in Asia.

---

[35] Khin Ma Ma Myo, "ASEAN Cooperation in Transportation Towards Regional Integration," *MAAS Journal*, no. IX (2011): 86.

Myanmar has various transport projects bilaterally and multilaterally. Its domestic transport network has continuously improved although it is not very efficient. Its participation in the regional transport plans supports its transport sector including funding, facilities of ports, road transport technical skill, border check points, conservation of inland water resources, dry ports and the establishment of deep sea ports. On the other hand, its cooperation in all modes of transport definitely contributes to a transport network between China and ASEAN.

Both China and ASEAN countries outline regional plans for the development and well-being of people. Good connectivity can bring about fruitful outcomes including extensive market, trade surplus, investment, infrastructure support, people-to-people contact and mutual understanding. However, it can also increase socioeconomic issues such as illegal trade, transnational crime, money laundering, human trafficking, etc. States and regional institutions concerned should jointly plan to tackle negative impacts and make united efforts to prevent non-traditional issues for mutual interests.

The overall picture of these projects can be drawn as a spider-web of transportation routes that can fulfill the plans of ASEAN community and China's BRI. Myanmar's strategic location has made it a key transit route for the region especially in the opportune time of regional integration of ASEAN and grand plans of China. Its transport network and strategic location and topography make Myanmar a key to seamless and sustainable regional connectivity. It is definitely an integral link in the physical connectivity of ASEAN and China. It is possible that Myanmar would also gain advantages from the integrated and efficient network of connectivity in Asia.

Chapter

10

Leveraging Industry 4.0 Toward a Sustainable Belt and Road Initiative: Evidence, Prospects and Challenges

Jovito Jose P. Katigbak and Darlene V. Estrada

Center for International Relations and Strategic Studies of the Foreign Service Institute of the Philippines, Philippines

Introduction

The Second Belt and Road Forum for International Cooperation held in April 2019 in Beijing, China, is an important milestone in the Belt and Road Initiative's (BRI) short history as it explicitly directs the project's path toward sustainability, or a future wherein BRI mechanisms and parties exercise "openness, greenness, and cleanliness".[1] Indeed, this is an arduous and ambitious undertaking given its magnitude and extent, which encompasses more than 120 countries and

---

[1] Tan Dawn Wei, "China Will Keep Belt and Road Sustainable, Clean, and Green: Xi Jinping," *The Straits Times,* April 26, 2019, https://www.straitstimes.com/asia/east-asia/china-will-keep-belt-and-road-sustainable-clean-and-green-xi-jinping.

almost 30 international organizations. Although the Chinese government has already put forward proposals to jump-start the road toward a more sustainable BRI, it is crucial to acknowledge that the initiative operates within an economic environment that is driven by Industry 4.0 or the Fourth Industrial Revolution. For its part, the Chinese government has introduced the Digital Silk Road and the Made in China 2025 strategy into the overall BRI strategy to account for the sweeping effects of Industry 4.0. Hence, this chapter postulates that participating countries along the Belt and Road may follow China's lead and leverage the technological breakthroughs cultivated under the ambit of Industry 4.0 to promote a sustainability-oriented BRI.

It is divided into five sections. The first part provides a description of the Fourth Industrial Revolution. It is succeeded by a brief review of tech-centric initiatives under the BRI and a discussion on the potential application of Industry 4.0 innovations. The third portion focuses on the challenges which may be encountered by countries opting to adopt 4IR-related technologies. The next segment outlines lessons for the Association of Southeast Asian Nations (ASEAN) as they concurrently advance regional connectivity through the Master Plan on ASEAN Connectivity (MPAC) 2025. The learning points for ASEAN are perceived as possible building blocks for closer cooperation between the BRI and the MPAC 2025. The final section highlights key insights and perspectives on two primary areas, namely: (1) the trajectory of the BRI toward sustainability; and (2) the nature of collaboration between BRI and MPAC 2025 in the near to medium term. The exploratory nature of this chapter highlights the immense potential of conducting future research in emerging areas.

Characterizing the Fourth Industrial Revolution

The Fourth Industrial Revolution (or Industry 4.0) can be aptly portrayed as a technological revolution that blurs the delineations and boundaries between the physical, biological and digital worlds (Schwab, 2015).[2]

---

[2] Klaus Schwab, "The Fourth Industrial Revolution: What it Means and How to Respond," Foreign Affairs, December 12, 2015, https://www.foreignaffairs.com/articles/2015-12-12/fourth-industrial-revolution.

The unfettered velocity, extensive networks and profound impacts brought by the present technological breakthroughs are poised to transform how people, firms, industries and governments produce goods and services, manage resources and exercise governance. Further, the advancements in areas such as the Internet of Things, robotics, 3-D printing, artificial intelligence, quantum computing, nanotechnology, energy storage, biotechnology and materials science are perceived as accelerators of the mentioned changes. The commonly used term to describe the environment perpetuated by Industry 4.0 is VUCA, which stands for volatility, uncertainty, complexity and ambiguity.

Notably, connectivity seems to be the core feature of the Fourth Industrial Revolution as smart technologies, cloud computing and big data enable the integration of machines, processes and humans. Several industries have already begun using generative design and 3D printing to create products quicker and at cheaper costs. Industry 4.0 technologies are likewise deployed in various stages of supply chain. The adoption of sensor-enabling equipment in factories results in a comprehensive, real-time view of the status of machines, work cells and systems. To illustrate one of its benefits, digitization of the manufacturing sectors is highly regarded by industry players since estimates show that this trend will generate USD 10 trillion in value for the global economy by 2025. In addition, a highly digitized manufacturing sector can raise the country's annual productivity growth by 1% to 1.5%.[3] Moreover, the use of information and communication technology (ICT) to spur precision medicine, gene editing and early disease detection can disrupt health care and other related industries.

Industry 4.0 is similarly transforming another traditional industry which is the financial sector. The emergence of financial technologies (Fintech) is viewed to have a substantial impact on the financial system as it fuels the disaggregation of financial services, disintermediation of incumbents and decentralization of networks. Fintech likewise presents a handful of benefits such as lower costs, greater accessibility

---

[3] Stephen Ezell, "The Coming Digital Technology Landscape, Breakthroughs, and a Glimpse into the Future," presented at the *2018 PIDS Annual Public Policy Conference* held on 19 September 2018 at EDSA Shangri-La, Manila, Philippines, https://pidswebs.pids.gov.ph/CDN/EVENTS/ezell_appc.pdf.

and better efficiency and convenience.[4] Despite its projected benefits, Fintech players in many countries must still deal with a number of impediments to entry such as access to incumbent financial institutions, access to government regulator data, outdated regulations, and restrictive standards and standards processes.

On the flip side, the Fourth Industrial Revolution poses three main challenges to governments and industries around the world.[5] First, the emergence of frontier technologies and Industry 4.0 is projected to result in the loss of over five million jobs by 2020. The developing countries are the hardest hit as around 66% of all jobs are susceptible to automation. Estimates reveal that 44% of workers with low education are at risk to automation by mid-2030s. The effects of job displacement not only focus on the economic aspect but also encompass the social dimension. Next, the existence of digital divide hinders the rise in the level of technology adoption by individuals and households as 52% of the world's population still do not have access to the Internet. Other key factors such as lack of access to ICT infrastructure and low research and development (R&D) expenditure contribute to the slow rate of Industry 4.0 and frontier technologies adoption. Lastly, the proliferation of 3D bio-printing, gene editing, Internet of Things (IoT) and artificial intelligence (AI) generate a host of moral, ethical and legal issues that are inadequately covered by the current laws, policies and regulations of many countries, especially in the developing world.

Acknowledging the massive gains to be reaped by adapting to the Fourth Industrial Revolution, a number of countries have already employed Industry 4.0-centric initiatives. Specifically, ICT companies in Germany and the United States (U.S.) took the lead in crafting

---

[4] Francisco Dakila Jr., "Leveraging on Fintech Innovations for Financial Inclusion," presented at the *5th Annual Public Policy Conference* held on September 19, 2019 at Sofitel Philippine Plaza Hotel, Manila Philippines, http://www.microsave.net/files/pdf/Leveraging_Technology_for_Meaningful_Financial_Inclusion_in_Asia_2.pdf.

[5] Mia Mikic, "Better Future for All: Responsible Polices for Smart Economies," presented at the *2018 PIDS Annual Public Policy Conference* held on September 19, 2018 at EDSA Shangri-La, Manila, Philippines, https://pidswebs.pids.gov.ph/CDN/PUBLICATIONS/pidsbk2019-appc2018.pdf.

"maturity indices" and "model use cases" to underpin the digital transformation of manufacturing companies. "Pilot fabs" that demonstrate smart-manufacturing techniques on active production lines have also been introduced in Germany, Australia and the U.S. In Austria, Italy and South Korea, small and medium-sized enterprises (SMEs) have benefited from tax credits to facilitate equipment upgrades as well as access to cloud-based, high performance computing-powered design, modeling and simulation software.[6] Singapore and Malaysia can be considered as leaders in Southeast Asia as they have already crafted and began implementing their respective national strategies concerning Industry 4.0.[7]

Capitalizing on Industry 4.0: Evidence and prospects for the BRI

Recognizing that a new round of technological revolution is at place, the Chinese government has made corresponding calibrations to its domestic and foreign policies. The BRI, for one, has declared the creation of a subset called the Digital Silk Road to enhance digital connectivity between China and BRI countries.[8] Moreover, the BRI has been complemented with the industrial policy called *Made in China 2025* designed to comprehensively upgrade Chinese industries.[9] In his speech during the 2018 Annual Meeting of the

---

[6] *Ibid.*

[7] Samyukta Raman, "Singapore's Advanced Manufacturing Avatar "Industry 4.0," *EDB Singapore*, July 10, 2017, https://www.singaporebusiness.com/2017/singapores-advanced-manufacturing-avatar-industry.html; Bernama, "MITI Hopes to Announce National Industry 4.0 Policy before Mid-Year," *The Malay Mail Online*, January 10, 2018, http://www.themalaymailonline.com/money/article/miti-hopes-to-announce-national-industry-4.0-policy-before-mid-year.

[8] Clayton Cheney, "China's Digital Silk Road: Strategic Technological Competition and Exporting Political Illiberalism," Council of Foreign Relations, September 26, 2019, https://www.cfr.org/blog/chinas-digital-silk-road-strategic-technological-competition-and-exporting-political.

[9] Scott Kennedy, "Made in China 2025," CSIS Critical Questions, June 1, 2015, https://www.csis.org/analysis/made-china-2025.

New Champions, Premier Li Keqiang acknowledged that Industry 4.0 is changing the world by ushering more spaces and possibilities for innovation and that China is ready to take on the challenge of harnessing the Industry 4.0 to bring prosperity to all peoples.[10] This is demonstrated by China's increasing and aggressive turn toward innovation as a new source of economic growth and the essential application of available Industry 4.0 solutions to development concerns.

Examined individually, each of the innovation-themed initiatives such as the Made in China 2025 and the Digital Silk Road provide nuanced and focused prioritization. While the Made in China 2025 is a domestic policy, it nonetheless involves international implications. On the other hand, the Digital Silk Road takes on an outward orientation in spurring growth by helping BRI countries develop technologically and promoting win–win engagements through the cooperation model of BRI. Together, these undertakings provide a picture of how the opportunities and solutions brought about by Industry 4.0 are incorporated to China's BRI to make the BRI sustainable and future-proof.

Accordingly, the State Council launched the industrial policy *Made in China 2025* in May 2015. It draws inspiration from Germany's *Industry 4.0* plan, and focuses on intelligent manufacturing to transform its own manufacturing sector.[11] The policy recognizes that China has long been known for being the world's factory and seeks to address the prevailing perceptions that Chinese companies manufacture low-quality products.[12] Under this policy, the Chinese government aims to upgrade the quality of consumer goods and build globally reputed brands.[13] The government has likewise

---

[10] Li Keqiang, "Full Text of Premier Li Keqiang's speech at the Opening Ceremony of the Annual Meeting of the New Champions 2018," September 19, 2018, http:// english.scio.gov.cn/topnews/2018-09/20/content_63674597.htm.

[11] *Op. cit.*, Kennedy (2015).

[12] Li Hui, "Made in China 2025: Chinese Manufacturing to Get a Makeover," *CKGSB Knowledge*, May 21, 2015, http://knowledge.ckgsb.edu.cn/2015/05/21/ policy-and-law/made-in-china-2025-chinese-manufacturing-to-get-a-makeover/.

[13] "Higher Quality Aimed for Homemade Goods," *China Daily*, August 30, 2016, http://english.www.gov.cn/policies/policy_watch/2016/08/30/content_ 281475429181659.htm.

expressed interest to introduce compulsory quality standards on identified sectors.[14] More specifically, Made in China 2025 focuses on the following sectors: (i) aviation and aerospace equipment; (ii) electrical power equipment; (iii) new materials; (iv) new generation information technology; (v) railway transportation; (vi) agricultural equipment; (vii) new energy vehicles; (viii) bio-medicine and advanced medical apparatus; (ix) high-end robotics; (x) maritime engineering.[15] China hopes to be a leader in an innovation-led manufacturing industry by underpinning high-tech industries.[16]

In addition, the Chinese government is working on building an environment conducive for innovation and new technologies. Thus, it has provided Chinese technology companies significant support in the form of sponsored tech-zones and innovation hubs to help them in developing key industries and technologies.[17] Tech companies in China are similarly able to enjoy exceptional growth due to the country's massive domestic market, access to data and societal welcoming of new innovation.[18] It is also in this context that several digital tycoons such as Baidu, Alibaba, Tencent and Xiaomi have emerged and eventually ventured onto the global stage.

The Digital Silk Road is another vital component of the BRI. It was first mentioned in China's 2015 BRI blueprint through the Information Silk Road which aims to "advance the construction of cross-border optical cables and other communications trunk line networks, improve international communications connectivity".[19]

---

[14] "Quality Revolution Needed for 'Made in China'," the State Council, August 29, 2016, http://english.www.gov.cn/policies/policy_watch/2016/08/26/content_281475426397196.htm.

[15] *Op. cit.*, Kennedy (2015).

[16] *Op. cit.*, Hui (2011).

[17] Grzegorz Stec, "The Invisible Silk Road: Enter the Digital Dragon," EIAS EU–Asia at a Glance, May 2018, http://www.eias.org/wp-content/uploads/2016/03/EU_Asia_at_a_Glance_Stec_DSR_2018.pdf.

[18] *Ibid.*

[19] "Vision and Actions on Jointly Building Silk Road Economic Belt and 21st-Century Maritime Silk Road," National Development and Reform Commission, March 23, 2015, http://en.ndrc.gov.cn/newsrelease/201503/t20150330_669367.html.

In 2016, the State Council declared the construction of an Online Silk Road as one of the priority actions as indicated in its 13th Five-year Plan for National Informatization.[20] In 2017, during the first Belt and Road Forum held in Beijing, President Xi Jinping officially used the term Digital Silk Road for the first time, and called for the incorporation of Industry 4.0 technologies such as artificial intelligence, nanotechnology, quantum computing, big data, cloud computing and smart cities to BRI in order to prompt an innovation-driven growth.[21] While the evolution in nomenclature might seem trivial, it nonetheless demonstrates the evolution of the initiative's coverage. The Digital Silk Road has widened its scope from improving international communications to incorporating wider set of tools including 4IR solutions to BRI overall objectives.

Evidently, the Made in China 2025 and the Digital Silk Road complement each other in such a way that the domestic strategy of developing key technologies and industries forms an integral part in an international undertaking that would later promote such technologies and products globally. At present, the Chinese government, in partnership with leading ICT firms, is working to link technological solutions to existing BRI projects and investments.

Stec provided a handful of examples that demonstrates China's use of key technologies to promote better implementation of the BRI.[22] One example is the use of e-commerce and customs automation to resolve lengthy custom procedures and security checks and that cause delays.[23] This solution has already been introduced in Malaysia which together with Alibaba established a Digital Free Trade Zone. Another example is in the case of telecommunications infrastructure. China's state-owned enterprises (SOEs) such as Telco,

---

[20] Lan Suying, "China releases 13th Five-Year Plan for National Informatization," *National Business Daily*, December 28, 2016, http://www.nbdpress.com/articles/2016-12-28/592.html.

[21] Hong Shen, "Building a Digital Silk Road? Situating the Internet in China's Belt and Road Initiative," *International Journal of Communication*, no. 12 (2018), 2683–2701, https://ijoc.org/index.php/ijoc/article/view/8405.

[22] *Op. cit.*, Stec (2018).

[23] *Ibid.*

Unicom and Mobile have been developing overland cable links in BRI routes while Huawei is developing telecommunications infrastructure in Africa. ZTE is likewise bringing fiber optic technology into Afghanistan.[24] The cited firms are also working for the development of 5G technologies.[25]

Further, Alibaba has established data centers overseas. To support its e-commerce, Alibaba launched its own cloud computing arm, Alibaba Cloud, in 2009.[26] It then expanded internationally and erected data centers in Dubai, Frankfurt and Sydney, but it was the BRI that paved the way for the construction of data centers in BRI countries and the access to markets along the BRI route. Since then, its service has reported a 400% growth in overseas markets.

In terms of artificial intelligence, Alibaba, Baidu, Tencent and Cambricon Technologies have enjoyed financial support from the Chinese government to develop AI-related research projects such as surveillance technologies and other customized products.[27] The BRI markets are similarly experiencing greater presence of Chinese technological solutions for online payment. This is evident in the presence of Alipay, the online payment platform of Alibaba, in BRI countries such as the Philippines, Indonesia, South Korea and Malaysia.[28]

Blockchain is another key technology that is being explored in the realm of financial technology. Among the well-known blockchain players are Alibaba (AliPay), Tencent (owner of WeBank and WeChat Pay) and Baidu. Through blockchain technologies, these firms are working to "de-bank" their industries, or institute the "removal or minimization of central authorities, intermediaries and overhead

---

[24] *Ibid.*

[25] Kristin Shi-Kupfer and MareikeOhlberg, "China's Digital Rise: Challenges for Europe," *MERICS Papers on China*, April 2019, https://www.merics.org/sites/default/files/201904/MPOC_No.7_ChinasDigitalRise_web_4.pdf.

[26] *Op. cit.*, Shen (2018).

[27] *Op. cit.*, Shi-Kupfer and Ohlberg (2019).

[28] The Economist Intelligence Unit, China's Digital Silk Road, (n.d.) https://www.business.hsbc.com/belt-and-road/chinas-digital-silk-road.

functions" in transactions.[29] Hong Kong's Secretary for Finance and Treasury mentioned that blockchain technologies would be beneficial for BRI countries as it could create a trade finance platform.[30]

Indeed, China's development in the fields of 5G, cloud computing, artificial intelligence, blockchain among others, emphasizes the country's commitment to adapting to the Fourth Industrial Revolution. More importantly, its implementation of the Made in China 2025, as well as Digital Silk Road, illustrates the nation's foresight of capitalizing on Industry 4.0 solutions to nurture more sustainable BRI projects and investments. Thus, BRI participating countries are enjoined to leverage on the aforementioned technologies and solutions, which is easier said than done as persistent challenges await them.

Roadblocks for BRI countries

Countries along the Belt and Road seeking to follow China's footsteps are bound to face the same obstacles encountered by nations seeking to transition in the Fourth Industrial Revolution. The only difference is that projects are to be executed within the mechanisms and arrangements deemed valid under the BRI. The BRI participating countries must therefore be prepared in addressing these challenges, specifically, low level of innovation, outdated legal and regulatory frameworks, job displacement, and cyber security and data privacy.

First, the aversion to innovate may be cited as one of the main barriers to the effective adoption of Industry 4.0 technologies and solutions. The Global Innovation Index (GII) 2019 reveals that Singapore, Israel, Republic of Korea and China are the only BRI

---

[29] Paul Fox, "One Belt, One Road, One Blockchain," *Medium*, October 22, 2018, https://medium.com/@ozpaulfox/on-belt-one-road-one-blockchain-9e5dd 36219c4.

[30] Brady Dale, "Hong Kong Official Touts Blockchain for China's 'Belt and Road' Plan," *Coindesk*, November 14, 2017, https://www.coindesk.com/hong-kong-trade-finance-belt-and-road.

participating countries which entered the top 20.[31] Numerous parties to the BRI cracked the top 50, but it is vital to note that majority of these innovative nations are either located in Europe and Northern Africa and Western Asia, or falling between high-income and upper-middle income brackets. Southeast Asian countries in the top 50 include Singapore, Malaysia, Vietnam and Thailand, while nations belonging in the lower-middle income group are Vietnam, Ukraine and Georgia. While the results of the GII 2019 paint an encouraging picture, it may be derived upon closer examination that the ability of BRI countries to maintain their innovative capability stems from two factors: (1) their economic position which enables them to invest heavily in research and development; and (2) inter-generational penchant to venture into science and technology.

Hence, low-income and lower-middle income BRI countries may be the thrust of efforts and initiatives aiming to enhance the level of innovation. These groups include Yemen, Burundi, Togo, Guinea, Zambia, Zimbabwe, Madagascar, Mozambique and Burkina Faso among others. The provision of technical and financial support to these types of nations may prove to be instrumental in their effective transition toward Industry 4.0. Moreover, governments may encourage investments in ICT infrastructure. The installation of next-generation digital infrastructure (e.g. 5g technology) coupled with digital literacy programs in public schools and adult workforce retraining systems can substantially support the transition of actors and stakeholders toward a highly disruptive environment. A large portion of the populace with competent ICT skills is an indispensable asset in the near future where humans exist and work alongside machines and digitized processes.

Second, the existence of restrictive laws and regulations is perceived as a major impediment to the efficient uptake of Industry 4.0 technologies by public sector and private sector organizations. Evidence in Northeast (e.g. Japan) and Southeast Asia (e.g. Singapore,

---

[31] "The Global Innovation Index 2019: Creating Healthy Lives — The Future of Medical Innovation," Cornell University, INSEAD, and WIPO, accessed September 29, 2019, https://www.globalinnovationindex.org/gii-2019-report.

Philippines) indicate the wide gap between Internet and/or platform-based services and regulatory mechanisms, unable to catch up with the accompanying disruption. As a result, governments are often constrained to shoehorn Industry 4.0-related innovations into traditional regulations. The presence of outdated legal and regulatory measures may adversely affect the BRI through its three priority areas of cooperation, namely, financial integration, unimpeded trade and people-to-people bond. This is due to current laws and regulations stifling the growth of Fintech, e-commerce platforms, and tourism-oriented platforms and applications.

In this vein, BRI participating countries may re-assess and/or amend their extant legal and regulatory measures to promote innovation and the adoption of Industry 4.0 technologies. A viable policy option is the simultaneous development of both formal, national digitization strategies and sector-specific approaches for the deployment of Artificial Intelligence (AI), Internet of Things (IoT), cloud computing, big data analytics among others.[32] As possible models, they may review the experiences of two Southeast Asian countries: (1) the Singaporean government's continuing effort of ensuring fair market competition and social protection of workers engaged in the transportation sector; and (2) the Philippine government's application of regulatory "sandboxes" to new and upcoming Fintech. Certainly, the effective enforcement of people-centered, innovation-friendly laws and regulations within and among countries along the Belt and Road is crucial to the realization of a vibrant Digital Silk Road.

Next, the issue of job displacement is related to two types of technologies ushered in by Industry 4.0, which are enabling and replacing. On one hand, enabling technologies are applied to improving the productivity of manual labor and providing cheaper goods and/or services. On the other hand, replacing technologies have the possibility to totally displace humans in a particular task. The introduction of these technologies into a specific industry/sector may result in lower wages, weaker labor demand and reduced overall employment. Displacement effects exacerbate the undesirable

---

[32] *Ibid.*

labor market conditions when new technologies fail to generate new jobs. This is characterized by displaced workers with skills not suitable to other jobs and the possibility of retooling them to be employed in other sectors is unattainable. Nevertheless, both types of technologies may lead to displacement and productivity effects and organizations must ensure that productivity effects are greater than the displacement effects.

A 2018 study about the future of work highlights that developing countries in Asia should adopt a positive outlook on job prospects amid technological breakthroughs.[33] A major reason is that new technologies often only automate specific tasks associated with a job. Workers that perform manual, routine jobs have the highest risk of being replaced by machines, while researchers and managers face the lowest risk of job automation. Furthermore, industrial robots are concentrated in capital intensive sectors with low employment shares such as electrical and electronics, automotive and metal industries. The rising demand for digitally enabled products and services across the developing Asia is also viewed to offset job displacement driven by automation. The biggest winner in the Fourth Industrial Revolution is the non-routine, cognitive category as new occupations and higher wages are being witnessed by industry players and laborers.

In the context of BRI, the integration of machines into work processes may be expected in areas such as infrastructure projects, conduct of trade, (e.g. online customs procedures, use of block chain) and quality of commodities (e.g. digitization of manufacturing). Thus, governments may opt to provide ICT-oriented education and training to their labor force, enforce favorable labor regulation and social protection measures and enact ICT-friendly tax policies. Governments may likewise facilitate skills development and job-matching and efficiently deliver public goods and services through

---

[33] "The Future of Work: Regional Perspectives," African Development Bank, Asian Development Bank, European Bank for Reconstruction and Development, and Inter-American Development Bank, 2018, accessed September 15, 2019, https://www.adb.org/sites/default/files/publication/481901/future-work-regional-perspectives.pdf.

Industry 4.0 technologies.[34] In addition, a key tenet that must be embedded by governments and firms into their processes and initiatives is that new skills and competencies will continuously and rapidly emerge amid the Fourth Industrial Revolution.

Lastly, countries along the Belt and Road should always strive to safeguard the security of cyber systems within their localities as well as the data privacy of their entire population. This foremost risk is being magnified due to the availability of tons of data utilized for transactions and the proliferation of hackers, terror groups and money launderers well-trained in launching cyber-attacks against governments, firms and banks. The incessant cross-border flows of data for a multitude of purposes further complicates the challenge of preserving the integrity and privacy of citizen's personal information. In this regard, governments should proactively craft and implement cyber security and data protection measures at the national and regional levels. The creation of a BRI-wide regulatory framework or guidelines for cross-border data flows may be a policy option for China and participating countries as they cultivate an open, inclusive and secure Digital Silk Road.

Key takeaways for ASEAN

The fundamental objective of the MPAC 2025 is to establish a connected region that will serve to deliver tangible benefits to the ASEAN citizens. The MPAC 2025 also recognizes that disruptive technologies such as mobile internet, big data, cloud technology, the Internet of Things, the automation of knowledge work and the Social-Mobile-Analytics-Cloud (SMAC) are important developments that could bring in increased efficiency, new products and services and in turn, generate gains for the entire region.[35] Given the parallelism with that of the BRI objective of enhancing connectivity between and

---

[34] Ibid.

[35] The ASEAN Secretariat, *Master Plan on ASEAN Connectivity 2025* (Jakarta: ASEAN Secretariat, 2016), 8, https://asean.org/storage/2016/09/Master-Plan-on-ASEAN-Connectivity-20251.pdf.

among regions, both ASEAN and China are poised to benefit from synergizing efforts under the domain of the initiatives and promoting 4IR technologies.

Aside from the geographical advantage that situates ASEAN and China as neighbors, both parties can make the most of its long-standing good relations, and the existing extensive cooperation dialogue mechanisms spanning areas such as connectivity, finance, agriculture, ICT, human resources development, investment, energy, culture, tourism, public health, environment and sub-regional development.[36]

Moreover, ASEAN may tap BRI networks and institutions such as the Asian Infrastructure Investment Bank in pushing forward its digital innovation projects and undertakings. It may likewise maximize the current state of expertise possessed by China to support ASEAN Member States (AMS) in upgrading their skills and capacities, respectively. The achievement of this goal may be supported substantially by enhancing the readiness in adopting Industry 4.0 technologies and the absorptive capacity of AMS and their communities. In addition, ASEAN nations should promote transparency, pursue higher levels innovation, enact appropriate and innovation-friendly legal and regulatory frameworks and enforce data protection measures to systematically address persistent barriers.

Way forward

The previous sections underscore that digital dimension is a critical strategic value of the BRI. For Winston Ma Wenyan of the World Economic Forum, the value of BRI's digital dimension lies in its five main purposes, namely: (1) long-term constructive role in making infrastructure development more viable, efficient and sustainable; (2) capability to bring advanced IT infrastructure to BRI countries; (3) capacity to capacitate MSMEs through smarter cross-border

---

[36]"China and ASEAN are Close Partners for BRI Cooperation," *Belt and Road News*, April 13, 2019, https://www.beltandroad.news/2019/04/13/china-and-asean-are-close-partners-for-bri-cooperation/.

logistics system; and (4) use of big data as a solution option for environmental challenges; and (5) capacity to address the digital divide.[37]

Hence, a handful of considerations should be kept in mind in keeping with the goal of promoting a sustainable BRI. For BRI participating countries, it is important to note that harnessing its Industry 4.0 opportunities entails intensive efforts through talent development, the use of transparency mechanisms, undertaking legal and regulatory reforms, and due regard for all concerned stakeholders whether it be MSMEs or members of local communities. Certainly, partner countries should keep in mind that reaping the full benefits of 4IR technologies requires strategic planning, integrated policies and targeted government interventions.

Conversely, China continues to play an important role in seeing through how Industry 4.0 technologies may be leveraged to foster inclusive societies and realize sustainable development along the Belt and Road. It may therefore consider cultivating partnerships to bring Industry 4.0-led industries to interested BRI countries and localities while judiciously monitoring related developments, emerging innovations and attendant challenges. The fulfillment of these functions is viewed to steer the BRI toward a future that is open, green and clean.

---

[37] Winston Ma Wenyan, "Could a Digital Silk Road Solve the Belt and Road's Sustainability Problem?" *World Economic Forum*, September 19, 2018, https://www.weforum.org/agenda/2018/09/could-a-digital-silk-road-solve-the-belt-and-roads-sustainability-problem/.

https://doi.org/10.1142/9789811234316_0011

Chapter

11

Mainstreaming Sustainable Principles into BRI Projects: Notes from the Philippine Experience

Jovito Jose P. Katigbak*

Foreign Service Institute, the Philippines

On April 25–27, 2019, the Second Belt and Road Forum for International Cooperation was held in Beijing, China, which brought together several world leaders and around 5,000 representatives from 150 nations to hold dialogues about the possible trajectory of the ambitious Belt and Road Initiative (BRI). Although the discourse

---

*Mr. Katigbak presented this chapter at the NACT Working Group Meeting on "Regional Connectivity and Sustainability: Connecting the Belt and Road Initiative (BRI) and the Master Plan on ASEAN Connectivity (MPAC) 2025" on April 29–30, 2019 held in Langkawi Island, Malaysia.

The views expressed in this chapter are of the author alone and do not reflect the official position of the Foreign Service Institute, the Department of Foreign Affairs, and the Government of the Philippines.

largely focused on the personalities who were present, an equally newsworthy topic was President Xi Jinping's pronouncement of aligning the BRI operations in congruence with the principles of "openness, greenness, and cleanliness".[1] Accordingly, this move can be viewed as the Chinese government's response to calls for reforms regarding BRI-related processes, amid reports and allegations of corruption, debt trap diplomacy, low absorptive capacity of recipient countries and failed implementation of projects. With BRI activities adopting sustainability as their main guiding principle and perhaps their ultimate objective, what can China and the participating countries learn from the Philippine experience concerning the application of sustainable principles into infrastructure projects?

Hence, this chapter outlines key policy considerations and options for the parties involved in BRI projects, as they seek to effectively address economic, social and environmental facets simultaneously. Furthermore, it has five sub-sections. The first segment provides a review of the Initiative's objectives and scope while the second section discusses the nature of Philippine participation in the BRI. The third section tackles the progress and setbacks of the BRI while the fourth section expounds on the main takeaways from the Philippine experience in fostering sustainable infrastructure projects. The last segment describes a way forward for the initiative.

A Review of BRI's Objectives and Magnitude

Chinese President Xi Jinping announced the country's plan to launch the Silk Road Economic Belt (SREB) at a speech in Nazarbayev University, Kazakhstan, in 2013. A month later of the same year, President Xi, in his speech to the Indonesian Congress, expressed China's ambition to build the 21st Century Maritime Silk Road (MSR). Both comprise what turned out to be the BRI. Subsequently, the Vision and Actions on Jointly Building SREB and 21st Century

---

[1] Tan Dawn Wei, "China Will Keep Belt and Road Sustainable, Clean, and Green: Xi Jinping," *The Straits Times*, April 26, 2019, https://www.straitstimes.com/asia/east-asia/china-will-keep-belt-and-road-sustainable-clean-and-green-xi-jinping.

MSR was released in March 2015 and stipulates that the funding for projects of the BRI will be accessible through investments, syndicated loans and bank credits. The main financing mechanisms are the Asian Infrastructure Investment Bank (AIIB), BRICS New Development (NDB), Shanghai Cooperation Organization (SCO) Bank and the Silk Road Fund.[2] The issuance of bonds in Renminbi and in foreign currencies by Chinese financial institutions and companies is also encouraged to raise funds for the BRI. The BRI approximately covers 40% of the world's gross domestic product (GDP) and 65% of the total population.

The initiative is guided by five principles: (1) in line with the purposes and principles of the UN Charter and upholding the Five Principles of Peaceful Coexistence; (2) open for cooperation; (3) harmonious and inclusive; (4) following market mechanisms; (5) promoting mutual benefits. It likewise espouses four main concepts, namely, "peace and cooperation, openness and inclusiveness, mutual learning, and mutual benefit". Furthermore, the BRI will nurture a community that is founded on shared interests, a common destiny and a collective responsibility underpinned by "mutual political trust, economic integration, and cultural inclusiveness".

In terms of geographic scope, the Belt and Road will link two major circles: one comprising the dynamic East Asia economic circle; and the other composed of the developed European economic circle. To be specific, the Belt seeks to connect China via three routes: (i) Central Asia, Russia and Europe (the Baltic); (ii) Persian Gulf and the Mediterranean through Central Asia and West Asia; and (iii) Southeast Asia, South Asia and the Indian Ocean. The creation of a new Eurasian Land Bridge and the development of economic corridors are identified as crucial elements of the BRI. The China–Pakistan Economic Corridor and the Bangladesh–China–India–Myanmar Economic Corridor are vital to the BRI as well as the construction of other economic corridors such as China–Mongolia-Russia, China–Central Asia-West Asia and China-Indochina Peninsula.

---

[2] Darlene V. Estrada, "The Belt and Road Initiative and Philippine Participation in the Maritime Silk Road," *CIRSS Commentaries*, no. 7(7) (2017): 1–2.

International transport routes and economic industrial parks are labeled as concrete mechanisms for the advancement of cooperation platforms related to the BRI. At the sea, the Road will traverse two routes: (a) from China's coast to Europe via South China Sea and the Indian Ocean; and/or (b) from China's coast to the South Pacific through the South China Sea.

Moreover, the BRI has five key priority areas for cooperation. These are policy coordination, facilities connectivity, unimpeded trade, financial integration and people-to-people bond. In terms of facilities connectivity, the Belt and Road urges for the building of international trunk passageways and the development of an infrastructure network linking all sub-regions in Asia, and between Asia, Europe and Africa. In addition, the cited initiative seeks for the development of land–water transportation channels and port cooperation as well as a comprehensive civil aviation platform which is necessary for the eventual establishment of a regional aviation hub. Enhancing connectivity in the sectors of energy and international communications are also noted as one of the priority programs. For financial integration, the Belt and Road aims to expand the coverage and size of bilateral currency swap agreements with participating countries and introduce a bond market in Asia.

Huang underscores that China's decision to launch the BRI is motivated by two aspects, specifically, economy and politics.[3] The reference to the first dimension is grounded on the country's current shift from an export-oriented, fixed assets-centric investments type of economy toward one that is heavily reliant on services and high-value added sectors. The BRI is viewed to upgrade China's technological capacity and industries and underpin a sounder financial system and state-owned enterprises (SOEs) management. Observers similarly contend that the mentioned undertaking may be used to export the country's excess steel, coal, shipbuilding and other construction materials to underdeveloped regions in the world. Aside from the economic rationale, the Initiative is perceived by experts as China's

---

[3] Yiping Huang, "Understanding China's Belt & Road Initiative: Motivation, Framework and Assessment," *China Economic Review*, no. 40 (2016): 314–321.

opportunity to play a greater role in shaping the international economic governance system, given its rising status and position in the Asian region.

Aboard the China-led Ship: Philippine Participation in the MSR

The Philippines officially joined the BRI upon signing of the Memorandum of Understanding (MoU) on BRI Cooperation with China in November 2018. The MoU lays out that both parties must enforce projects that abide by the "strictest respect for national laws, rules, regulations, and policies" and the principles of "complete transparency" and "mutual respect for territorial integrity and sovereignty".[4] It is non-binding and has an effectivity of four years which can be renewed for another four years. Other deals that were concurrently signed in November include areas such as oil and gas development, basic education, cultural exchanges, infrastructure projects and foreign exchange.[5]

More recently, the Duterte administration inked 19 business agreements with Chinese companies worth USD 12.16 billion on the sidelines of the Second Belt and Road Forum for International Cooperation. These deals are projected to create more than 21,000 jobs in sectors such as infrastructure, telecommunications, energy, tourism and economic zones.[6] However, it is important to stress that the Philippine government has yet to release an official list of agreements which falls under the BRI basket, despite several reports claiming otherwise. Estrada emphasized that the country's participation in

[4] Daryl John Esguerra, "READ: PH-China MOU on Belt and Road Initiative," *Inquirer.net*, November 27, 2018, https://globalnation.inquirer.net/171728/read-ph-china-mou-on-belt-and-road-initiative.

[5] Nestor Corrales, "PH, China Sign MOU on Oil and Gas Development, 28 Other Deals," *Inquirer.net*, November 20, 2018, https://globalnation.inquirer.net/171449/ph-and-china-sign-mou-on-oil-and-gas-development-28-other-deals.

[6] Arianne Merez, "PH Inks P633 Billion in Trade, Investment Deals with China," *ABS-CBN News*, April 26, 2019, https://news.abs-cbn.com/business/04/26/19/ph-inks-p633-billion-in-trade-investment-deals-with-china.

the BRI is more likely through the MSR which would focus on port development.[7]

It may be stated that the Philippines' interest in partaking in the BRI is catalyzed by two forces, namely, the need for additional financing mechanisms for the "Build, Build, Build" (BBB) program and the diversification of relations in pursuit of an independent foreign policy. The first factor pertains to the Duterte administration's vision of leading the country toward a "golden age of infrastructure" by spending about PhP 8–9 trillion (over USD 150 billion) over the period 2016–2022. BRI projects are thus expected to complement the BBB program via infrastructure development encompassing energy, information and communication technology (ICT) and water resources. The second element relates to the Philippine government's move toward a more balanced network of bilateral ties with non-traditional and emerging partners such as China. To illustrate, the Philippines–China relations entered a new chapter after the inauguration of President Rodrigo Duterte in June 2016. Consequently, this resulted in the conclusion of a Six-Year Development Program (SYDP) which provides further exploration of partnerships between the two parties in areas encompassing trade, investment, agriculture and fisheries, infrastructure and tourism among others.[8] The BRI is hence an opportunity for the country to carry out more exchanges with China at a bilateral level.

In spite of the apparent benefits to be reaped, the Duterte administration must still address and contend with a handful of domestic issues. For instance, a poll in December 2018 revealed that 60%, or 6 out of 10 Filipinos, still distrusted China mainly because of the West Philippine Sea/South China Sea dispute.[9] This has implications on the Philippine government's actions concerning the BRI as the

---

[7] *Ibid.*

[8] Jovito Jose P. Katigbak, "Bridging the Infrastructure Investment Gap through Foreign Aid: A Briefer on Chinese ODA," *CIRSS Commentaries*, no. V(11) (2018): 1–3.

[9] "Six of 10 Filipinos Distrust China; US Enjoys 84% Support–Survey," *Inquirer.net*, January 15, 2019, https://newsinfo.inquirer.net/1073144/six-of-10-filipinos-distrust-china-us-enjoys-84-support-survey.

success of projects hinges on the buy-in of Filipino citizens. Other equally vital subject matters are the low absorptive capacity and delays and failures in the implementation of infrastructure projects due to financial and political factors.

Progress and Tales of Caution

Since 2013, the BRI has attained substantial progress in advancing trade among the participating countries. By the end of October 2019, China had entered into 197 cooperation documents with 137 countries and 30 international organizations. Russia, Kazakhstan, Pakistan, South Korea and Vietnam are the top countries with the largest number of BRI-related cooperation projects, while Russia, Philippines and Cambodia are the leading parties in terms of policy exchanges with China. The trade volume of goods between China and BRI countries has likewise surpassed the USD 6 trillion mark over the period 2013–2018. China's main exports to markets along the Belt and Road are electromechanical products while its primary imports are electrical equipment and fossil fuels. Private firms comprise 43% of the total trade volume and Central Asian nations capitalized on this development more than the others.

In terms of facilities connectivity, China has opened new ship routes with over 600 ports in more than 200 countries and signed 62 bilateral inter-governmental air transport agreements with nations along the Belt and Road. By the end of March 2019, China–Europe freight trains have exceeded 14,000 trips, which traverse between China and 50 cities in 15 European countries.

Moreover, the AIIB has approved investments for BRI projects worth more than USD 5.3 billion while the Silk Road Fund has already committed approximately USD 87 billion. The AIIB has already taken on the task of "greening" its portfolio by approving loans of 34 infrastructure projects as of April 2019. Association of Southeast Asian Nations (ASEAN) member states such as Indonesia, Myanmar and Lao PDR have secured funding for their respective "green" infrastructure projects under the AIIB. For its part, the Philippines availed of a USD 207.6 million loan for its Metro Manila

Flood Management project. China has likewise signed currency swap agreements with 20 countries and 102 Chinese-funded banks were also established in 24 countries.

Tourism similarly prospered as statistics showed that 60 million travelers moved between China and BRI nations, along with the blossoming of 1,023 sister cities. More specifically, the number of Chinese visitor arrivals in ASEAN countries has been on an upward trend, jumping from just 4,201 in 2009 to 25,284 in 2017.[10] Thailand, Singapore and Malaysia are the top three destinations of Chinese tourists over the period 2007–2016. Conversely, the volume of ASEAN tourists to China has steadily hiked from over 5 million in 2009, to more than 21 million in 2017. Of this figure, the large chunk of ASEAN travelers comes from Malaysia, Thailand and Myanmar. Citizens from Vietnam and Laos have also exhibited greater enthusiasm in exploring various parts of China during 2009–2017.

In terms of educational exchanges, there were about 120,000 Chinese students in Singapore, Thailand, Indonesia and Vietnam in 2015. On the other hand, there were over 70,000 students from Thailand, Indonesia and Vietnam who opted to further their education in China during the same period. The Chinese government has also provided scholarships to citizens of countries along the Belt and Road such as Pakistan, Mongolia, Russia, Vietnam, Thailand, Laos, Kazakhstan and Nepal. Furthermore, it established around 31 Confucius Institutes and 29 Confucius classrooms in ASEAN countries. Thailand hosts the largest number of the facilities at 15 and 20, respectively, while the Philippines caters to 4 institutes.

Nevertheless, a number of cases linked to the BRI raise fears and anxieties of citizens of participating countries.[11] In particular, several

---

[10] Xia Liping, "China–ASEAN People-to-People Exchanges Against the Background of the B&R Initiative," presented at the *6th Network of ASEAN-China Think Tanks (NACT) Annual Conference on "Enhancing Inclusive and Sustainable Economic Development*," June 14, 2019, Bangkok, Thailand.

[11] "China's Belt and Road Initiative, Five Years In," *Stratfor*, June 22, 2018, https://worldview.stratfor.com/article/chinas-belt-and-road-initiative-five-years.

energy and transportation projects in Bangladesh, Kazakhstan, Myanmar and Pakistan have either been delayed or canceled due to financial incapacity and political instability. Allegations of corruption and use of funds for personal benefit are likewise the foremost risks in countries such as Djibouti and Venezuela. More importantly, concerns about a debt trap diplomacy coupled with changes in political leadership have resulted in the review of several BRI projects, specifically, the Kyaupku port in Southern Myanmar and the East Coast Rail link in Malaysia. It can be observed that the present administration of both countries would likely alleviate any domestic polarization and avoid the experiences of Sri Lanka and Pakistan, who have leased their Hambantota port for 99 years and Gwadar port for 40 years to China, respectively, due to challenges in debt repayment. Notably, the Chinese government has employed various kinds of debt relief and forgiveness measures to nations with high external debts such as Djibouti, Kyrgyzstan, Laos and Montenegro.

The last issue associated with the Initiative is environmental degradation.[12] A study by the Worldwide Fund (WWF) reveals that projects along the BRI may result in biodiversity loss as they will affect 256 threatened species such as giant pandas, gorillas, endangered tigers and Saiga antelopes, to name a few.[13] To illustrate, the USD 1.6 billion hydroelectric powerplant being developed in the Batang Toru forest highlands in Sumatra, Indonesia, is perceived to disrupt the habitat of the Tapanuli orangutan, which is the world's rarest great ape.[14] In addition, the primary BRI corridors are projected to

---

[12] Elizabeth Losos, Alexander Pfaff and Lydia Olander, "The Deforestation Risks of China's Belt and Road Initiative," *Brookings*, January 28, 2019, https://www.brookings.edu/blog/future-development/2019/01/28/the-deforestation-risks-of-chinas-belt-and-road-initiative/.

[13] World Wildlife Fund, "The Belt and Road Initiative: WWF Recommendations and Spatial Analysis," *WWF Briefing Paper*, accessed on May 6, 2019, http://awsassets.panda.org/downloads/the_belt_and_road_initiative___wwf_recommendations_and_spatial_analysis___may_2017.pdf.

[14] Jason Thomas, "China's BRI Negatively Impacting the Environment," *The ASEAN Post*, February 19, 2019, https://theaseanpost.com/article/chinas-bri-negatively-impacting-environment.

directly traverse through and impinge on more than 1,700 important bird areas, 46 biodiversity hotspots and globally 200 Ecoregions. Another research discovers that the BRI could facilitate the introduction of over 800 alien invasive species into the native ecosystems of Southeast Asian countries.[15]

Hydropower projects along the Mekong River, which encompasses Cambodia, Laos, Myanmar, Thailand and Vietnam, are also cited as catalysts of river flow changes and blocked migration of fish. These lead to reduced solid fertility and lower fish stock, thus threatening the livelihood of fisher folks and communities around the coastal areas.[16] A similar key environment-related issue is deforestation. The removal of forests along the path of massive BRI infrastructure projects such as the Pan Borneo Highway, connecting Malaysia, Indonesia and Brunei, is expected to contribute to more occurrences of landslides, floods and other related disasters.[17]

Fostering Sustainable Infrastructure: Insights from Philippine Initiatives

As a response to calls for reforms by participating countries and observers due to reports and allegations that were previously discussed, President Xi Jinping signified the need to align BRI operations in congruence with the principles of "openness, greenness, and cleanliness" at the recent Belt and Road Forum. More specifically, the Joint Communique of the Leaders' Roundtable of the 2nd Belt and Road Forum for International Cooperation demands for the construction of "high-quality, reliable, resilient and sustainable infrastructure" that is "viable, affordable, accessible, inclusive and broadly beneficial over its entire life-cycle". It similarly pushes for green

---

[15] Xuan Liu, Tim Blackburn, Tianjian Song, Xianping Li, Cong Huang and Yiming Li, "Risks of Biological Invasion on the Belt and Road," *Current Biology*, no. 29(3) (2019): 499–505.

[16] Maizura Ismail, "What's At Stake for the Mekong's Fishery," *The ASEAN Post*, November 14, 2018, https://theaseanpost.com/article/whats-stake-mekongs-fishery.

[17] *Ibid.*

development, open and transparent procurement processes, anti-corruption practices and participation of private firms and local companies. A debt sustainability analysis framework was likewise available for interested parties. Hence, with the BRI heading toward a more sustainable future, China and the participating countries may perhaps acquire some key takeaways from the Philippine experience.

Accordingly, the main sustainability-related principles can be categorized into two levels: (i) partnership and (ii) project cycle. At the partnership level, governments must ensure policy stability. A report by PwC underlines that BRI projects are vulnerable to geopolitical risks which may come about due to lengthy gestation periods which are subjected to political cycles, developments in bilateral ties and cross-border spats which influence project enforcement.[18] The Philippines is no stranger to these forces as local elections are held every three years while the President and Vice President along with the top 12 senators are voted into office every six years. The remaining 12 Senators have a fixed term of three years and are up for re-election for another three years. Recognizing that entering into BRI-related deals is a political as much as — or many times more than — an economic decision, participating governments should uphold policy continuity to prevent delays and cancellations of projects.

In addition, the widely publicized West Philippine Sea/South China Sea dispute has contributed to negative perceptions by Filipino citizens toward China, which certainly affects the government's dealings with the aforementioned countries. In this regard, the role of effective public diplomacy targeted toward the Filipino masses becomes a crucial component of the continued cooperation between the Philippines and China, especially through the BRI.

Another consideration is the provision of an enabling environment for two purposes: (1) convenient implementation of projects; (2) optimal use of built infrastructures. A practical example is less cumbersome customs and border procedures for consultants and import equipment necessary for BRI projects. To maximize the

---

[18] PwC, "Repaving the Silk Road," May 8, 2019, http://www.pwc.com/ee/et/publications/pub/pwc-gmc-repaving-the-ancient-silk-routes-web-full.pdf.

constructed facilities, governments must then pursue enhanced trade facilitation measures as well as better trade logistics networks. For the Philippines, the enactment of Republic Act (RA) No. 10863, otherwise known as the Customs Modernization and Tariff Act (CMTA), in May 2016 mandated the shift toward a modern, more efficient administration of customs standards, rules and processes. It prescribes the upgrading of the Bureau of Customs' (BoC) capacity in efficiently managing customs procedures and control through the use of ICT. The Duterte administration has also signed into law RA No. 11302, or Ease of Doing Business and Efficient Government Service Delivery Act, in May 2018. The salient provisions of the new law include the development of a Central Business Portal to process applications related to business transactions, the creation of a Philippine Business Databank to store information on all registered firms, and the installation of automated business one-stop shops across localities. These measures are expected to increase the competitiveness of local firms at the global level while simultaneously encouraging seamless cross-border trade, which is one of the primary areas of cooperation of the BRI.

At the project cycle level, the sustainability of BRI projects may be advanced through transparent and competitive procurement processes and sound environmental impact assessments (EIAs) during the initiation and planning stages. These steps can facilitate the involvement of suitable firms which offer the most rational proposals both economically and environmentally. The Philippine Government Procurement Reform Act of 2003 (RA 9184) may serve as a case study for other interested governments as it espouses the principles of transparency, competition, harmonized rules and regulations, accountability, and checks and balances. Companies are required to register and place their bids on the Philippine Government Electronic Procurement System (PhilGEPS) which can be monitored by civil society organizations (CSOs). Public bidding is designated as the default mode of procurement and penal and civil liabilities can be levied against violators of legally established rules and regulations.[19]

---

[19] Adoracion M. Navarro and Juan Alfonso O. Tanghal, "The Promises and Pains in Procurement Reforms in the Philippines," *PIDS Discussion Paper Series No. 2017–16,*

To promote environmental preservation, the Philippine government mandated the conducting of environmental impact statements for activities with significant environmental effects, since 1977 via Presidential Decree (PD) 1151. The creation of a Philippine Environmental Impact Statement System (EISS) was formalized in 1978 through PD 1586 and stipulated that "no person, partnership or corporation shall undertake or operate any environmentally critical project (ECP) or locate a project within an environmentally critical area (ECA) without first securing an Environmental Compliance Certificate (ECC)". These laws underwent permutations over several decades but continue to be a vital component of the regulatory regime concerning infrastructure development.

Subsequently, implementing agencies may incorporate the principles of stakeholder participation and involvement of local communities to augment the success rate of project execution. The partaking of the private sector and local government units (LGUs) in BRI projects may result in economic and social gains for these actors such as job creation, income generation and social cohesion. The Philippine Public–Private Partnership (PPP) Center has been capacitating LGUs nationwide in crafting business cases for community projects which can be undertaken with the private sector.[20] This initiative is instrumental in improving the capacities of both actors in carrying out community-based programs.

A similarly crucial element in the effective implementation of projects is the participation of empowered communities. A model program which has substantially helped in attaining this objective is the Kapit-Bisig Laban sa Kahirapan-Comprehensive and Integrated Delivery of Social Services, or Kalahi-CIDSS. It is founded on the community-driven development (CDD) approach and empowers communities of targeted municipalities to govern and to design,

---

April 2017, https://pidswebs.pids.gov.ph/CDN/PUBLICATIONS/pidsdps1716. pdf.

[20] Czeriza Valencia, "LGUs Urged to Build Cases for PPP Project Proposals," *The Philippine Star*, April 17, 2019, https://ppp.gov.ph/in_the_news/lgus-urged-to-build-cases-for-ppp-project-proposals/.

execute and monitor poverty reduction activities. Kalahi-CIDSS was likewise redesigned to assist communities in their post-disaster rehabilitation after being affected by Typhoon Haiyan in 2013.[21] Evidently, the buy-in of local communities can substantially contribute in mainstreaming the sustainability aspect of BRI projects.

Lastly, the safeguarding of effective, impartial monitoring of projects during the performance and control stage may be achieved by engaging third-party actors such as CSOs and non-government organizations. An illustrative case is the Bantay Lansangan or Road Watch project in the Philippines which sought to monitor the performance of the country's Department of Public Works and Highways (DPWH) in fulfilling its mandate of making available quality road sector infrastructure and services to the citizens. The initiative was launched in 2007 and lasted for only 30 months but was successful in cultivating partnerships among government agencies, private sector, NGOs and CSOs, and development partners to ensure the effective delivery of public services to the citizens.

Given the abovementioned principles that may be integrated into the processes of the BRI to nurture sustainability, it is paramount to highlight that the enforcement of "open, clean, and green" BRI projects is a shared responsibility between China and the recipient countries. Thus, leaders and representatives of both parties must practice good governance ideals such as transparency, participation and accountability to effectively address and respond to interests and concerns of their constituents.

Realizing BRI's Legitimacy through Isomorphism?

To conclude, the previous sections have demonstrated that China's move toward the adoption of international standards and best practices for BRI processes and projects can be perceived as a response to

---

[21] "2014, a Year of Accomplishments for Kalahi-CIDSS, Development Partners," Department of Social Welfare and Development, March 12, 2015, https://www.dswd.gov.ph/2014-a-year-of-accomplishments-for-kalahi-cidss-development-partners/.

the criticisms and questions associated, both directly and indirectly, with the BRI's credibility and legitimacy. Hence, if the recent pronouncement of President Xi is to be taken as a valid indicator of the BRI's trajectory in the near future, it would therefore be imperative for countries along the Belt and Road to adopt principles and practices that foster sustainability. It is crucial to emphasize that the pace and success of BRI's move toward sustainability are heavily dependent on the participating countries' reception of the proposed reforms.

In addition, a development worth perusing is the warmer relations between BRI institutions and established multilateral development banks such as the Asian Development Bank and World Bank. Will this scenario result in closer collaboration between the two parties and what direction will this partnership take? More importantly, how will the mounting pressure from various groups and "peers" affect BRI *vis-à-vis* conformance to institutional prescriptions and standards present in the wider environment?

The study of new institutionalism may thus prove to be useful in addressing these inquiries. Specifically, the central tenet of this theory is that institutions are deeply enmeshed in social and political environments and that the former's structures and practices are either mirror images or responses to norms, beliefs and rational myths embedded into the larger environment. The existence of peer pressure from organizations within the built circle influences institutions to conform to standards to augment their chances of survival and eventually establish legitimacy.[22] Eventually, similarity across organizations, or what is known as isomorphism, emerges. In the BRI's case, the source of legitimacy is the recipient countries.

Finally, nations along the Belt and Road recognize that China's growing power and influence in Asia and elsewhere subject the latter to accompanying duties and responsibilities as well as risks. In this regard, the BRI may serve as a litmus test for China in taking a leadership role in steering the global economy toward sustained growth. This arduous task is compounded by larger factors at play, namely,

---

[22] Mark C. Suchman, "Managing Legitimacy: Strategic and Institutional Approaches," *Academy of Management Review*, no. 20 (1995): 571–610.

the U.S. economic presence and visibility in the region and Asia's marching toward greater regional integration.

Accordingly, observers and analysts note that the lingering U.S.–China trade war may produce negative repercussions on the recovery of the global economy, while simultaneously creating opportunities for alternative market destinations such as ASEAN countries. At the regional level, cooperation between China and ASEAN may be deepened through highlighting the complementarities, as well as developing pathways toward more extensive collaboration, between the ASEAN Master Plan on Connectivity (MPAC) 2025 and the BRI. A caveat to China, however: upon comprehensive and careful examination, these endeavors should be explicitly identified as either warning signs or guideposts along its journey as an emerging bastion of free trade amid persistent calls for protectionism due to discontents expressed by apparent "losers of globalization". The role of reliable partners is therefore paramount in this ambitious and oftentimes taxing undertaking.

Chapter

12

A Tale of Two Regional Integration Connectivity Projects: Harmonizing China's Belt and Road Initiative with the ASEAN Master Plan on Connectivity

Aaron Jed Rabena

Asia-Pacific Pathways to Progress Foundation Inc., Philippines
University of the Philippines, Philippines

Introduction

China and the Association of Southeast Asian Nations (ASEAN) are two entities that have ambitious regional integration connectivity initiatives. China's Belt and Road Initiative (BRI) has five major areas of cooperation (AOC): (1) policy coordination; (2) trade and investment facilitation; (3) infrastructure connectivity; (4) financial integration; (5) people-to-people ties and connectivity. ASEAN's Master Plan on ASEAN Connectivity (MPAC) 2025 (as part of the ASEAN Community Vision 2025), on the other hand, likewise has

Table 1   BRI–MPAC Policy Matching Matrix.

MPAC	BRI	
Seamless logistics	Infrastructure connectivity/Trade and investment connectivity	
Sustainable infrastructure	Infrastructure connectivity	
Digital innovation	Financial integration	AOC
Regulatory excellence	Policy coordination	
People mobility	People-to-people ties and connectivity	

five AOCs: (1) sustainable infrastructure; (2) digital innovation; (3) seamless logistics; (4) regulatory excellence; (5) people mobility. The two initiatives share a lot in common and cover both soft and hard infrastructure. Needless to say, the BRI and MPAC possess a wide area for potential collaboration. During the 22nd China–ASEAN Summit, a Joint Statement was issued which formally stated the integration of the BRI with the MPAC.

BRI and the MPAC can be synergized by drawing parallels between the BRI and MPAC's AOCs and by starting with BRI's first and primary AOC, that is, policy coordination. This is because policy coordination is the starting point or the framework upon which cooperative measures could be made.

Many things have already been done on the trade front considering that China is ASEAN's — and for many individual ASEAN countries — largest trade partner. However, trade deficit also persists with many ASEAN member states (AMS) and therefore there is a need to correct the trade imbalance. One area where China could further increase its presence in ASEAN is in its investments (see Table 1).

The Parallels in BRI and MPAC Policy Issue Areas

Apart from forging the *2016–2020 Plan of Action to Implement the Joint Declaration on the ASEAN–China Strategic Partnership for Peace and Prosperity* (more recently the ASEAN–China Strategic Partnership Vision 2030) and pledging joint efforts on Smart City Cooperation Initiative, Connecting the Connectivities Initiative,

Initial Rolling Priority Pipeline of Potential ASEAN Infrastructure Projects, Lancang–Mekong Cooperation (LMC), the Greater Mekong Sub-region (GMS) and the ASEAN–Mekong Basin Development Cooperation (AMBDC), the Ayeyawady–Chao Phraya–Mekong Economic Cooperation Strategy (ACMECS), and the Brunei Darussalam–Indonesia–Malaysia–Philippines East Asian Growth Area (BIMP-EAGA), there is a need for specific supplemental mechanisms and frameworks to identify how cooperation should proceed between the BRI and MPAC. One major way is by complementing ASEAN's already existing mechanisms, efforts and initiatives.

Policy coordination

To ensure the progress and legitimacy of the BRI and MPAC integration, China can employ its Third-Party Market Cooperation (TPMC) mechanism (e.g. with Japan, France, Italy, UK, Canada, Singapore, Spain, Netherlands, Belgium, Australia, European Investment and Development Bank).[1] Doing this, especially with Western powers, would dispel notions and allay fears that China seeks to dominate its regional backyard and that the BRI is a one-way street. Moreover, by getting developed countries on board, targeted projects would gain prestige and credibility. This is especially crucial when BRI projects are widely reported to be "debt traps" and are non-compliant to environmental rules and regulations, or are environmentally unsustainable.

With policy coordination, China would be able to show that it abides by high standards regarding economic and commercial engagement (e.g. managerial expertise, project management rules). In addition, applying the TPMC model would indicate that the BRI is indeed inclusive and is open for every interested country or stakeholder. In this respect, it is important to note that China has signed BRI cooperation agreements with around 30 international organizations. Relatedly, TPMC would further align with ASEAN's consistent

---

[1] In March 2019, the TPMC was mentioned in the Report on the Work of the Government. In August 2019, TPMC guidelines were released by the National Development and Reform Commission (NDRC).

mantra of "ASEAN Centrality", which means inclusiveness or open engagement with all. Thus, as with the Sino-Japan Third-Party Cooperation Forum, a China–ASEAN Third-Party Cooperation Forum could also be put in place. There are several examples of combining the comparative advantages of China with those of other countries. As a study by a consulting firm puts it:

> China overseas infrastructure development advantages lie in strong financial strength, short construction cycle, strong government support and high cost-performance ratio. However, the risk management and control mechanism of Japanese infrastructure enterprises are more mature and well developed. They have obvious advantages in project operation and management, but... face issues such as labor shortage and long construction cycle. Therefore, third-party market cooperation between the two countries... is highly complementary...[2]

In fact, American companies have already taken part in the BRI, including AECOM (Engineering Procurement and Construction [EPC]), Black and Vetch, Caterpillar, Honeywell, GE, Citigroup, and Goldman Sachs.[3] Apart from these, China can utilize the ASEAN+ frameworks (e.g. ASEAN+3, ASEAN+6, ASEAN+8, ASEAN+3 Cooperation Work Plan) in advancing TPMC (through government and private entities) with other ASEAN dialogue partner countries (e.g. U.S. Overseas Private Investment Corporation [OPIC], Australia's Department of Foreign Affairs and Trade [DFAT], Japan Bank for International Cooperation [JBIC], Japan International Cooperation Agency [JICA], French Development Agency [FDA],

---

[2] "Borderless win–win cooperation in building the Belt and Road," EY Belt and Road Navigator, 2019, http://files.chinagoabroad.com/Public/uploads/content/files/201911/Navigator%203rd%20issue%20-%20Borderless%20win-win%20cooperation%20in%20building%20the%20Belt%20and%20Road_final.pdf.

[3] See "Chapter 3: China and the World: Section 1: Belt and Road Initiative," https://www.uscc.gov/sites/default/files/2019-10/Chapter%203%2C%20Section%201%20-%20China%20and%20Continental%20Southeast%20Asia_0.pdf.

Export Finance Australia, Nippon Export and Investment Insurance, Export Credit Guarantee Corporation of India).

Similarly, TPMC involving multilateral institutions should be encouraged (i.e. with Asian Development Bank, World Bank).[4] According to an Organization for Economic Cooperation and Development (OECD) Report:

> The OECD has a number of regional initiatives underway ... The Central Asia Competitiveness Initiative ... aims to help countries to enhance productivity by supporting entrepreneurship, private sector development, inclusiveness and the building of suitable knowledge-based economies ... Countries work with OECD Committees covering a number of areas such as corporate governance, foreign direct investment, competition, bribery and corruption, pensions, the environment, social policies and taxation.[5]

Other specific measures for strengthening TPMC in ASEAN could include the alignment of the BRI with Japan's Partnership for Quality Infrastructure (PQI). In fact, TPMC is also being done by the U.S. in its Free and Open Indo-Pacific (FOIP) Vision (e.g. Japan–U.S. Strategic Energy Partnership, Japan–U.S. Strategic Digital Economy Partnership, MoU between USAID and Korea International Cooperation Agency [KOICA], U.S.–India Clean Energy Finance Task Force, U.S.–Japan Mekong Power Partnership, U.S.–Singapore Third Country Training Program, U.S.–Thailand International Law Enforcement Academy). Apart from the Joint Statement between ASEAN and China on Further Deepening the Cooperation on Infrastructure Connectivity and Joint Statement on Production Capacity Cooperation, China and ASEAN should sign MoUs explicitly supporting ASEAN Community Blueprints 2025, ASEAN sectoral work plans, the Initiative for ASEAN Integration (IAI)

---

[4] TPMC already implicitly exists between ADB and AIIB.

[5] "China's Belt and Road Initiative in the Global Trade, Investment, and Finance Landscape," OECD 2018, https://www.oecd.org/finance/Chinas-Belt-and-Road-Initiative-in-the-global-trade-investment-and-finance-landscape.pdf.

Work Plan II and ASEAN Strategic Transport Plan 2016–2025, as these are all related to MPAC.

The MPAC 2025's National Focal Points that would be in place in each ASEAN member state is to "establish a regular (e.g. semi-annual) consultative process with private sector entities (business associations and business councils) to update on progress of initiatives under the ASEAN Connectivity work plans" which should be widened to include China. The MPAC's plan to develop an ASEAN Connectivity website (which contains clear description of vision, strategies and regular updates on progress, contact person for questions/media requests) should be extended to those projects that are being done by or with China. China's Belt and Road Customs Clearance Cooperation Action Plan may also be synergized with ASEAN's customs standards, regulations and policies. This could not be done at a more proper time as more Chinese companies have decided to relocate their business operations in the wake of the trade war with the U.S.

All these policy coordinating measures, particularly the TPMC are important. The ASEAN Outlook on the Indo-Pacific (AOIP) has noted the following elements: a perspective of viewing the Asia-Pacific and Indian Ocean regions, not as contiguous territorial spaces but as a closely integrated and interconnected region, with ASEAN; playing a central and strategic role; an Indo-Pacific region of dialogue and cooperation instead of rivalry; an Indo-Pacific region of development and prosperity for all; and the importance of the maritime domain and perspective in the evolving regional architecture.[6]

Since China's provinces also play pivotal roles in the BRI, they should have designated partner-country/countries in ASEAN in order to optimize their industrial comparative advantages and opportunities to link with Southeast Asian markets. Coordinating and harmonizing policies should be done through the ASEAN Connectivity Coordinating Committee (ACCC) and the Chinese Working Committee of the China–ASEAN Connectivity Cooperation Committee (CWC-CACCC).

---

[6] AOIP, 2019, https://asean.org/storage/2019/06/ASEAN-Outlook-on-the-Indo-Pacific_FINAL_22062019.pdf.

By working with multiple countries, China is integrating the BRI with the regional strategies of other countries (e.g. Japan's FOIP, India's Act East Policy, South Korea's New Southern Policy, USAID and ADB partnership for energy projects in the Indo-Pacific). China can also come up with a "BRI Transparency Initiative" which would hold to account people and companies that go against standards of ethical behavior in order to send a message that the BRI is not a recipe for corruption-laden and debt trap deals. To improve the image of Chinese state and non-state enterprises, the Chinese government should reward those entities that show outstanding Corporate Social Responsibility (CSR) in the communities where they operate (e.g. human capacity building efforts, medical missions, school construction, etc.).

Trade and investment facilitation

China can set up a regular summit or forum for stakeholder engagement that would involve business associations and civil society groups as a form of consultative mechanism with non-state stakeholders (e.g. MSMEs, investors, businessmen, international institutions, government officials). This may be complemented by establishing a China–ASEAN Public–Private Center in order to easily convene and converge the agendas of public and private stakeholders in generating two-way investments between China and ASEAN. One added advantage of this arrangement is that after every regional or global financial crisis, coordinating investments for economic recovery would be much easier. This can additionally be carried out in conjunction with the Comprehensive Asia Development Plan (CADP) 2.0 by the World Bank and the Economic Research Institute for ASEAN and East Asia (ERIA). The ASEAN Coordinating Committee on MSMEs (ACCMSME) could also be transformed into ASEAN–China Coordinating Committee on MSMEs, and the BRI integrated with China's ASEAN Strategic Action Plan for SME Development (2016–2025).

Against this backdrop, a paper published by the Singapore Institute of International Affairs makes a good case of how China is advancing in ASEAN markets — which can be done with multinational companies from developed countries:

> ... Chinese tech-related investments through companies such as Alibaba, JD.com and Tencent have quadrupled in 2017. These include Didi Chuxing and Softbank's USD 2 billion investment into Grab, as well as Alibaba's USD 4 billion investment into Lazada. Tencent is also the largest stakeholder in Singapore-based Internet platform provider SEA... In Indonesia, Alibaba led a USD 1.1 billion investment in Tokopedia and Go-Jek, the country's other unicorn, has also raised capital from Tencent. China has also spent approximately more than USD 100 billion in Malaysia, Indonesia and the Philippines to support their smart city initiatives.[7]

Infrastructure development and connectivity

The Digital Silk Road should be harmonized with the ASEAN Broadband Corridor. China may also opt to participate in the ASEAN Telecommunications Senior Officials Meeting (TELSOM) and work with ASEAN on the ASEAN ICT Master Plan 2020 through the Working Committee on Financial Inclusion (WC-FINC) and Working Committee on Payment Systems and Settlement (WC-PSS). This is a good opportunity for China to share its remarkable best practices on e-commerce and Fintech. This consequently would expedite economic activities not only within AMS, but also between ASEAN and China. It will be valuable if China can organize a China–ASEAN Forum on data privacy and cross-border data sharing to compare and/or integrate data management frameworks, and come up with a combined digital data governance framework.

Concerning hard infrastructure, the ASEAN-RORO Network may be included within the China-BIMP-EAGA Cooperation since it is mostly the maritime ASEAN countries that are in need of the

---

[7] "Making the Belt and Road Initiative Work for ASEAN," Singapore Institute of International Affairs, August 2018, http://www.siiaonline.org/wp-content/uploads/2018/08/Summary-Report_Making-the-Belt-and-Road-Initiative-work-for-Asean.pdf.

maritime shipping network. As stated in the MPAC, China can help in the "construction of a database covering the ASEAN land transport network and conducting time release studies to measure the time required for the goods vehicles crossing the border".

Assessing compatibilities in TPMC can be done through: the need for a database for the identification of trade lanes or economic corridors for the prioritization of certain commodities and the role of the private sector in targeted recipient countries.[8] One can also take a look at France's expertise in terms of nuclear energy and China's inadequacy in the same; and China's strides in renewable energy and France's initial stage in the same.[9] Similarly, French companies have a strong foothold in high-speed rail technology while China has made accomplishments in high-speed rail in terms of construction period and cost.[10] As for China and the UK, in terms of infrastructure development, the UK has strong points in design, law, consulting and engineering management, while China is efficient in construction, technological innovation in engineering, cost performance, cost control and supply chain management.[11]

Financial integration and connectivity

A paper by EY consulting firm gives an idea how China can expand its financial integration advances in ASEAN through TPMC: "... major third-party market cooperation between China and Japan in financial sector mainly involves China's policy banks and state-owned enterprises, with Japan's three major banks in investment, loans and insurance areas. In the future, we expect more diversified cooperation, and small and medium-sized financial institutions will gradually "go abroad" so that the two countries will broaden their cooperation..."[12]

---

[8] *Op. cit.*, EY Belt and Road Navigator (2019).
[9] *Ibid.*
[10] *Ibid.*
[11] *Ibid.*
[12] *Ibid.*

In addition, the following can be replicated in ASEAN: first, China and France's desire to create a mutual investment for providing financial assistance for tripartite cooperation; second, the establishment of a bilateral dialogue and coordination mechanism that can accommodate the financial institutions in project investments; third, the formation of a steering committee between China's NDRC and the French Treasury for the setting up of a demonstration project list for the identification of cooperation areas; and fourth, the prospects of China–UK complementarity (e.g. green finance) given that the UK has an impeccable track record in international finance with strong ties with various ASEAN countries.[13] Besides, what China has done in Malaysia in the case of the Alibaba Business School in training 15,000 digital talents can also be applied in other ASEAN countries.

People-to-people ties and connectivity

In this respect, it is important to build a China–ASEAN University Network (similar to the ASEAN University Network), which would strengthen and systematize institutional ties and linkages between Chinese and ASEAN universities and could in turn lead to joint programs, research projects and activities (e.g. conferences, workshops). China may also complement the ASEAN Work Plan on Education 2016–2020 which emphasizes the development of technical vocational education and training (TVET).

This is relevant because vocational graduates in China have reportedly exceeded 90% in 2019 and have played crucial roles in promoting rural development and poverty reduction. "Chinese vocational colleges attracted 17,000 overseas students in 2018, with countries along the Belt and Road being the major sources for international students".[14] Private Chinese companies could therefore lead the way

---

[13] *Ibid.*
[14] "Employment Rate of Chinese Vocational Graduates Exceeds 90 Percent: Report," *Xinhuanet*, June 21, 2019, http://www.xinhuanet.com/english/2019-06/21/c_138159683.htm.

by establishing vocational academies. This effort would be substantial in helping address ASEAN's skills gap.

The Silk Road Think Tank Network may also be linked with ASEAN universities (including university-based research centres) in order to strengthen institutional linkages and project collaboration. Similarly, the Belt and Road News Association should be incorporated within ASEAN frameworks and mechanisms to foster better media-to-media relations between China and ASEAN. This is significant in monitoring and coordinating media coverage of BRI initiative and efforts. And just as with Japan's FOIP Vision, China can help the legal system development of ASEAN (e.g. legal and judicial development project, project for promoting the Development and Strengthening of the Rule of Law in the Legal Sector).[15]

Conclusion

In sum, there are many cooperation opportunities in integrating the BRI and MPAC as both have parallel AOCs (policy coordination, trade and investment facilitation, infrastructure connectivity, financial integration, people-to-people ties/connectivity *vis-à-vis* sustainable infrastructure, digital innovation, seamless logistics, regulatory excellence and people mobility). China would be able to rebrand South–South Cooperation into a broader North–South Cooperation within the BRI framework through TPMC by taking into account the comparative advantages and experiences of advanced economies and their industries. There are several ways how TPMC can materialize. Examples include: supply cooperation, joint bidding, co-investment, co-financing, promote high-quality development, increase transparency, establish TPMC cooperation funds.[16] The active application of TPMC is strongly advised given that ASEAN member states are

---

[15] The Government of Japan, *Towards Free and Open Indo-Pacific* (November 2019), https://www.mofa.go.jp/files/000407643.pdf.

[16] Youyi Zhang, "Third Party Market Cooperation under the Belt and Road Initiative: Progress, Challenges, and Recommendations," *China International Strategy Review*, no. 1 (2019): 310–329, https://doi.org/10.1007/s42533-019-00026-7, 311.

predominantly developing countries and are politically unstable, have pervasive red tape issues, and are ridden with social conflicts.[17] China has already engaged in TPMC with various countries across different continents. It is only a matter of doing the same in ASEAN considering that there is much negative publicity about BRI projects and initiatives in the region.

---

[17] *Ibid.*, p. 325.

Chapter

13

Connecting Master Plan on ASEAN Connectivity 2025 and Belt and Road Initiative: Singapore's *Infrastructure Asia* as a Platform

Kong Tuan Yuen

East Asian Institute, National University of Singapore, Singapore

The Master Plan of ASEAN Connectivity 2025

Southeast Asia is the third largest market in the world with a population of 642 million in 2017, almost double that of 1980.[1] There is a huge expansion compared with other regions such as European Union in this period. The youth and productive working-age population remains high, accounting for 35.4% below age 20 and 50.1%

---

[1] The ASEAN Secretariat, "ASEAN Key Figures 2018," (Jakarta: ASEAN Secretariat, 2018), p. 1, https://www.aseanstats.org/wp-content/uploads/2018/12/ASEAN-Key-Figures-2018.pdf.

among the age group of 20–54. With the tremendously increasing population, Southeast Asia has become the seventh largest economy in the world and it may move forward to stand as the fourth by 2050. The total GDP of ASEAN was about USD 2.8 trillion in 2017, almost four and a half times the level of 2000, and the average growth rate of GDP in the region remained over 5% between 2000 and 2017, far better than the global average. Moreover, most of the ASEAN member states have increased or maintained a high level of the net enrollment rate in secondary education as well as educational and health expenditure to GDP. In short, the fast-growing economic development and demographic dividend with increasing educational and health expenditure to GDP in ASEAN countries make Southeast Asia one of the most attractive investment regions in the world.

To tighten the regional linkage for strengthening mutual cooperation and meeting the future challenges, ASEAN countries adopted the Vientiane Declaration on the Adoption of the Master Plan on ASEAN Connectivity (MPAC) 2025 in 2016 on the occasion of the 28th ASEAN Summit. MPAC 2025 is the latest revision of the Master Plan on ASEAN Connectivity 2010 for encompassing the physical, institutional and people-to-people connection in order to achieve the economic and socio-cultural pillars of an integrated ASEAN community.[2] MPAC 2025 promotes competitiveness, inclusiveness and a greater sense of community through a seamlessly and comprehensively connected and integrated ASEAN. It emphasizes the strategic areas such as sustainable infrastructure, digital innovation, seamless logistics, regulatory excellence and people mobility.

There is some significant progress in ASEAN physical connectivity based on the assessment report of MPAC 2010.[3] The ASEAN Highway Network has fully been planned and the narrow two-lane

---

[2]The ASEAN Secretariat, "Master Plan on ASEAN Connectivity 2025," (Jakarta: ASEAN Secretariat, 2016), p. 8, https://asean.org/storage/2016/09/Master-Plan-on-ASEAN-Connectivity-20251.pdf.

[3]By the assessment of MPAC 2010, there are 39 completed and 52 uncompleted initiatives in MPAC 2010.

road with double bituminous treatment (Class III), which is one of the connectivity indicators, has largely been reduced.[4] Many third parties have been actively involved in the implementation of rail link between Singapore and Kunming, even though there is just a small section in Cambodia under construction. Nine power interconnection projects under the ASEAN Power Grid, for example, the Sarawak–West Kalimantan, and 13 bilateral gas pipelines under the Trans-ASEAN Gas Pipeline have been completed in order to fulfill the energy need in the region. The ASEAN Broadband Corridor has also been initiated in 2013 to provide a suggestive framework for the governments of ASEAN member states to instruct the potential players for broadband establishment.

Accompanied by the increasing economic growth, Southeast Asian countries apparently heavily require infrastructure funds as well as disruptive technologies to support their domestic development. The Asian Development Bank has expected that ASEAN countries need about USD 3 trillion in infrastructure investment between 2016 and 2030.[5] It has been estimated that the governments of ASEAN countries are just able to pay half of the infrastructure spending, causing the total infrastructure gap of over USD 100 billion, so they need to find long-term financing and support for projects from outside the region. Besides the ASEAN budget, many ASEAN countries do not have alternative capital sources to fulfill their own long-term infrastructure investments.

The prominent economic performance of ASEAN countries may draw attention from foreign investors to get involved in the ASEAN infrastructure projects, but the ASEAN countries need to persuade investors in terms of return on investment. Many mega infrastructure projects can highly benefit the local society, but they lack in profit

---

[4]The ASEAN Secretariat, "ASEAN Transport Strategic Plan 2016–2025," (Jakarta: ASEAN Secretariat, 2015), p. 21, https://www.asean.org/storage/2016/01/11/publication/KUALA_LUMPUR_TRANSPORT_STRATEGIC_PLAN.pdf.

[5]Eijas Ariffin, "Financing ASEAN's Infrastructure Demand," *The ASEAN Post*, July 15, 2018, https://theaseanpost.com/article/financing-aseans-infrastructure-demand.

incentives for private investment. Private sector prefers the short-term projects that can quickly get the reward; many resources have been allocated for these kinds of investments. In terms of financial barriers, the fiscal shortage with limited budget of particular countries has left them with no choice but to prioritize their resources on current needs, such as health care and education. In addition, some projects in ASEAN countries have not fully been uncovered yet to the outside capital sources, especially the road projects of ASEAN Highway Network in remote villages.

ASEAN countries also lag behind in applying disruptive technologies, including big data, cloud technology and artificial intelligence, to speed up the ASEAN connectivity. The disruptive technologies may not only create new opportunities for the economic growth of individual countries but also enhance the cross-border cooperation in a more efficient mode. However, most of the disruptive technologies' application for ASEAN connectivity cannot be carried out without the high-efficient network infrastructure such as fiber connection. Finally, ASEAN policymakers may return to the very beginning puzzle: whether ASEAN countries are able to source funds and then the technologies to develop ASEAN connectivity.

The Growing BRI

BRI, combining "the Silk Road Economic Belt" (SREB) and "the 21st Century Maritime Silk Road" (MSR), as one of the important Chinese master plans to closely connect with foreign countries, has been widely discussed in academia and media since Chinese President Xi Jinping's promotion in 2013. By inland, the SREB plans to connect China with countries in the continental Eurasia region. By maritime, the MSR starts from coastal China, one route is from the South China Sea to the Indian Ocean, then extending to Europe and the other route also passes the South China Sea but goes through the South Pacific Ocean. Southeast Asia is under the third route of SREB that links the mainland Southeast Asian countries, including Cambodia, Laos, Myanmar, Vietnam, Thailand, Malaysia and Singapore to China. The Southeast Asian countries also act as a bridge in the second route of MSR, especially the Strait of Malacca located in an irreplaceable position for trade with contemporary China.

Southeast Asian countries are the key partners of China in BRI not only because of the externally geographical and economic consideration but also because of the internal Chinese industrial development. Geographically, Southeast Asia is a hub for China to connect with Southern and Western Asian countries. The Strait of Malacca is one of the busiest shipping lines around the world. In addition, Southeast Asian countries have had political and economic connections with China since a long time ago. With the rapid economic development after opening up, China has become the largest trading counterpart. Of most of the Southeast Asian countries, there are many Chinese clans and diasporas who distributed in Southeast Asia and assumed an important part of the local communities. The communities form the main element of ASEAN–China economic relations. They export the local products such as Myanmar's wood and jade products to China and import the cheaper and more convenient daily supplies, for example, clothes and shoes, now electric products, even vehicles, from China.

Southeast Asia has been deeply engaged in the BRI development in terms of infrastructure project, economic and trade cooperation zone, port construction and industrial cooperation. The mainland Southeast Asian countries, particularly Cambodia, Laos, Myanmar, Vietnam and Thailand, have participated in the development of China–Indochina Peninsula Economic Corridors. There are at least nine cross-national highways built up across the China–Indochina border. In view of facility construction, the rail link between Kunming of China and Singapore has been discussed frequently for a long time, even though the progress is slow-paced. China also participates in many port construction projects such as the Western Rakhine State Port in Myanmar and industrial park establishment, for example, Malaysia–China Kuantan Industrial Park, in the Southeast Asian region.

The more important thing is that the Asian Infrastructure Investment Bank (AIIB), influenced by China in policy-making, can support BRI projects in many ways. AIIB is a multilateral development bank and functions with the aim of improving the social and economic outcomes in Asia by investing in infrastructure and other productive sectors, and connecting people, services and markets for a better life.[6] It was launched in Beijing in 2016 and consists of 100 approved members around the world so far. AIIB has signed a co-financing agreement with the World Bank to increase the financing opportunities among the potential infrastructure projects. Besides, AIIB has signed several memoranda of understanding (MoU) with the regional development banks, such as the African Development Bank and the Asian Development Bank, and collaborated with private financial institutions to create multilateral cooperation in infrastructure development.

Since 2016, AIIB has approved 45 projects and eight of them belong to the Southeast Asian countries (Table 1). Some of the ASEAN countries have truly benefited from the AIIB financing, including Indonesia (4), Myanmar (1), the Philippines (1), Lao PDR (1) and Cambodia (1). The sectors involved in the projects are mainly related to energy (including water) and urbanization. For example, Indonesia got approval of Strategic Irrigation Modernization and Urgent Rehabilitation Project in 2018 to rehabilitate Indonesia's irrigation system by increasing participatory development, improving service levels and upgrading infrastructure and sustainable management. The World Bank is co-financing the project and acting as a leading financier to guide loan management, including procurement, disbursements, environmental and social compliance, and project monitoring and reporting.

In addition, there are six projects that were approved under the AIIB Project Preparation Special Fund for the International Development Association recipients. For instance, the projects of Lao PDR: National Road 13 Improvement and Maintenance received USD 128 million from the Special Fund financed by AIIB loan, the World Bank, Nordic Development Fund and Counterpart Fund to improve the road condition, safety and climate resilience in the Laos National Road 13. The Special Fund will benefit Laos's almost 60 km

---

[6]Asian Infrastructure Investment Bank, (n.d.), "Introduction: Who We Are", https://www.aiib.org/en/about-aiib/index.html.

Table 1   The AIIB's Approved Projects for ASEAN Countries.

Name	Sector	Approval date
1. Cambodia: Fiber Optic Communication Network	Digital Infrastructure	July 12, 2019
2. Lao PDR: National Road 13 Improvement and Maintenance Project	Transport	April 04, 2019
3. Indonesia: Mandalika Urban and Tourism Infrastructure Project	Multi-sector	December 07, 2018
4. Indonesia: Strategic Irrigation Modernization and Urgent Rehabilitation Project	Water	June 24, 2018
5. The Philippines: Metro Manila Flood Management Project	Water	September 27, 2017
6. Indonesia: Dam Operational Improvement and Safety Project Phase II	Multi-sector	March 22, 2017
7. Myanmar: Myingyan Power Plant Project	Energy	September 27, 2016
8. Indonesia: National Slum Upgrading Project	Urban	June 24, 2016

Source: AIIB Website: https://www.aiib.org/en/projects/approved/index.html.

of road and some of them will be extended from two lanes to four lanes. The project will not only improve the landlocked Laos's domestic transport system and logistic situation but also increase the trans-border trading within and beyond the Southeast Asian countries.

Singapore's *Infrastructure Asia* Bridging MPAC 2025 and BRI

Southeast Asian countries need more funding and disruptive technologies outside the region to support the development of ASEAN connectivity under MPAC 2025 while China actively promotes infrastructure connectivity with domestic financing sources, for example, government BRI funding, and internationally mutual collaboration such as AIIB and the World Bank. Even though there is the demand and supply of connectivity cooperation, a platform established to bridge both MPAC 2025 and the BRI, and avoid resource mismatch, is necessary. The platform may need to fulfill some special requirements: first, it highly supports MPAC 2025 and BRI, and will be the beneficiary of both projects. Thus, the intuition is that it would come from Southeast Asian countries or China; second, it is an ASEAN-based rather than a China-based platform. The reason is that Southeast Asian countries more or less support China's BRI development, and naturally the MPAC 2025, but China is not the member of MPAC 2025. Simply put, ASEAN countries are more relevant to both projects; and third, the platform has sufficient knowledge and experience in terms of financing and technology to form the cooperation.

Singapore is one of the ASEAN member states that have adopted the MPAC 2025 along with other members. Singapore took the ASEAN Chairmanship in 2018 and identified three priority deliverables regarding MPAC 2025. The first one is that ASEAN supported by the World Bank has launched a priority pipeline of infrastructure projects to attract more public and private investment. The second one is that ASEAN has formed a development template to mitigate urban challenges with the support of the ASEAN–Australia Development Cooperation Programme (AADCP) Phase II. The third one is that the Economic Research Institute for ASEAN and East Asia supports a study to adopt digital technology by micro, small, and medium-sized enterprises to strengthen their capacities for the fourth industrial revolution.[7] On the other hand, Singapore has a strong relationship with contemporary China, especially there are three government-to-government projects having been implemented in Suzhou, Tianjin and Chongqing of China. There are also several BRI related agreements that have inked Singapore and China to

---

[7]The ASEAN Secretariat, "The Master Plan on ASEAN Connectivity 2025 Deliverables for 2018 and ASEAN Connectivity Microsite Launched," November 13, 2018, https://asean.org/master-plan-asean-connectivity-2025-deliverables-2018-asean-connectivity-microsite-launched/.

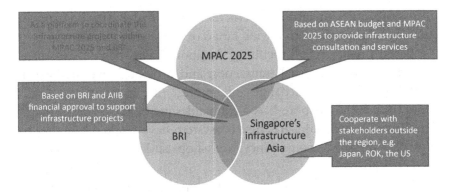

Figure 1 The Overlapping Relations among MPAC, BRI and Singapore's *Infrastructure Asia.*

facilitate the collaboration, particularly in infrastructure investment, financial services cooperation, and technology and innovation.[8]

Obviously, Singapore is a reasonable candidate to provide a platform to connect MPAC 2025 with BRI (Figure 1). Singapore not only is one of the adopters of MPAC 2025 and the supporter of BRI development, but it also has good practices on international infrastructure collaboration in terms of project management, financing and legal service provision, and technical and engineering consultancy. In 2018, two Singapore government agencies, Enterprise Singapore and Monetary Authority of Singapore, worked together to establish *Infrastructure Asia* (IA) to zoom into the development of infrastructure projects in Asia. The entity acts as a platform to call for all the players in the infrastructure value chain, including infrastructure developers, institutional investors, multilaterals, and legal, accounting, and financial services providers, irrespective of whether these are foreign firms, governments or the expertise in Singapore, to fulfill Asia's growing need for infrastructure. In addition, it will serve

---

[8] "Singapore, China ink deals on trade, Belt and Road projects," *The Strait Times*, April 30, 2019, https://www.straitstimes.com/asia/east-asia/singapore-china-ink-deals-on-trade-belt-and-road-projects.

in a more efficient and competitive way to match the demand of Asia's infrastructure with a wide range of infrastructure talent.

Based on the AI's brochure, Singapore-based banks have managed about 60% financial transaction and provided diversifying risk solutions of foreign exchange and interest rate in Southeast Asia.[9] More than 300 Singapore-based companies including 17 best-in-class firms in Singapore infrastructure ecosystem have worked together to provide professional consultancy, workshops and seminars to meet the market needs.

IA is continuously seeking partnerships to explore the infrastructure cooperation opportunities. In Singapore, IA signed an MoU with Singapore Business Federation to share information with Singapore-based companies. Internationally, IA has inked three MOUs since 2018 with World Bank group, Canada Department of Foreign Affairs, Trade and Development, and U.S. Overseas Private Investment Corporation to strengthen the capacity for the collaboration of infrastructure projects.

In view of IA, an infrastructure project can be simply classified into three stages: project development, project management and execution, and operation and maintenance. At the stage of project development, a project will be initiated with further feasibility studies and plan structuring, and the legal and financial sources will be checked to facilitate project execution and risk management. The stage of project management and execution is related to project engineering, material procurement and physical construction with leveraged equity and debt financing. The infrastructure will be operated and maintained by the owner or expertise team at the final stage.

With the previous experience and ongoing capacity building, IA has identified six fields where Singapore can cooperate with other partners to support Asia, especially the Southeast Asia infrastructure demand. The first one is project development. Singapore has many world-renowned developers contributing their services on project

---

[9]Infrastructure Asia Brochure, "Making Infrastructure Happen," June 2019, https://www.infrastructureasia.org/-/media/InfraAsia/About-us/IA-Brochure.

structuring and management with workable financing around the world. For example, two Singapore-based developers, Sunseap Group and InfraCo Asia, have jointly worked to build a solar energy farm in Vietnam. The second one is financing and risk management. Singapore-based banks have frequently participated in the international loan financing activities to reduce the stakeholders' risk. Recently, international development banks and Singapore-based financial institutions such as Clifford Capital have jointly provided a loan to develop one of the largest independent power plants in Myanmar (Case 2, Table 2). The third one is legal services. Most of the influential international accounting firms, especially the Big Four, have established headquarters or international centers in Singapore to get involved in regional infrastructure practices. The fourth one is technical and engineering services. Along with the existing transnational professionals in infrastructure project, Singapore continues to give related training and internship programs to enlarge and deepen the talent pool in technical and engineering terms. The fifth one is the formation of the multilateral collaboration, as in the Myanmar case, and the sixth one is regular organization of international events. Singapore holds the Asia–Singapore Infrastructure Roundtable, World Bank–Singapore infrastructure Finance Summit and the Asia Infrastructure Forum to provide platforms for stakeholders to share expertise, knowledge and catalyze potential infrastructure projects.

Table 2 *Infrastructure Asia*'s Featured Projects.

Name	Sector	Approval date
1. Singapore: Keppel Seghers Tuas Waste-To-Energy Plant	Power	2006
2. Myanmar: Sembcorp Myingyan Independent Power Plant	Power	October 2018
3. The Philippines: Northgate District Cooling Plant	Urban solution	September 2017
4. Singapore: Infrastructure Take-Out Facility	Financing	July 2018

Source: Infrastructure Asia.

For the collaboration with China's BRI, IA helps to set up the China–Singapore Co-Investment Platform, which funds USD 500 million, to develop the greenfield infrastructure projects in Southeast Asia by providing equity and debt financing. The funding is provided by Singapore-based infrastructure consulting firm, Surbana Jurong, and the Chinese government-supported Silk Road Fund.

Policy Recommendations

ASEAN and China have much room to form cooperation in terms of infrastructure development. There are many common motivations and tasks in both MPAC 2025 and BRI, especially physical connectivity. ASEAN may demand more outside funding sources and disruptive technologies to develop ASEAN connectivity while China is willing to supply financing and technological assistance through BRI. Moreover, China has accumulated much experience despite success or failure of the implementation of infrastructure projects and provided practices in applying disruptive technology for connectivity. Apparently, ASEAN and China could build up long-term regional partnership by sharing information, flexible financing, reliable technology, harmonized communities and win–win solutions.

The ASEAN has approximately 370 million (58% of population) internet users while China has 580 million (41% of population). However, e-commerce has become a main driver of China's economic growth in recent years. The total value of China's e-commerce was close to USD 500 billion in market value in 2017 while the ASEAN has just reached USD 18 billion.[10] Simply speaking, China has nearly 28 times of ASEAN's e-commerce market value with (less than) double internet users. There are two interesting things in digital development. First, the application of disruptive technology in trading including online shopping, e-payment, as well as food and beverage ordering which are supported by internet infrastructure has expanded the market in a new form. Second, the relationship between the

---

[10]We Are Social, 2018, "Global Digital report 2018," https://digitalreport.wearesocial. com.

market value creation and the number of internet users multiplies the effect. ASEAN–China community may work together to develop collaborative platforms including infrastructure project development, management and execution, and operation and maintenance. Singapore's IA could bring together local and international partners across the value chain, including infrastructure developers, institutional investors, and legal, accounting, and financing providers, to support the Asian regional infrastructure project. IA may also invite other partners such as Chinese network infrastructure companies to join the platform to provide affordable, reliable and sustainable services for regional infrastructure development.

Based on the assessment report of MPAC 2010, only 39% of the projects are implemented with proper momentum. The failure or delayed cases need to be investigated by international infrastructure project experts, for example, the team formed by Singapore's IA, to give advice for MPAC 2025 and BRI. On the other hand, there are also many controversial BRI cases that need to borrow solutions from the completed or uncompleted initiatives in MPAC 2010. The information sharing can provide both sides with an alternative joint initiative for regional connectivity development.

The budget and expertise as well as motivation of BRI and MPAC 2025 have different bases. ASEAN–China community needs to study how to utilize and mobilize the resources of BRI and MPAC 2025 for each other. Besides, the regional infrastructure development should open to other players outside the region to maximize the utilization of capital and technology. For example, Japan has more experience in the development of Greater Mekong Sub-region (GMS). ASEAN–China community can also encourage bilateral or multilateral cooperation with a third party. For example, Singapore–China cooperation in Cambodia industrial park development. This model may not only create more cooperative opportunities among the members of the region but also bring together the economic development experience through the third party.

Last but not least, BRI projects have been criticized frequently by citizens of recipient countries apprehensive that they may fall into debt trap and sovereignty conflicts, as well as face environmental destruction. The local job opportunities being taken away is another raising issue. However, the infrastructure construction from MPAC is rarely claimed as a troublesome project. Thus, BRI may learn the investment model from MPAC to alleviate the political impact of economic growth-based infrastructure projects. Based on the scope of BRI, the projects of bilateral or multilateral regional connectivity may develop beyond the vision of ASEAN. ASEAN countries need to absorb the ingredients from BRI cooperation and safeguard the centrality of ASEAN as well.

© 2021 World Scientific Publishing Company

https://doi.org/10.1142/9789811234316_0014

Chapter

14

Aligning the BRI and MPAC 2025: A Perspective from Vietnam

Chu Minh Thao*

*Center for Security and Development,
Institute for Foreign Policy and Strategic Studies,
Diplomatic Academy of Vietnam, Vietnam*

Introduction

ASEAN and China have maintained a traditional and friendly relationship for the last 30 years. At this point of time, the two parties have a great opportunity to strengthen the bilateral relationship through joint efforts to build a more integrated regional connectivity, especially infrastructure connectivity as China has been implementing the Belt and Road Initiative (BRI) since 2013, while ASEAN

---

* Disclaimer: The views and opinions expressed in this chapter are those of the author and do not necessarily reflect the official policy or position of the Diplomatic Academy of Vietnam.

has been implementing its Master Plan on ASEAN Connectivity 2025 (MPAC 2025). A careful preparation for cooperation in the connectivity will bring economic development, growth and prosperity for the region. In that context, this piece of research provides a preliminary view about how to align the BRI and MPAC 2025 from Vietnam's perspective. This chapter argues that a successful alignment of the BRI and MPAC 2025 depends first on the current foundation of strong bilateral relationship, and identification of opportunities and challenges posed for the relationship, and then suitable objectives and principles for cooperation. The chapter is structured with the first section identifying key foundations to build the alignment, and then discussing opportunities and challenges, and finally some recommendations for alignment between the BRI and MPAC 2025.

Positive Dynamics for Connecting the BRI and MPAC 2025

Strong political will of ASEAN and Chinese leaders

The Southeast Asian countries and China have had a long and traditional relationship for about 30 years, which lays a basic firm foundation for future cooperation in general and cooperation in infrastructure connectivity in particular by aligning the BRI and MPAC 2025. ASEAN and Chinese leaders have already made commitments to synergize common priorities identified in MPAC 2025 and China's BRI as stated in the Joint Statement of the 19th ASEAN–China Summit to Commemorate the 25th Anniversary of ASEAN–China Dialogue Relations in 2016.

Vietnam has already signed in November 2017 the Memorandum of Understanding (MoU) on the joint implementation of the BRI and Vietnam's "Two Corridors and One Economic Circle" on the occasion of President Xi Jinping's state visit to Vietnam. The commitments focus on key areas such as infrastructure construction, production capacity, and cross-border economic cooperation zones and focus on major projects.

Existing ASEAN–China cooperation in connectivity

ASEAN and China would be able to enhance regional connectivity by exploiting ASEAN's existing and planned connectivity networks and bilateral relationships between China and ASEAN members as well as the multilateral relationships between China and ASEAN. Multilaterally, ASEAN and China have deepened the cooperation on infrastructure connectivity by signing a joint statement in 2017 Transport Connectivity, which is part of upgrading the ASEAN–China Free Trade Area (FTA), through connecting ASEAN with Guangxi Zhuang Autonomous Region (GZAR), and Yunnan of China. Currently, there are four highways connecting China and ASEAN countries. In addition, some major BRI–ASEAN projects have been designed to connect China with Southeast Asia, for example, the railway routes connecting Kunming, China and Laos, Thailand, Malaysia and Singapore, the other routes connecting Kunming and Vietnam, Cambodia and Thailand and the last one passing through Myanmar to Thailand. The Greater Mekong Sub-region (GMS) also set top priority to transportation connectivity among six ASEAN member countries and China.

Bilaterally, there are many large infrastructure projects between China and ASEAN countries. Some projects aim to boost ASEAN's digital economy, in line with China's vision for a digital silk road, such as Philippines's "Build, Build, Build" program, Indonesia's Global Maritime Axis Vision, Thailand's Eastern Economic Corridor, Malaysia's Digital Free Trade Zone, East Coast Rail Link and two gas pipelines, Logistics and Trade Facilitation Master Plan (2015–2020). In 2017, Vietnam has already implemented the two economic corridors, the Kunming–Lao Cai–Ha Noi–Hai Phong–Quang Ninh corridor and the Nanning–Lang Son–Ha Noi–Hai Phong–Quang Ninh corridor to improve connectivity between Yunnan and Guangxi (China) and Vietnam.

These multilateral and bilateral infrastructure projects are the strong foundations for further cooperation. The coordination between MPAC 2025 and BRICS will help to upgrade the current cooperation to a higher level, i.e. greater connectivity among existing sub-regions and sub-regional programs.

Mutual benefits of cooperation

The cooperation between ASEAN and China is expected to create synergy for implementation of regional connectivity plans. The interests of ASEAN countries are determined by the need for more sources of capital, transfer of technology, creation of jobs, skills from China to the Southeast Asian region, making the region more competitive with more opportunities for development. On the other hand, China is able to carry out its global dreams of connecting with the world, increasing global influence. The two parties will greatly benefit from efficient and cost-effective mobility and reduced inequality within and between the countries, as Adam Smith says in *An Inquiry into the Nature and Causes of the Wealth of Nations*.

Meeting demands for connectivity

The Southeast Asian region is among the world's most dynamic economic region, which has increasing demands for infrastructure for smooth mobility. ASEAN's annual infrastructure needs have increased to USD 110 billion. ASEAN also has high demands for digital economy, which is expected to add USD 1 trillion to ASEAN's current GDP.[1]

The BRI fits well with Vietnam's advocates for regional economic connectivity and cooperation. Vietnam has set the target for the country to become the region's tiger by maintaining the annual GDP growth rate to be around 7% and attracting foreign investment and enhancing competitiveness. The infrastructure system is one of the key strategic breakthroughs set by the government for sustained socioeconomic development in the future. To meet this end, Vietnam's annual demand for investment in infrastructure is about USD 25 billion/year.[2] By 2020, Vietnam will need USD 480 billion

---

[1] "BRI Can Boost ASEAN's Infrastructure, Connectivity," *China Daily*, April 29, 2019, https://www.chinadailyhk.com/articles/0/136/168/1540889222856.html.
[2] World Bank, "World Bank Ready to Help Vietnam Meet Growing Infrastructure Demands," February 25, 2019, https://www.worldbank.org/en/news/press-release/2019/02/25/wb-ready-to-help-vietnam-meet-growing-infrastructure-demands.

for infrastructure. The Vietnamese government has been spending about 5.7% of annual GDP for investment in infrastructure, the highest in Southeast Asia.[3] It is clear that the Vietnamese government itself fails to meet this need, given the public debt ceiling set by the National Assembly at 65% GDP; hence, it will need to mobilize resources from private sectors and foreign donors and partners.

Given the context, Vietnam will need infrastructure improvement internally as well as connectivity externally. Vietnam can tap into the potential regional connectivity projects such as those within ASEAN, and currently China's BRI. Vietnam pays attention to road and rail infrastructure that improves regional connectivity. Due to the aforementioned demands in the investment gap in connectivity, Vietnam welcomes the cooperation with private sectors, development partners and international initiatives.

Meanwhile, China attaches special importance to ASEAN, which is among China's top trading partners and foreign policy priorities. The BRI with the aim to build trade and infrastructure networks will act as an effective means for deepening the bilateral relationship. The BRI and ASEAN hence share similar ideas and focus on improving infrastructure, facilitating economic and trade cooperation. China has promised to provide USD 70 billion in investment and USD 400 billion in loans for the BRI overall. The BRI thus serves well as an alternative source for traditional foreign donors such as Japan, South Korea (see Figure 1).

The benefits of infrastructure connectivity go beyond meeting only infrastructure needs to include connecting economic hubs, improving the living standards of the people, accelerating the economic growth, trade, investment, tourism, and creating jobs, better business conditions and open markets. The transfer of the technology, know-how and knowledge and raising awareness of the people would definitely change the image of China among the ASEAN people, thus contributing to enhance China's soft power in the region, reducing

---

[3] "Vietnam Among Leaders in Asian Infrastructure Race," *The Straits Times*, March 24, 2017, https://www.straitstimes.com/asia/se-asia/vietnam-among-leaders-in-asian-infrastructure-race.

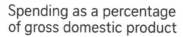

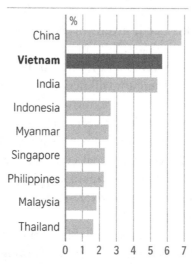

Figure 1   Biggest Infrastructure Spenders in Asia.

Note: Data includes public- and private-sector investment.

Sources: Asian Development Bank, Bloomberg Straits Times Graphics.

the people's sentiment about China's threat, thereby increasing the trust among people.

However, to meet these benefits, certain conditions should be created such as clean, green, sustainability, good governance, transparency and good regulatory frameworks in line with international standards, and regular structured dialogues for proper inter-regional plans.

Complementarity between MPAC 2025 and the BRI

The two plans focus on strengthening hard infrastructure like transportation system and soft infrastructure like harmonization of standards, and at the same time boosting people-to-people connectivity. The MPAC 2025 and the BRI share similarities in the objective of strengthening connectivity. While the five strategic objectives of

MPAC 2025 focus on (i) Sustainable Infrastructure; (ii) Digital innovation; (iii) Seamless Logistics; (iv) Regulatory Excellence; (v) People Mobility, the five major cooperation priorities of BRI are: (i) Policy Coordination, (ii) Connectivity of Infrastructure; (iii) Unimpeded Trade; (iv) Financial Integration; (v) Closer People-to-People Ties. As such, ASEAN and China are covering a large scope, not only hard and soft physical infrastructure connectivity but also an overall environment for sustainable development, hence the connectivity also covers people-to-people exchanges.

The coordination for the implementation of the BRI and MPAC 2025 will definitely strengthen the relationship in a constructive manner. The common goals of the BRI and MPAC will ensure the sustainable connectivity for the region, contributing to sustainable economic development and prosperity for the region. The BRI will then provide greater efforts and forums to constructively building existing regional integration processes, and provide funds for ASEAN to meet the infrastructure needs, realizing ASEAN Community Vision 2025 and MPAC 2025.

Thus, given the strong political, economic and social relationship for over 30 years, deepening the relationship through enhancing connectivity by promoting complementary and common solutions will benefit both sides.

Challenges of cooperation

Despite the long and traditional relationship, Chinese infrastructure projects implemented in Southeast Asia still face certain difficulties, though may be less severe than other regions such as South Asia. Across the world, general concerns about China's BRI projects are related to geopolitical concerns, governance, transparency and inclusiveness, which could cause unsustainable financial debts — the so-called "debt traps" with China due to Sri Lanka's handing its port to a Chinese company after failing to pay its debt. Such concerns also influence the ASEAN countries. For example, Malaysia has to renegotiate the project cost and downscale the BRI projects.

While MPAC 2025 also pays attention to institutional connectivity, the BRI has not identified this as a key component. This difference is one of the main reasons for challenges in the implementation of the BRI due to the lack of uniform rules and regulations in the implementation of the BRI. In addition, forms and criteria for a BRI project/program are not yet clarified, which create ambiguity for the countries' deep involvement in the BRI. This difference should be dealt with for successful implementation of the BRI without causing distress to the local people. Despite the differences in approach and areas of cooperation, due to their shared interests, China and ASEAN could work well together not only bilaterally but also multilaterally to create synergy and promote further commonalities and reduce the differences.

In Vietnam, general concerns about cooperation with China in infrastructure projects are multifold in all economic, political and social aspects. Economically, Vietnam faces certain risks relating to borrowing loans from China. First, loans with high interest rates: Vietnam has upgraded to become a middle-income country; hence, ODA has been greatly reduced. Instead, Vietnam has considered borrowing from various sources, including that from China. However, Chinese interest rates are high, added by several fees, with loan's annual interest being 3% compared to 0–2% (South Korea), and 1.7% (India).

Secondly, China's projects create an impression of delay, low quality, accelerated investment and low investment inefficiency. China wins contracts with low bidding price (maybe only ½ market price), but then increases costs later during the implementation process, which makes the overall costs higher than other partners due to delays and slow work, no guarantee of quality, thus reducing investment efficiency.[4] Vietnam has been heavily indebted to China in many areas such as electricity, energy, coal power plant, which has caused environmental pollution, creating discontent in the society. The

---

[4] "Debt and Inefficiencies Come with Chinese Infrastructural Investments in Vietnam," *Asia News*, April 28, 2019, http://www.asianews.it/news-en/Debt-and-inefficiencies-come-with-Chinese-infrastructural-investments-in-Vietnam-46557.html.

so-called debt traps are not yet seen in Vietnam's case, however the loans and incurred costs due to the delay could contribute to high level of investment, which in turn create pressure on the macro-balance and overall development.

Politically, people are concerned that the economy cannot be self-reliant due to overdependence on Chinese loans, which will cause threats to losing the ownership of land, thus causing risks to economic and political security. In addition, as the Chinese firms are too familiar with Vietnamese politics and its political system, there is a higher chance for corruption in Chinese projects than with other countries; the commission (or in fact corruption) sometimes can reach 50%. Moreover, the general sentiments take root from complicated political relationships between Vietnam and China, especially the South China Sea territorial disputes that would cause the most severe negative impacts on BRI projects implementation in Vietnam.

Socially, the public's concerns are more severe due to possible social disorder risks with a large number of Chinese laborers coming to work in Vietnam and creating isolated Chinese communities in the localities. In addition, Vietnamese are now concerned more about potential negative impacts on the environment and are not ready to trade development and economic benefits for environmental damage. This change of increased awareness of negative impacts on the environment could be seen with the Formosa environmental disaster when people became highly alert due to the incident of mass dead fish found across the country's coast due to the toxic discharge from the Formosa Ha Tinh Steel Corp. The previous infrastructure projects implemented by China have created a negative impression on the Vietnamese as China's investment projects are often delayed, politically distorted and come with low technology, which has generated concerns among both the people and local authorities to engage in more infrastructure projects with the Chinese enterprises.

Other reasons for these challenges are not mainly from China and other partners, but also from Vietnam's side. Vietnam's authorities lack capacity to negotiate the loans with appropriate terms and conditions, as well as capacity to supervise the infrastructure and ensure the loan efficiency and good governance to prevent corruption. Thus, different from infrastructure projects sponsored or loaned by other development donors, China's infrastructure projects are quite sensitive due to complicated political relationships.

How Should the Engagement Between the BRI and MPAC 2025 Be Like?

Despite potential political, economic and social challenges from the BRI, it is necessary to manage, control and mitigate the challenges and difficulties while finding ways to take advantage of the great benefits from the BRI. The engagement between the BRI and MPAC 2025 is one of the best ways for cooperation for implementation of the BRI and regional connectivity strategy for mutual benefits of China and ASEAN member countries. By aligning the BRI with MPAC 2025, i.e. finding convergence points of connectivity between the two parties, ASEAN countries could utilize China's financial and technical support while at the same time save resources by relying on each country's institutions and policies regarding the implementation of MPAC 2025. Meanwhile, China can promote the implementation of the BRI more effectively with the support of the region, gaining the legitimacy of the BRI in the region, and diluting controversial features of the BRI. The two parties hence could help increase trade, and create more opportunities for enterprises, by deepening the mutual beneficial cooperation and by creating a cooperative framework on the basis of these two initiatives and plans.

To meet this end, such an engagement should be based on the current status of cooperation, as well as future plan of connectivity of ASEAN and China, tapping advantages and overcoming challenges and differences in the objectives of the two parties. As both sides expect to build a strong partnership for regional prosperity, it is essential to map out joint efforts to promote the cooperation between the MPAC and the BRI for mutual benefits. It is expected that the implementation of the BRI in alignment with MPAC 2025 would speed up the implementation of MPAC 2025 by first of all providing additional financial and technical support for regional infrastructure projects, while at the same time handling negative impacts of the infrastructure on environment and society.

Objectives

The common objectives of the alignment of BRI and MPAC 2025 should be a connectivity that is of high quality, green and clean, sustainability, affordability and efficiency.

Principles

Vietnam supports the connection with the BRI, which must respect peaceful cooperation, equality and mutual benefits, respect independence, national sovereignty, territorial integrity of the nations, and be in line with the international regulations, the United Nations' Charter, United Nations Sustainable Development Goals 2030, and build a prosperous and peaceful world. Such principles have been mutually agreed by China and ASEAN leaders in various documents, and thus act as guidelines for all cooperation activities between the two parties.

An effective coordinating mechanism

A coordinating mechanism is needed to ensure smooth cooperation and coordination between China and ASEAN. Currently, the cooperation for the implementation of the BRI is mainly on bilateral relationships. Hence, a multilateral mechanism is necessary to create a negotiation platform for coordinating regional projects, serving co-development and co-existence of regional countries. Such a platform/mechanism is significant, given the diversity in development gap, different types of institutions, regulations and standards among countries.

The coordination mechanism should work with China and ASEAN to ensure efficient connections and networks between the BRI and MPAC 2025. Such cooperation should focus on certain works. Firstly, the coordination mechanism should be tasked to serve as a platform for the two parties, China and ASEAN member countries, to facilitate further effective dialogue, communication and exchange of knowledge and ideas regarding the BRI projects; set regional agenda and regional vision; discuss high standards relating to the substance, requirements for the BRI projects. By doing so, such a mechanism also coordinates to narrow down the differences relating to environmental, societal and economic regulations, to ensure the sustainability of the infrastructure, good governance and transparency.

As China has already set up very high standards in these areas, once the BRI is implemented, such regulations or international standards should be considered for application in ASEAN countries in case the local areas lack high-standard regulations or have lower standards than China. Currently, ASEAN member countries, such as Vietnam, Myanmar, Laos and Cambodia, have lower quality of infrastructure than China. Hence, it is greatly beneficial for these countries in terms of the application of the BRI's higher standards of environmental protection and high-quality infrastructure to ensure fiscal, environmental, social and economic sustainability, thus gaining the support of the ASEAN people, and creating a level playing field and equal opportunities for all parties.

Given the ambiguity of BRI projects, the mechanism would also coordinate the assessment for BRI projects in terms of project scope, economic and financial viability, risks, and negative impacts, terms and conditions, interest rates, and ensure transparency and good governance. It would provide a framework for assessment, setting principles for development planning, implementation, monitoring and assessment and accountability. Hence, a transparent governance mechanism for the implementation of joint projects between China and ASEAN countries will reassure the relevant stakeholders over the objectives of sustainable development of the projects.

Secondly, it is recommended to map out a proper plan for efficient connections and networks between the BRI and MPAC 2025 at the regional level, rather than at the bilateral level as has been the case. An overall plan for China to negotiate multilaterally with ASEAN as a whole will help to synergize the resources, avoid duplication and ensure the ASEAN centrality. At the same time, the overall plan would identify priorities and sequencing, focusing on the weakest links in the regional air, sea and land transport. Such cooperation and a well-mapped Master Plan will avoid fragmentation and create synergy of different projects and initiatives. Next, an action plan should identify priorities, goals and optimal sequencing of projects. Some key priorities should be planned in advance, such as digital connectivity, infrastructure connectivity and people-to-people connectivity. Such a carefully mapped out plan would be able to mitigate negative impacts on local society, community and environment, and prevent conflicts and biodiversity loss.

Some considerations for alignment

Sustained connectivity

For the infrastructure connectivity to be sustained, at the policy level, it is necessary to first, apply holistic, comprehensive and intersectoral policy for the regional economic development. It is necessary to bridge Chinese and Southeast Asian communities by ensuring the social and environmental sustainability of the infrastructure projects. To avoid isolation of BRI projects from local people and region, the BRI projects should generate jobs and livelihoods, transfer technology, train skills for local people, not just for Chinese laborers but for local laborers as well. It is important that the local people, especially small and medium enterprises, can join the huge projects, first for economic profits; second, for capacity building. This will contribute to a harmonious society and inclusive social development when Chinese projects are implemented in the regional countries, contributing to people-to-people connectivity and ensuring the sustainability of the projects. To meet these ends, complimentary policies between China and regional countries are necessary to improve labor mobility, worker education and training, creating fair opportunities for the workers to find appropriate jobs and increasing their income.

The issue of environmental sustainability should be paid attention to balancing economic development and environmental protection, rather than seeking environmental trade-offs for economic benefits.

Hence, the issue of maintaining the biodiversity and ecological system in the region and reducing negative impacts caused by environmental pollution should be among the criteria to be considered in effective environmental impact assessments as well as the environmental requirements, serving as the basis for consideration of building an infrastructure project. In addition, the focus on renewable energy development will create an alternative for fossil fuel development, contributing to realizing green BRI. This issue is important given the concerns that the BRI project portfolio of coal and hydropower plant could cause environmental degradation, especially with regard to Mekong region. Thus, we need to handle the clean and green resources for development while at the same time tackling climate change.

Second, the infrastructure connectivity should ensure the link between the BRI projects and regional economic centers, energy and services hubs to maximize benefits, promoting the economic development and growth of the region. The cooperation between the BRI and MPAC, though focusing on infrastructure connectivity, should expand to institutional connectivity and people-to-people connectivity, ICT connectivity, energy, trade, agriculture and tourism-related infrastructure among the regional countries as an integrated and comprehensive, cross-cutting approach to regional development. Such an approach will generate an overall sustainable development for the region. So far the number of tourists visiting China and ASEAN countries has increased remarkably in recent years, which could be further improved with increasing cultural exchanges between the two sides, contributing to generating more understanding among the people, and reducing the concerns regarding BRI projects.

Sustainable finance

The huge amount of money for infrastructure projects is risky not only for debt recipients to pay back the money but also for the debt owner to avoid risks of bankruptcy. With the aim to achieve financial sustainability of infrastructure projects, it is expected that BRI projects:

(i)   Provide more favorable terms and conditions, and commercial interests rates. The BRI projects should be provided with market-based, yet more favorable, interest rates in competition with other projects funded by other sources with lower interest rates, such as Japan (0.9% in 2017),[5] South Korea (2–4%)[6] and India (8–10%),[7] and longer loan periods.

(ii) Be more transparent and inclusive. The transparency is especially important given the corruption in developing countries like Vietnam, although the relevant governments have made great efforts to fight against corruption. High standards regarding transparency for the BRI projects will create leverage for the reformers to suppress domestic interest groups that are taking advantage of legal loopholes and insufficient technical standards regarding good governance.

(iii) Use more diverse financial tools and mobilization of resources through the participation of private sector, and/or international partnerships. It is essential to increase the involvement of private sector as the public sector needs to maintain public debt ceiling that limits further borrowing to avoid macro-economic risks. At the same time, the mobilization of social sources will request the relevant countries to create favorable business and investment climate for doing business, and to ensure the protection of investor's benefits by implementing more transparent and more open procurement processes. These requirements are in line with domestic policies of the countries in their efforts and priorities to attract foreign direct investment and support domestic enterprises involved in large infrastructure projects.

---

[5] The World Bank, https://data.worldbank.org/indicator/FR.INR.LEND?locations=JP.

[6] The World Bank, https://data.worldbank.org/indicator/FR.INR.LEND?locations=KR.

[7] The World Bank, https://data.worldbank.org/indicator/FR.INR.LEND?locations=IN.

At the same time, the BRI and MPAC 2025 should work with other initiatives, mechanisms and partners to mobilize diverse sources of funds and create synergy. For positive spillover effects, the infrastructure projects should be coordinated through existing regional and multilateral organizations to facilitate trade, business environment and regional economic integration, thus attracting further investment. Such sustainable finance through cooperation with various stakeholders will help complete the infrastructure as scheduled, rather than delay the works and cause incurred cost that can be harmful to the national public expenditure budget. As a framework for cooperation with about 70 countries, the BRI itself is an open system for collective action and cooperation. Similarly, ASEAN has traditional relationship with various development partners such as WB, ADB, JICA and dialogue partners. Thus, both the BRI and ASEAN could make efforts to implement activities in cooperation with external partners to meet the local demands for connectivity and sustainable development.

Conclusion

In conclusion, it is necessary and timely to map out how to combine the BRI and MPAC 2025 to create synergy for successful implementation of the BRI and MPAC 2025. Such a close cooperation would definitely bring mutual benefits for both sides, responding to local development needs, creating an impetus for regional economic integration and sustainable development, most importantly contributing to handling the strategic political concerns and building mutual trust. A careful preparation for future cooperation in infrastructure projects to connect China and Southeast Asia by aligning the BRI and MPAC 2025 will help to tap into the full potential and avoid possible tensions and frictions. The most important factor would be the state leaders of both sides, China and ASEAN need to provide full support for the implementation of the BRI, focusing not only on economic benefits but also social and environmental sustainability, thus creating a harmonious society and sustainable development in the end.

Printed in the United States
by Baker & Taylor Publisher Services